THE DEFERRED REVOLUTION

A Social Experiment in Church Innovation
in Holland, 1960—1970

The Deferred Revolution

A Social Experiment in Church Innovation in Holland, 1960—1970

Walter Goddijn

 ***Elsevier***

Amsterdam — Oxford — New York — 1975

ELSEVIER SCIENTIFIC PUBLISHING COMPANY

335 Jan van Galenstraat
P.O. Box 211, Amsterdam, The Netherlands

and

52 Vanderbilt Avenue
New York, N.Y. 10017

Library of Congress Card Number: 74—83313

ISBN: 0-444-41228-X

Printed in The Netherlands

Contents

CHAPTER I

Holland in Focus

World press and ecclesiastical circles have, of late, paid much attention to previously unnoticed Holland where a new tourist attraction has developed, the changes in the Roman Catholic Church. Dutch Catholicism has become a problem; it is an *enfant terrible*, a sign of contradiction after Vatican II. Even a serious newspaper like *The Times* (20 March 1973) takes a negative view of the situation: "The forces of change after the reign of Pope John were in fact so powerful that it would have taken and did take strong executive organization to prevent the Vatican being disrupted in the way that the Roman Catholic Church has in fact been disrupted in The Netherlands or in many parts of the United States." Others, however, think more positively about the state of the Catholic Church in The Netherlands: the Dutch are practical; they will try to adapt the old church institution, in the spirit of Vatican II, to modern society; you can leave it to them without worry, for they are very faithful to the Pope in Rome.

In this chapter we shall study the "Dutch case" from various angles, in an effort to find the most adequate point of focus and method of research.

1. The Unknown Netherlands

Up to the Second World War Holland was scarcely noticed in the world forum. If anything was written about The Netherlands it was usually written by the Dutch themselves. But this does not increase the self-knowledge of a nation, nor does it promote the objective reporting of what is happening within its borders. Not until 1967 was a systematic study of "Dutch Society" published in the U.S.A., this as well written by a Dutchman (Goudsblom, 1967). "Owing to its location and its small size, the country has always been open to foreign influences," Goudsblom writes. These foreign influences created for The Netherlands a blurred image of its national and cultural identity. The country was looked upon as a kind of Germany-on-sea, a "Germania Inferior," the latter term referring not to its culture but to the lowness of the land, which is in certain places below sea level. Nevertheless, its borders worked as a filter: foreign influences were not admitted indiscriminately. Presently the percentage may be a little lower, owing to the immigration of people from Indonesia, Surinam, and migrant workers, but even as late as 1960 96% of all Dutch people had been born in the country. Therefore, in spite of its size and location, The Netherlands does have its own image, character and customs.

However most observers are usually at a loss when trying to describe these. One of the first Roman observers, the historian Tacitus, had this to say about the Batavians, then the inhabitants of our estuarine regions: "They are a Germanic group with a very high standard of civilization but with extremely bad manners" (De Baena, 1968). Johannes Huizinga repeats this indictment, describing Dutch national culture as homely both in its virtues and its vices: "Lasciviousness, impoliteness, stinginess. Our national character consists of tidiness (we have at least eight words for it), respect for the rights and opinions of others, very little room for illusions and rhetoric, pertinacity as regards ideas once accepted, *esprit de clocher*, lukewarm reaction to enthusiasm, political indifference, and antipathy towards national self-glorification. We are open to, and even prefer, acknowledging the value of everything that comes from abroad." The Duke of Baena, who was Spanish Ambassador to the country for several years, collected many quotations of this kind, and has taken the trouble to record his ideas and assessment of the people in his book *The Dutch Puzzle*. For him the Dutch were increasingly enigmatic and in this respect he resembles the Frenchman Henri Asselin, who in 1921 wrote a book *La Hollande dans le Monde* in which he had to admit that he could not possibly pass a definitive judgment on the Dutch.

The Duke of Baena has this to say to his Dutch readers:

Since you are passionately devoted to freedom and as meekly submit to convention, since you are republican citizens and also loyal monarchists, since you are tender and even sentimental in your feelings and at the same time rude in your behavior, since you are both tolerant and fanatical, since you are basically mean in daily life and generous in all sorts of human disaster, since you are as magnanimous as you are petty-minded, since you are excessively prudent and terribly indiscrete, since you are inveterately materialistic and extremely pious, since you are no less sensual than puritanical, since you are sober and realistic and at the same time given to romantic dreaming, since you are both sensitive and impertinent, you will have to agree there is a mystery, an inextricable knot of contrasting elements, difficult to explain in everyday terms. I myself think it could be explained as follows: by nature you are a peaceful race of bourgeois realists with a tendency towards stinginess, work and love of ease, but your nation's history has forced you to fight, has obliged you to resist not only the superior forces of raiding enemies from abroad, but also the forces of nature, especially the everlasting threats of the North Sea; and to complete the picture, there is your unremitting struggle with the Calvinist Reformation.

The Netherlands is an enigma both to itself and to others. People see what we do, but often they do not understand why we do it. Holland is still scarcely known abroad. Those who know it, face a riddle. Unknown, and therefore unloved. Some familiarity did grow, however, after the period 1940—1945, when American, British and Canadian soldiers came to liberate the country. Especially in the west, where the big cities of Amsterdam, Rotterdam and The Hague are situated, they found a starving population. Starved by the German occupational forces who had come to know The Netherlands all too well. Many countries, especially the U.S.A., organized large campaigns to aid the ravaged land. Then in 1953, nearly ten years later, The Netherlands was struck by a new catastrophe, precipitated by its hereditary enemy, the water. because of a remarkable coincidence of climatic circumstances, the dykes which serve to protect the polders against the water of the North Sea were weakened; there were hundreds of victims in the flooding that followed and incalculable damage. From all over the world supplies were sent to Holland. It was a serious blow to the fame of the Dutch as builders of dykes and canals, a fame even referred to by Dante in his *Divina Commedia* (Inferno, Canto XV, 4) where he compares the sturdy dyke surrounding the slough of hell with the Cadzand sea-dyke. It is unlikely that this is connected with the remark supposedly made by the Duke of Alva, Spanish despot over The Netherlands: "Holland borders on hell!."

J. Huisman writes that the Dutch image has long been that of clog-wearing fishermen and thrifty burghers, even after rapid changes had taken place. Within a hundred-year period the population increased five fold. Within the same period the average Dutchman grew significantly taller: a study by G. Kenntner, concluded in 1963, reported an average increase in height of 13.5 centime-

3

ters, a development found nowhere else. At every congress abroad they talk about "those tall Dutchmen" (J. Huisman, 1966).

Another remarkable fact also turned attention towards Holland. In his United Nations sponsored study of the population development of Europe between the two World Wars, Dudley Kirk (1946) observes: "The Netherlands is the exception to the rule of low birth-rates in Western Europe, an exception not yet adequately explained." Later, Dutch sociologist F. van Heek (1954) would attempt to explain this remarkable phenomenon by the historical minority position and the spiritual élan of the Dutch Roman Catholics.

2. The Unknown Dutch Catholics

Somewhere in his *History of the Popes* J. Schmidlin reportedly has said that only after diligent searching do Vatican sources yield some morsels of information which allow a reconstruction of Dutch relations with Rome. Dutch church historian L.J. Rogier (1970), referring to this comment, thinks Dutch Catholicism may have acquired some fame because The Netherlands supplied more Zouaves or soldiers to Pope Pius IX for the defence of the Vatican State than any other country in the world. "To be sure, this did not induce the Holy See to give The Netherlands any part in military command, but strikingly Pius IX often spoke of *mes bons Hollandais* who obeyed without criticism and even without asking questions. Well-behaved children that didn't cause Papa any trouble."

Apart from an internal row between Utrecht and Rome, which later resulted in the secession of the Old Catholics, not much had happened to Dutch Catholicism. It is estimated that the percentage of Catholics in the areas now composing the Dutch territory went down from 47% to 38% between 1656 and 1809, decreased to 35% in the following period, and is now more or less stable at about 40% (J. de Kok, 1964). Yet this relatively high percentage in the national census did not give them much prominence. It was a clandestine Catholicism in The Netherlands, as in Europe in general: Holland was very often looked upon as a "Protestant nation."

Sometimes opinions from abroad were considered to describe the whole of religious life in The Netherlands. A recent book on the Dutch Church by J. van Laarhoven begins with a quotation

4

from Karl Barth concerning Holland: "Down there along the Rhine, there is a corner where it's smoky." Van Laarhoven (1973) comments:

> To be sure, in that estuary of large, slow rivers the fog of the low countries mingles with the smoke from the many many little houses where the Lord is invoked; and the theological gunpowder-smoke, often drifting in from elsewhere, lingers there persistently and, coming down with the drizzle, makes the soil fertile for a varied ecclesiastical crop. Nowhere are there so many theologians — sure of possessing the truth — as in this country of churches and conventions, of peaceful believers and stern debaters, of practical tolerance and impractical pedantry. Historians wishing to record the ecclesiastical history of the country lose heart at the sight of all the church steeples, they trip over many fences and pay their toll at many little religious drawbridges, for in this country where so much water flows, God's water, too, has been canalized and God's acre has been dyked in thoroughly and parcelled out minutely.

The Netherlands is known for its deep intermingling of religion and social life. Group formation along denominational lines seems to be a Dutch phenomenon: sociologists find it difficult to establish adequate terms and talk of "pillaring" or "vertical pluralism"; Yves Congar once characterized the country's Catholicism as *catholicisme sociologique*.

For at least ten years after the Second World War Dutch Catholicism — comprising only one percent of the world Catholic population — was unimportant. The periodical *Dokumente, Zeitschrift für übernationale Zusammenarbeit* devoted an entire issue to Catholicism in Europe (Heft 4, 1956), without a single comment on The Netherlands, not even in Friedrich Heer's leading article "Nationale und universale Aspekte des europäischen Katholizismus." Holland, Catholic Holland, was unknown, but the situation was not to last much longer.

3. International Interest in Dutch Catholics after 1960

After Pope John XXIII announced the great council of reform (January 1959) the Catholics of the Netherlands began to attract more attention. Fervent, Rome-oriented Holland proved able to provide news items for the world press. Repressed Dutch Catholicism had long struggled for emancipation and finally wrested itself free from the dominating Protestant influence, and Pope John's appeal for an *aggiornamento* was exactly in tune with the needs of those Dutch Catholics who wanted their church to function well

5

in a modern, urbanized and densely populated country. They got full support from the Dutch bishops. Even before and during the Vatican Council Dutch publications in foreign translations had given rise to differences of opinion between the bishops of The Netherlands and the central authorities in Rome.

After the euphoria of Vatican II, which has been called the "Prague Spring," the Roman Catholic Church experienced a change in 1968. On 8 December 1965 Pope Paul VI closed down Vatican II and then began, ever more obviously, slowing down the movement for renewal sparked off by Pope John, or, to put it more positively, steering it into well-ordered channels. It was especially in the later sixties that the Dutch bishops, led by Cardinal Bernard Alfrink, came into open conflict with Rome. During those years the international mass media threw full light on Dutch Catholicism. Journalists from television, radio and the press, from the United States, Great Britain, Canada, Spain, Italy, Germany, France, Switzerland and Belgium arrived in Holland to cover the story and hold interviews. They put The Netherlands on the front pages of the big newspapers, where conflicts between little Holland and big Rome, especially on questions such as obligatory priestly celibacy, made the international headlines. Besides journalists, professors from all over the world came to The Netherlands to talk with their colleagues. Groups of priests and ministers, seminary and university students arrived. The Netherlands became a tourist attraction, made the most of by foreign travel agencies. Even people from the field of politics, diplomats and high officials, presented themselves at the Foreign Office in The Hague, not to get introductions to the managers of Philips at Eindhoven or the port authorities of Rotterdam, but to ask where they could "see" Dutch Catholicism.

4. Questions for the Dutch Catholics

As is the case with all tourist visits, questions were asked. Why these rapid and unexpected changes in Dutch Catholicism? Had there been a gradual evolution of events in the fields of doctrine, the role of the clergy and of participation by the faithful in the government of the Church? Had all these things perhaps begun even earlier and could they have been predicted? Had the bishops been under pressure from certain groups or were they indeed forerunners of church renewal? Could one describe it as a sudden explosion, with a tremendous impact on the whole world church? Had there been, just as in the floods of 1953, a surprising and unexpected interplay of elements which had presented church leaders with a *fait accompli* and forced them to take emergency measures wherever the needs were greatest? Was this "church explosion" "to the benefit of the community of the faithful" or its undoing? Might it even be a disaster for which help from churches abroad should be sought? Was Rome going to take action? Would not there be a breach between The Netherlands and Rome?

Later on these questions were formulated in many articles, even books, about Dutch Catholicism that were published abroad. Dutch Catholicism, itself linguistically isolated, was "translated" into orderly and legible publications, studied by foreign scholars, bishops, even by Rome. Already controversy had begun within the Church in other places such as Germany, Italy, France and the United States. A sample of the titles of articles and books in a selected bibliography (Huysmans and Snabel, 1971) indicates the Dutch situation was viewed as the result of implementation of the ideas of Vatican II, in the course of which the good relations between Holland and Rome threatened to be disturbed. There are general titles such as "New Church Model," "The Risk-taking Church," "Through Reformation towards a New Church," "Evolution and Crisis," "Crisis of Growth," "New Bearings and Appeal," "Renewal", "The Quiet Revolution," "The Exploding Church." The conflict in the situation is brought out more clearly in titles such as: "Holland, Testing Grounds of God's Church," "The Holland-Rome Conflict," "The Netherlands, the Promised Land for Church Reform," "David and Goliath," "The Progress of the Dutch Experiment as opposed to Roman Conservatism," "Dutch Resisting Italization"; very obviously negative approaches are indicated in titles such as "Voices from the Dutch Wilderness," "Visiting Heretics," "On the Brink of Schism" and "Church in Need."

The enormous publicity surrounding the Dutch movement of renewal after Vatican II was to have its consequences. The Netherlands became an international "case," a public challenge addressed to those Vatican authorities who, after the closing of the Council, advocated very gradual renewal or even none for the time being. The renewal movement in The Netherlands was not given the opportunity to strive, unhampered, in the quiet required for experiments, towards a balance between historical continuity and reform in the spirit of Vatican II. Reactionary minority groups, disavowing their own bishops, found mysterious support in Vatican circles.

Rome began to interpret negatively the developments in The Netherlands and had its answers to the many questions internationally asked about Dutch Catholicism all ready.

5. Rome's Answer

Rome's answer was first heard in the inner sanctums of the Vatican. It is December 1969, shortly before the fifth plenary meeting, to be held the following month, of the Dutch Pastoral Council, the national consultative body of bishops, priests and laity. One of the draft reports prepared for the Council deals with the position of the priesthood. The International Documentation Center in Rome, established during the Second Vatican Council and since then working under Dutch management (IDOC), has already circulated in Rome a French translation of the report and the draft resolutions, yet to be discussed at the meeting, on the status and function of the priest in the Roman Catholic Church. Throughout the world press reports are circulating that Dutch bishops are going to permit their priests to marry. After talking with Cardinal John Wright, recently appointed head of the Vatican department for questions concerning the priesthood, "Father" he says when I have already said goodbye, "keep the finger in the dyke." He alluded to the legend, especially popular in the United States, that a little Dutch boy once saved The Netherlands from a flood disaster by courageously putting his finger in a hole in a dyke thus stopping the water. Only later did it dawn on me that this open and honest Vatican leader was interpreting the Dutch renewal movement as a flood which was threatening to destroy the dykes of ecclesiastical authority.

In the period that followed, observers from the Vatican were invited several times to attend meetings of the Dutch Pastoral Council but even an unofficial visit was not allowed: the Vatican representative in The Netherlands stayed away from the January session of the Pastoral Council in protest. In March and July of 1970 Cardinal Bernard Alfrink had talks in Paris and Rome with superior Vatican authorities. But the real, public answer from Rome was still to come, and it came, at the end of 1970, in the appointment by Rome of a new bishop to the vacant See of Rotterdam. The Pastoral Council had been closed in April of 1970. Intensive study was now underway about the means for establishing a new, permanent form of consultation through which the faithful would be stimulated to share in the responsibility for pastoral policy. The Rotterdam appointment was legal, but was it legitimate? It had been made without any form of open and trusting consultation between Rome and the Dutch bishops. Solidarity between bishops and the faithful was put under heavy pressure by this appointment, for at the Pastoral Council the appointee, Ad Simonis, had clearly emerged as the spokesman for a small minority group which constantly attempted to undermine the authority of the Dutch bishops.

6. The Dutch Answer

As archbishop of the "local church" of The Netherlands, Cardinal Alfrink was to give an answer that would bring the conflict with Rome out in the open, and at the same time show how the differences of opinion among the Catholic faithful, previously latent, had now become of utmost importance. For Cardinal Alfrink this "breach" within the Dutch Catholic community was a "schism" that had been in fact thrust upon it. It was he who, with great patience, had constantly tried to keep communications open between Holland and Rome. Now, as the leader of the Roman Catholic Church in The Netherlands, he felt repudiated by the highest authority in Rome.

At the ordination of Bishop Simonis the cardinal gave his answer to Rome. The now-exposed conflict was described by him as

... a clear sign — on both sides — of feelings that had been offended, unacknowledged and ignored by those from whom confirmation, hope and trust was expected. All this has done much damage to the Church, and it has undermined confidence in church authorities. The most regrettable thing of all is perhaps that the situation could have been avoided if other ways had been chosen; a repetition must be avoided at all costs. I think that anyone, who has the future of the Dutch Church at heart, must regret it and must realize that the mission of the episcopacy, to be true pastors to everyone, has been made more difficult. Bishops of a church province cannot identify with only a certain group from among their faithful. God has commissioned them to be shepherds of the entire flock.

This reply from The Netherlands voiced by Cardinal Alfrink, fell flat when, just over a year later, Rome again announced an episcopal appointment which reflected its unfavourable opinion of the renewal movement within Dutch Catholicism. Bishop Gijsen of Roermond, ordained in Rome by the Pope himself, had openly, in various publications, attacked the bishops who now became his colleagues. And even after his ordination, a critique of the Dutch renewal movement appeared in a German publication, which had previously been sent to press. It contains the following assessment of the Dutch situation, quite different from that by Cardinal Alfrink:

> Only a few people had the courage and the power to work for a proper and moderate implementation of the decisions of Vatican II; their voices were almost lost amid the shouts of exaltation with which public opinion received the ideas of the "progressives." A growing uncertainty spread, nourished by lack of strong leadership. The limited knowledge of the principles of Catholic thinking, on the one hand, and the love-of-ease caused by the new ideas, on the other, became the main causes of the lethargy which slowly but surely hallmarked the Catholics of The Netherlands (Haarsma, 1973).

7. Desirability of Further Inquiry

When, within such a relatively short time, two people, both at least formally competent to give an opinion, can offer such completely contradictory assessments of the religious and ecclesiastical situation in Holland then further enquiry is certainly desirable. One authority is of the opinion that Rome is undermining the prestige of bishops who started a movement of renewal in complete harmony with Vatican II. The other thinks that the vitality of Dutch Catholicism has withered to a state of lawlessness, uncertainty and lethargy and that the church leaders who introduced changes after Vatican II have badly failed. When Dutch "insiders" can disagree to that extent about the whys and hows of the changes in their own Catholic Church, how then can we hope to explain to foreign readers what is happening in Holland.

In 1971 the Dutch sociologist J. Thurlings published a historical-sociological study of Dutch Catholicism "between assimilation and pluralism." The book discusses the period of change within Roman Catholic organizations that started at about the same time, 1960, as the renewal movement, against the background of recent dynamism in Dutch Catholicism. "Since the Reformation never has such an acute crisis presented itself to Dutch Catholics." In the last pages of his extensive study he asks many questions he himself is unable to answer.

Are we moving towards a kind of all-assimilating secularism from which only a small group of extreme "orthodox" conservatives can keep itself free? Are we heading for an ecumenism in which Catholic and Protestant Christians, while recognizing each other's interpretations of certain aspects of the Evangelic Message, will talk together, and perform together certain acts of worship, sacraments included, and simultaneously acknowledge for the time being each other's autonomy? Or are we travelling towards a Catholic Church which allows numerous movements to be burnt by their own fire and then, politely and systematically, gets into touch with people of different persuasions, in select areas of interest? In which of these alternatives the threat of a schism with the Church Universal, or at least with the Pope, might become a reality, is a question we will not discuss here for practical reasons. But even in this simplified form the above questions are extremely relevant for the Catholic Church in The Netherlands. Here is an urgent problem that will have to be discussed and mastered within, let us say, a decade.

Nobody has better formulated the desirability of further study. In a previous publication we have offered an extensive analysis of the sociological relations between the Catholic status-minority in The Netherlands and the dominating Protestantism (W. Goddijn, 1957). The Dutch Roman Catholics have survived domination by the process of Protestantization. The work of J. Thurlings links up with some results of this study, but he concentrates mainly on the next phase of the history of Dutch Catholicism: the process of secularization. The third phase, the conflict between Dutch Catholicism and the "Roman" dominant is given special attention in the present study: here we have a process of assimilation and estrangement which clearly shows continuity with the older but still partly operative processes of Protestantization and secularization (W. Goddijn, 1973).

It is desirable to gain insights, by means as precise and systematic as possible, into the most relevant aspects of the recent changes in Dutch Catholicism. The relevance of what happened and is still happening in The Netherlands can only be made clear if general internal and external elements can be summed up alongside more specific ones. There is an urgent need to relativize recent events by comparing them with situations elsewhere and with similar situations in the past. Each era tends to think highly of itself, and feelings of national pride and self-respect always play a big role. Our innate idiosyncrasy of supposing that our own period is a time of crisis, and that at this exact moment renewal is especially needed, must not keep us from our task of learning from the past (von der Dunk, 1972). In the last analysis our ambitious purpose is to find out whether or not a comprehensive analysis of the Dutch situation can provide a "blueprint for survival" which could be of use to both national and international church leaders, especially in the Roman Catholic Church. As long as one tries to stay free from emotional prejudice with regard to the intentions of the Dutch Catholics, one can gain better insight through a systematic description of the facts and the application of a scheme of interpretation that is theoretically adequate. This improved insight, free from the sensational deformities of reality, is the purpose of this study. It is not meant to be propaganda for the view point of one local church or one particular country, but an attempt to offer a systematic and intelligible synthesis of knowledge and experience.

This brings us to a further description of the sociological approach.

8. Sociological Approach

Using the empirical data at my disposal, collected mainly through direct observation and participation, I shall try to explain the institutional changes in the Roman Catholic Church of The Netherlands during the period 1960—1970. Special attention must be paid to the rapidity and the unpredictability of these changes.

More specifically, the study concerns a local or particular church within the multinational Roman Catholic Church. Within its scope falls the relationship between The Netherlands and the central clerical authorities in Rome. The Roman Catholic Church has a multinational character, and a number of rules govern the relations among the various local churches themselves and their relations with the top; it maintains its role as an international system with its own identity by means of certain forms of centralized government, a uniformity of measures, and a definite subordination of various lower figures in the hierarchy. Conflicts between The Netherlands and Rome may be ascribed to defective communications, insufficient understanding of the motives behind Dutch renewal, and differences of opinion as regards ability for and the nature, extent and temporization of renewal, in comparison with other local churches. Furthermore, the study describes institutional changes which are in fact comparable with the general processes of development in any large social institution. We should not ascribe these changes to the character of Dutch Catholicism, nor call them specifically Dutch, when they have in fact an international character or have already occurred elsewhere in the past.

Even though Ernst Troeltsch has said that universal churches are conservative by definition, it is a fact that the history of the Roman Catholic Church is a history of change.

The institutional approach we have chosen is not much favoured in sociology of religion circles since Thomas Luckmann justly criticized a too one-sided approach to the sociology of religion as resulting in a sociology of church participation (H. and W. Goddijn, 1967; Th. Luckmann, 1963). The question asked by A. Greeley (1972) at the end of his study *Unsecular Man. The Persistence of Religion* remains very relevant: "Will the churches — that is to say, institutionalized religion in its present manifestation — survive.... If one means by a 'church' merely a human organization concerned primarily with religion, then one would be vastly surprised if a complicated and highly structured world like our own was able to produce a religion that did not turn into 'church.' To talk about 'institutionless' religion is at best naive romanticism. Whether the existing churches will survive or not is, of course, another matter." Cannot the changes within the Roman Catholic Church of The Netherlands be characterized as an attempt to give the church as an institution the opportunity to survive in modern society?

When studying the ecclesiastical renewal movement in The Netherlands we shall, as a matter of fact, also come upon doctrinal questions. If necessary, reference will be made to theological expositions. More than once it will appear that the theological approach is influenced by social change, even to such an extent that we can speak of the social characteristics of certain theological trends. The sociologist should avoid overstepping the boundaries of his profession. But on the other hand one can wonder if in the assessment of the changes in the great Christian churches there is not a continuous "theological reductionism," as James Gustafson calls it, of which not only church leaders but also theologians are guilty. Institutional forms do not necessarily create the conditions for a personal experience of faith. They can also hamper it. "The identity of the inner life as Christian depends upon the proper functioning of the institutional forms. One cannot conceive of the continuation of the communal, inner aspects of Christian Church life without proper external institutional forms" (J. Gustafson, 1961). Very little, and sometimes nothing at all, is known about the standard, the quality, the frequency and the deeper attitudes of Christian life in The Netherlands because no research has been done and because there are no adequate research techniques. Generalizing judgments in this field are usually *a priori* or based on unsystematic and prejudiced observations.

9. Our Methods of Inquiry

From the viewpoint of methodology it is not sufficient to limit ourselves to a chronological survey of facts concerning the history of the Roman Catholic Church in The Netherlands between 1960 and 1970. Even within this limited field the problem of selecting and ordering these facts would exist.

But we are examining more explicitly a characteristic specific for this period of Dutch Catholicism, namely the rapid changes within a population group which had seemed to be almost immobile within the international structure of the Church of Rome. We are concerned about changes in the church as an institution and probably in that type of church that is most resistant to change.

In the first part of our study — chapters II and III — we shall take a look at the origins and nature of the changes in the great Christian churches. It is a theoretical exploration which not only relativizes the changes in the Dutch Catholic Church, but also puts them into perspective. A subsequent description of church renewal in the present century brings out surprising parallels, in particular between church renewal in France and recent developments in The Netherlands. The fourth chapter ends with a typology of progress and regress, of renewal and stagnation. It is a hypothetical interpretation scheme, a model or paradigm, a synthesis of views of a part of reality (Lammers, 1973). According to a recent and rather spectacular study published in the U.S.A., history, and accordingly also church history, is increasingly studied with the help of those social patterns or models (Landes and Tilly, 1973). The particulars of Dutch Church renewal and the subsequent stagnation will be described in chapters V and VI. A final chapter then interprets these changes. Three factors will come forward which, in their relation to each other, prove to be very relevant for the problem under discussion, and which, in a further study, will probably appear to have a more general significance. The future is difficult to predict. But there is a method emerging of alternating progress and regress in the slow process of church renewal.

In short, the following hypothesis about progress and regress, about evolution and stagnation in church renewal will be tested out: When a church assimilates the three elements of democratic exercise — authority, free scholarship and modern publicity — and combines them in critical solidarity, there is progress. When these factors are dissociated through a more centralistic and authoritarian form of church government, which obstructs the mutual solidarity of local authorities (bishops), scholars (theologians) and publicists, then regress sets in.

Use has been made of the observations by various authors or groups of authors, and also of those observations of the present writer made during the period in which he served in a confidential position as advisor to the Dutch bishops, from 1963 till September 1972. Stressing the institutional aspects relevant for this kind of sociological study may sometimes obscure the insight into the ideas and opinions, in short, the "system of belief" of the Dutch Catholics. Without being exactly representative, the conclusions and resolutions of the national consultative body, the Pastoral Council, are a fair indication of the opinions of church leaders, priests and prominent lay people on many aspects of the Catholic Church. Only further study could make it clear in how far the resolutions, seconded by the great majority of the council members, really reflect the opinions of the Catholic community as a whole.

CHAPTER II

Structural Characteristics of Church Renewal

The search for possible explanations of the recent changes in Dutch Catholicism brings to light certain structural elements which have a far wider bearing. The historically oriented sociologist will attempt to discover this more permanent structure, in this case of the institution of the Catholic Church, and to explain from this basis the more dynamic and localized processes. Does what happened in The Netherlands fit into a historical pattern of reform movements within the Catholic Church? Only after studying this question can it become clear if there are, after all, indications that we are entering a new phase of development.

Evaluating structural elements is an indispensable preparation for the more concrete description of phenomena which are sometimes not yet quite clearly discernible. "It is a form of investigation inherent to man's perceptive powers: one must have a starting point with basic data in order to be able to trace and understand changes that occur" (A. Cohen, 1973). In the church, as well, renewers are little disposed to think historically. It seems as if they fear that their urge for radical renewal will be curbed by historical thinking. Their consideration of history starts just too late to relativize their own standpoints. At that moment they themselves have become a part of history, and the real opportunities for renewal have passed.

1. Church and Environment

While limited to the internal structural changes in the Catholic Church, this study is not meant to be of a church institution separate and isolated, independent of its environment. The great majority of church members live mainly "in the world," and only a small group work professionally as officials within the church institution. The church is world-directed, without merging with that world.

There are many technical and biblical terms describing this relation. Being present in the world, especially when fundamental decisions about the world are being prepared. Being averted from the world. Openness towards and seclusion from. Being sent into the world and adapting to it: Gentile among Gentiles, Jew among Jews, intellectual among intellectuals, native among natives (as priest-missionaries), worker among workers (as worker-priests), married among the married (as married priests). This interchange, this coming and going of people, of church representatives, can also be observed in the adoption or rejection of forms, groups, ideas, truths and values. There is a permanent dialectic between dissociation and conciliation, between pluralism and assimilation, between dissonance and congruence.

Traditionally this dialectic is expressed in images like the treasure in earthen vessels, the salt of the earth, the yeast in the leaven, the city on the mountain, the light on the candlestick. Their focus continuously changes as the "environment," the value system of the world, is seen as positive or negative for the survival and growth of the church. Sometimes the world is inimical, and the church retires into a secluded and stubbornly defended "Wounded Knee." Then again, the world is an ally and, like a chameleon, the church assumes worldly colours. The two extremes, between which the processes of change are oscillating, are continually either the complete merging with the surroundings, or the complete isolation without any possibility to function relevantly in the environment.

This fundamental interchange makes outsiders sometimes complain that with the church you never know "where you're at." The church appears unreliable; it always manages to save face. Change and renewal in the church are so difficult to interpret because both arguments, for openness and seclusion, have had their own respectable defenders. What one calls renewal, the other rejects as destructive.

The standards for the interpretation of renewal are changing with the times. The Roman Catholic Church as an institution has developed a great number of instruments to ensure its self-preservation and continuity. These vary as well between the extremes of the torture devices used by the Inquisition to a respectful dialogue with other churches that also acknowledge Jesus Christ as their Founder. In the pre-Tridentine period opposing groups that wanted to reform the powerful church institution from within were expelled in the numerous schisms. The Protestant Reformation symbolizes, as it were, that "reformation," is only possible after secession. Only when a group has existed for centuries can it expect an invitation to meet as an equal partner at the conference table. In some cases reform movements were integrated. Rome never took the initiative for religious reform movements such as those of the Franciscans or the Black Friars. But their survival as kind of tolerated sects within the Church depended on the approval of church authorities (W. Goddijn, 1962).

The heart of the post-Tridentine Church has continuously vacillated between safe immobility and risky pioneering. Internationally there existed an antithesis between openness and seclusion, both attitudes finding support among popes and theologians. "There have always been theologians who considered a wide spectrum of thinking within the church legitimate, alongside others who could only imagine the road to heaven as a narrow path, lined with the bleached skulls of beheaded heretics" (L. Rogier, 1970). Throughout history the progress of the church, penetrating into new cultures, has followed both narrow and broad paths.

2. A Few Theoretical Starting Points

Sociological studies about the changes in the Catholic Church as an institution are very limited in number. Only very few authors have dealt explicitly with the subject. For the rest, one must draw on general studies about social change, revolutionary phenomena, etc., and on works by historians and theologians.

The institution "church" does not necessarily change in order to suit its society or environment, but in certain circumstances has as well opposed society. In a recent book P. Zulehner (1972) says about this: "In the results of the Second Vatican Council, in papal encyclicals on social problems, and even more clearly in many modern ecclesiastical popular groups ideas are presented that indict, question and thereby exert a disintegrating influence on at least some aspects of actual social reality (e.g. war, underdevelopment, injustice, racial hatred, lack of freedom in social structures, etc.). Do not such phenomena demonstrate the inherent dynamism of religious reality and consequently also that of the churches?"

Most sociologists, however, look upon changes in the church as stimulated by society. Yet in spite of environmental changes and social pressure from outside, the institution of the Roman Catholic Church has existed for almost two thousand years. Permanent indoctrination, formal and informal, with a defined system of truths and values, rules and sanctions, group participation in numerous forms, and an executive body firmly bound to authority, has preserved the church despite nearly revolutionary changes. David Moberg (1962), the only sociologist of religion to write a book on "the church as a social institution," sketches a kind of ecclesiastical life cycle. The initial volunteer group has increasingly more formal rules imposed upon them. There is a growing bureaucracy and with it, a greater "efficiency." Then a kind of vicious circle develops: as the formalizing increases, the effectiveness decreases. The final stage he describes as one in which "...the institution may collapse, unless renewal occurs through relaxation of formal rules, increased stress upon informal relations, or other changes." Then the entire process can start over again. Theologians call this a re-sourcing (*ressourcement*), or confrontation with the structural elements of the first Christian community to be used as criteria for modern reform. Talking about the "volunteer church" is a part of the same development.

Besides this process Moberg also describes a kind of continuum of interrelated conflict groups within the great churches. The "parties" have the following names: fundamentalists, conservatives, moderates, liberals and modernists, the "pliable" and the "precise." It is fascinating to notice in the developments within the large Protestant churches numerous issues which only thirty or forty years later will arise in the Roman Catholic Church. Does not the following assessment remind one of church leaders who have to govern multiform churches? Large groups of church members can be progressive, but it becomes difficult when there are many different groups. "Such variability in a church, especially when no one viewpoint can claim a majority, creates many problems for leaders. It bears the seeds of internal dissension and strife if it is not wisely managed" (J. van Vleck Jr., 1937).

Conflicts within the church can work both positively and negatively. Negative consequences are an enormous waste of time, energy and material resources; certain public personalities may suffer severely from insinuations. A process of "overchurching" sets in,

19

and the stride toward common goals is impeded. But conflict can also be a source of renewal, through which the wishes of the faithful in a changing world can be met. "Much of the vitality of the church as a social institution is a direct result of conflict." Moberg's analysis of "internal church conflict" contains the following remarks about the Catholic Church: "Roman Catholicism is changing today, as in the past. It therefore can be expected to survive the impact of the vast social, technological and political changes of the twentieth century. The great diversity possible and permissible within it is, paradoxically, a source of both weakness and strength, of division and unity." This sociological judgment almost sounds like a paraphrase of "the gates of hell shall not prevail against it." Apparently the Catholic Church always finds opportunities to balance mystery and mysticism on the one hand, with institutional adaptation and the exercise of authority on the other (A. Zijderveld, 1971).

The above-mentioned structural elements of church renewal — conflict groups, pluralism, polarization (although the word is not mentioned), positive and negative effects of conflict, the need for good leadership in the various groups — can be applied in many ways on the present situation. In addition, detailed studies have been made about authority and power, such as that made by Paul Harrison for the American Baptist Convention, which contains sections directly comparable to the attempts in the Catholic Church to develop new authority relations. When their synods or conventions do not result in authoritative pronouncements (a permanent problem for the Dutch Pastoral Council) church leaders tend to become insecure and feel compelled "to conserve the gains they have made rather than risk the dangers of prophetic and imaginative leadership." With the American Baptists the risk-taking church thus became a conservative church (P. Harrison, 1959).

How the Anglican Church reacted to social change was described by K. Thompson (1970) in *Bureaucracy and Church Reform*. Of special interest is the phase in which local churches arrive at broader cooperation and the leadership must be organized into an assembly or synod. Thompson mainly concentrates on organizational aspects, on the tensions between pluralism and centralization, between adequate representation and a growing centralized organization. In the midst of all these adaptations the church must preserve its own identity: "In every stage of growth in the church's organization...both instrumental adaptation and the assertion of particular values were rendered subordinate to the maintenance of the basic identity of the Church of England, which rested on this comprehensiveness." The challenges mentioned by Thompson to indicate to which external factors the church must respond are: changes in population development, urbanization, competition with other churches, political changes (with consequences for the financial position of the church), the necessity for the church to remain certain of the support of the faithful, and, especially with a view to the middle classes, "to develop a sense of responsibility in its laity." Generally the "answers" to these challenges consisted only of organizational measures. Literally they suggest "improvement in the skills of organization — communications, transport, specialization, statistical and budgetary techniques." In view of the character of these reform measures the Anglican Church does not make the usual distinction between structural changes and religious directives. Even a good financial policy can further religious life.

Every conservative will take heart and many a radical renewer will start doubting when general sociology formulates the obstacles with which renewal has to contend. Usual factors impeding innovation are considered to be the high costs of renewal proposals, ignorance and lack of experience, the views of the older generation, the fear of what is new and of experiments, and respect for the past. Especially the established interests, who are better organized, act as the principal enemies of change. "The conservative tendencies in human nature are presumably stronger than the innovating tendencies." This generalization as stated by sociologists helps to explain better what is happening in the church (W. Ogburn and M. Nimkoff, 1946). We shall now take a closer look at the obstacles and limits to church reform.

3. Obstacles and Limits to Church Reform

The few theoretical starting points in sociological literature about church reform and church renewal give us additional insight into the recent developments in Dutch Catholicism. We recognize in the past very many things that in our present situation appeared unique. Although more characteristicly Dutch elements will certainly come to the fore, we are interested firstly in the structural obstacles and limits, in short, the restrictive context of reform movements in a church as old as the Roman Catholic Church.

There need not always exist a conscious desire to re-form. In its multinational character the church has had many forms of faith interpretation, of discipline, of organization, of liturgy etc. Accordingly as western society took over more and more ecclesiastical functions, and democratic freedom and cultural development increased, the leaders became more concerned about the inherent identity of the church. One often hears it put like this: the structures and forms of the church may change, but not the fundamental beliefs, the *depositum fidei*. In this way an attempt is made to define the boundaries within which reforms can be made. At one extreme is the museum-church, the preserve of a small group of tough rear guards, a national trust, morphological fundamentalism. At the other extreme is the destruction of established structures, a "floating in time," liquidation and blurring of the inherent identity for the sake of saving others. The church, as is bluntly stated in various documents of the World Council of Churches, is constantly defeating itself, its own mission. It is a "major hindrance to the work of evangelism." The continuous dynamism of reform can be typified as a continuous destructuring and restructuring in order to be maximally present in history and thus to support the people in the service of the church's real mission (J. Hoekendijk, 1963; C. Williams, 1963).

Characteristic of every reform movement are two questions: Where does the border lie between obligatory adaptation and obligatory non-adaptation? In a concrete case are only structural questions involved or fundamental beliefs as well? The first question is one for the theologians. It is a matter of interpretation, connected with the answer to the question whether or not "the environment" is threatening the self-preservation and survival of the church. In more technical terms, and as such the subject of an inquiry among West German Catholics: Is there a congruence or a dissonance between the value systems of society and church? (G. Schmidtchen, 1972). The second question is one for church authorities. Who makes authoritative, decisive pronouncements? Who decides if a reform measure, considered to be structural and as such accepted by the authorities, is in fact really carried out? These are typical of the questions regularly occupying the minds of people who are professionally connected with the church and of church members who are not indifferent, certainly at times when there is a generally felt need for church reform. Just over five years after Vatican II, G. Schmidtchen's inquiry among German Catholics showed that 45% valued unrest and striving towards reform positively. Between 15% and 18% regretted the unrest. The remainder had no clear opinion. The higher the level of cultural education and critical distance from the church, the more, this enquiry shows, reform was desired. Often both questions stimulate as well very emotional discussions. The reason is obvious: Neither question receives a clear answer. In many respects perhaps there are no clear-cut answers. We are only pointing out the factual results of reform movements which through collective lack of clarity are slowed down.

Another characteristic of church reform is: A completely new church is not built. There is rather talk of the reconstruction of the old one. Church authorities are more intent on continuity with the past than on risky pioneering for the future. Even the author of the best book "on reform" ever written by a Catholic theologian, Yves Congar (1962), warned against overdoing reform, shortly after Pope John had called for a world-wide *aggiornamento*. "One should keep in mind that the church is an existing institution, with a rich and long past...therefore one cannot begin work as if everything has to be done from the bottom up." Thus the question becomes: What can or must be renewed; and what must be preserved? The symbols of tearing down and building up have been used more often. The City of God must be cleaned up now and again, and the architects and rulers do not quite know how best to do it. Their indecision grows when the citizens, who after all have to live there, also offer suggestions. The discussions about these questions, with their side effects of polarization and insinuation, hang like a dark cloud over every reforming effort in a macro-church. L. Rogier (1968) expresses it poignantly as follows:

> Every renovation starts with demolition. Similarly it seems the church must demolish in order to be reborn. Sometimes it will seem as if a veritable demolition neurosis has overmastered leaders and followers, and then reacting against them, often grimly with foaming mouths, appear the champions of the status quo who get uneasy when confronted with so much renewal at once. Once again — by no means for the first time in the history of the church or the world — conservatism, weeping over every stone that is turned and every tree that is felled, firmly opposes a vandalism that seems to demolish for the sake of demolishing. For the rest it is easier to curb the zeal of the latter group than to convey to the former that the new generally has more sacred rights than the old. In the courtyard of the church stands a lot of dead wood, and if it is not chopped down in time, decay will eat into today's bloom and tomorrow complete decomposition will follow.

It is understandable that church leaders grow tired of all these discussions and would rather stick to what is customary. They often do not get clear advice, and they resent dicussions that, having become public, disturb the image of peace and brotherhood in the Christian church. Attempts at reconciliation usually lead to a restoration of the old situation. Church leaders are afraid of the total downfall of the church. "The ultra-conservatism of so much in the past is now counter-balanced by a kind of anarchy....Who can say where all this will end?" Thus American sociologist of religion Thomas O'Dea (1972) puts it in a recent study of the role of the Catholic intellectual in tradition. If he and many others are at a loss, how then can a comprehensive policy recommendation have a decisive influence on the bishops or the Pope in Rome? "Has the church started upon a course of deinstitutionalization that will lead to a new, more flexible, more adaptable, more creative, and more vital Catholicism? Is this deinstitutionalization the prelude to a new more appropriate institutionalization? Or has Catholicism entered upon a process of self-liquidation?" (Th. O'Dea, 1972). Elsewhere other religious sociologists already predict the end of the Roman Catholic Church: "...the loyalty is gone, the creativity is gone and the meaning is gone or at least going. The remarkable thing is that no outside foe destroyed us; we destroyed ourselves" (W. McCready and A. Greeley, 1972).

Not only church authorities quickly start hesitating when reform attempts are clearly continued. Where the "system of belief" itself, where religious life itself is concerned, creative theologians as well often begin to hesitate. Frequently they confine themselves to offering new ideas which are reconstructions of old concepts. Sometimes this is also done for tactical purposes, in order to get new thoughts across to church leaders more easily. A pluralism in structures and forms is more readily acceptable than a theological plurality. "There is certainly some truth in the well-known quip that a Catholic theologian first spends many years studying to discover something new, and then the same number of years to prove it is not new at all. Within the actual church structure a different attitude proved to have very few prospects" (T. Schoof, 1968).

Thus there are limits and obstacles to renewal movements in a universal church. To the general obstacles to renewal already mentioned can be added the following: leaving everything as it was is less tiring; new things cannot yet be demonstrated and have not proved their value; reformers usually do not agree on the methods to be used; after every "conciliar euphoria," as French authors characterized the mood during Vatican II, or after every "revival," a depression follows. It is interesting to consider whether every re-formation should be followed by a counter-reformation to restore the church's balance in its progress through history.

4. Conditions for Church Reform Without Schism

How can a macro-church like the Roman Catholic Church be reformed without having large groups withdraw or, through formal authoritative declarations, placing them outside the official church structure? Modern church leaders are more intent on fusions and ecumenical contacts than on schisms. All the same, this synopsis of questions in connection with structural characteristics of church renewal is important. There is also an informal kind of schism of groups and individuals who have drifted from actively participating church membership to an indifferent, alienated atti-tude. In quite a number of publications, especially in Italian news-papers, Dutch Catholicism was warned against a schism. The re-newal movement in The Netherlands was supposed to lead to a secession from the church universal. There are other church mem-bers who, despite feelings of uneasiness, the slowness of renewal, and the disappointing statements by church authorities, are willing to go on working for internal church renewal without running the risk of schism.

In 1950 French theologian Yves Congar published a book on true and false reform in the church. This Black Friar monk was both an ecumenic and ecclesiologist. In 1937 he published *Chrétiens Désunis* the first volume of the now-famous series *Unam Sanctam*, and up to the Second Vatican Council he had difficulties with ecclesiastical authorities. He bore them with great patience, and, as he once said himself, he was convinced of Lacordaire's words that "thunderstorm and unrest are the best times to sow and to plant." Summarizing Congar's conditions for reform, we reach the following conclusions.

The reformer should retain his solidarity with the church he wants to renew. Congar calls this the primacy of love, pastoral concern, being bound to the totality. He especially addresses him-self to people who either through personal or professional interest often reflect on the church: scholars and particularly theologians. They are used to taking a detached view of their subject. This is their habit as intellectuals. They objectivize. But it is exactly this objectivity which suggests aloofness, as if one does not belong to the church. He reproaches this type of reformer for having no feeling for the concrete church. Apostolic and pastoral concerns have, as it were, a regulating function and an orientation toward the lives of real people, towards their daily doings. They also require a sense of responsibility for the concrete consequences of rash action. Reformers are always biased. Progressivism is justified by the same reality in which it must find its rules and measures. Everything excessive and onesided, everything isolated from society as a whole, bears the seed of schism. To this Congar also attaches two conditions, patience and respect for delay. Impatience may completely spoil a reform movement. If a reform movement is to find its outlet within the church, it must be accompanied by a spiritual disposition of patience. Heresy is largely a result of purely intellectual attitudes, of too rash wording, the products of the dialectical mind. A real development of tradition is beyond one man's powers. It must always be the work of a generation and of the church as a whole. Real adaptation is not a mechanical process, that is completed from one day to the next.

Besides these conditions for intellectual involvement in church reform there is the relationship to authority. Congar clearly confirms our previous observation that ecclesiastical authorities primarily want to guarantee continuity with the past. Like all living things, the church is both continuous and changing. Recalling the distinction between the structure of the church and its life, one observes that the central organs and more particularly the hierarchy have as their primary task to safeguard the continuity of the church in its fundamental principles. The authority must always sanction the innovations that occur on the periphery. In order to prevent a reform movement, originating from the needs of a certain time or place, from moving in a deviating direction it must be given both the freedom to develop and the approval of authorities who test, direct, moderate and correct this movement. If this movement is really to become a movement within the church, it should develop along the fixed lines of church structure and be authorized by the central leaders, taken over by them and incorporated into the whole of church life. Ecclesiastical authorities also have obligations with regard to reform movements. The duty of submission, resting upon the reformer, is counterbalanced by the obligation of the church as such, and particularly of those in charge of its central government, to pay attention to the appeals directed toward them. St. Bernard told Pope Eugene III: "How long do you refuse to listen to the grumbling of the whole world?"

If Rome, or as Congar puts it, the *Urbs,* is to be open to the voice of the world, the *Orbis,* it is necessary that the central administrative organs really represent the great human values of the church and the great tendencies in the world.

Besides this role definition of authorities and intellectuals in the reform process, Congar also offers some suggestions for methodology: Be prepared for resistance; in the beginning there is always opposition. Give the authorities the freedom and the opportunity to take decisions themselves. Do not force these decisions by a *via facti,* through *faits accomplis.* Together with his remarks on patience and delay, Congar opts for the so-called "long way." But he admits that very many things that started *via facti,* have gained recognition in the church, then developed into customs, and finally were incorporated into the body of law. Too great and passive patience on the side of the authorities he considers reprehensible (Congar, 1950).

5. Central Elements in Church Renewal

What are the central elements, the hinges as it were, in the church as a whole that provide for continuity as well as change, for survival as well as permanent reform? The leaders, the authorities, the hierarchy on behalf of the entire community; the thinkers, the house intellectuals, especially the theologians, the ecclesiologists, religious sociologists, canon lawyers, who consider the church in its entirety. H. Schelsky (1965) mentions three levels of change in the church: changes in the church's organizational forms and methods, changes in the contents of the Christian doctrine, and finally changes in the religious experience of the church members themselves. J. Hadden (1970) speaks of a threefold crisis: the crisis in meaning and purpose of the church, the crisis of authority, and the crisis in theology. P. Berger (1967) sees a crisis mainly in theology, together with a crisis in the church's institutionalization. Strikingly these three modern sociologists of religion again stress the structural elements we found in earlier sociological studies and in Congar's concepts.

Every reform movement, concretely seen, will be confronted by these structural elements: decisions *and* interpretations about the role of the church in the world. In fact, the church authorities and ecclesiastical scholars must continually take a stand in relation to each other, in relation to the church as a whole, and in solidarity with the church as a whole. Every reform movement is a quest for truth or for a new aspect of reality. It is an evolution rather than a revolution, for a revolution renews through offering a completely new alternative. M. Blondel has described this process as follows: "The progress of religious truth is like running water seeking a bed, that in its innumerable meanderings encounters hundreds of obstacles, flows backward, rises higher and higher, breaks through repeatedly, and flowing on, unchecked, is driven by the very energy it collected at all those obstacles" (T. Schoof, 1968).

There is a kind of balance of power between the needs of the authorities for continuity and the creative endeavours of the scholars. They correct each other and, in case they do not sufficiently represent the church as a whole, processes of renewal start at the base of the church pyramid or, more geographically, on the periphery. But this periphery can as well be the slums at the foot of Vatican Hill as a diocese in Brazil. In this respect church reform appears to be democratic both ideally and by persuasion. If a man wants to belong to a large church, he must be simultaneously an individual Christian and a church member, an individual and a social being. There is always a tension between the greatest possible solidarity with the church and the greatest possible existential-cultural differentiation. The structural principles of church reform are so delicate exactly because they are balanced between solidarity, collegiality with the church universal and cultural, religious, theological pluralism (G. Szczesny, 1972).

This balancing, this continual task of digesting impulses from "right" and "left" slows down progress. Moderation and patience, a willingness to understand and compromise, and a dialogue in mutual loyalty seem to be more profitable for progress than radicalizing points of view. The church is an unremitting process. A procession! Not a matter of all or nothing, but a prudent walk through history. It is like the "jumping procession" at Echternach in Luxemburg: two steps forward (progression) and one step backward (regression), by which the motley cortege still moves slowly forward. In the last sentences of his study on reform movements in the Church of England, K. Thompson (1970) says that this church has only been able to preserve its own identity along with its internal pluralism by following a *via media* with respect to authority, doctrine and organization. This *via media* he calls " the crucial limiting factor." It may be the Way of the Cross.

CHAPTER III

Social Change and Church Renewal

The Catholic Church of The Netherlands does not live in a religious ghetto, but in the context of Dutch society. This society takes the form of a modern welfare state. The national government follows a moderately progressive socio-political policy; in the most recent period this trend has become even more accentuated. Many institutions and organizations follow a modern policy. The significant changes in society lay great stress on the conditions for good management in transition situations. It is noticeable that the processes of change and the reactions to them in civil government, in big enterprise, in educational institutions, in health services, in the administration of justice and in the military establishment, are, in a certain way, just as prevalent in the Catholic Church.

We shall first take a look at how the Catholic Church reacts to social changes in modern society. Then, we will pay further attention to church management. Finally we hope to compare the strategic manoeuvrability of multinational institutions and of the Roman Catholic Church.

1. Church and Society

The church does not only exist in society, but society also penetrates into the church. M. Lindqvist (1971) made a study for Europe of the "efforts for functional and organizational reform" in the various types of Christian churches. By means of interviews he also studied the situation in the Vatican and in the Dutch churches. Besides the increasing ecumenical cooperation among the churches, he mentions a second element which he encountered in all large churches. "The social situation is very similar in all the European countries. Industrialization, urbanization and rapidly increasing mobility within and across national boundaries are everywhere in evidence. Social problems have thus become common to all communities." But then he elaborates very systematically no less than twenty factors that are determinant for the crisis in European churches. Whoever wants to be convinced of the general and by no means specifically Dutch character of the church crisis, need only take a closer look at these factors. The steep decline in church attendance and other forms of ecclesiastical participation is very clearly related to the degree to which parishes have been urbanized. The churches have not succeeded in settling internal conflicts. Theological pluralism has significantly increased. Quite a number of basis groups have spontaneously arisen, which first worked for church reform but later on concentrated more on social problems. The role of priest and minister is unclear. The pastors are specializing more and more, but there is a great shortage of new manpower. In many churches, Lindqvist writes, the situation is very serious, and still continues to deteriorate. The laity must be reminded over and over that church membership also entails obligations. He also points to the growth of parishes, the increasing need for research and, naturally, the growing financial problems, among other things with regard to building churches.

Everyone who is familiar with the ecclesiastical situation in The Netherlands will agree: this survey fits exactly with the image of the Roman Catholic Church in The Netherlands. In fact it is a description of the predicament of the Christian churches in Western Europe.

What is now the tragedy here? These problems have been posed repeatedly. Innumerable studies have been devoted to them. As early as 1909 Austrian prelate Heinrich Swoboda started calling attention to the problems of the church in modern society, especially in the big cities of Western Europe. People kept sapping the reserves of the past without preparing for the task of the church in a new society. In all those years, which witnessed the birth of church sociology and later of a more fundamental sociology of religion, it seems that the church has not been able to find an appropriate answer to the steadily more pointed questions. The most traditional answer to all these questions has been an increasing isolationism. And this is exactly the island-situation which makes the distance between church and society ever more difficult to bridge. In his fascinating study of the church in the metropolis G. Winter (1963) mentions the extreme importance of breaking the church open, as it were, by social pressure and convincing it at last that it has lost all touch with the dynamism of modern society.

All this has been observed repeatedly. But alongside this phenomenon, which already has become something normal, has appeared a second type of change which in The Netherlands played an important role in the changes in the internal structure of the Catholic Church. This growing openness of organizations towards society can be characterized as follows. The openness with which organizations are now confronted is not so much a matter of whether or not the leaders decide to open themselves to the environment, but a "being broken open" by that environment. Organizations are hereby confronted by new groups not only from outside, but also internally. Even the most reliable and actively participating members formulate new demands for internal and external activities. The leadership is asked to take account of generally accepted social processes. This applies especially to the process of democratization. Its principal features are a flow of information from the top to bottom levels and vice versa; free access for everybody to leadership positions; the search for possibilities to involve all organization members in preparing and making policy decisions. An increasing number of people are taking an active part in these "breaking and entering" operations. "The traditional areas of activity, functions, methods and prerogatives of organizations are now questioned or challenged by people other than the organization's leaders. Those other people claim the right and the duty to break through the existing spheres of influence. This process of change towards openness is, moreover, occurring at a moment when many organizations, also within the existing framework of their own domain, are already facing fundamental and rapid changes and the need "to find adequate answers to them" (J. van Hoof, 1972).

Factors explaining this "activation" of organization members or outsiders are of a general nature, but also played an important role in the Catholic Church in The Netherlands. The Netherlands were becoming urbanized; the educational level rose; prosperity grew; leisure time increased. The need for a "coming of age" grew stronger; people wanted to be involved, to help make decisions. The leadership was criticized, and all kinds of important traditional values were relativized. All this makes it understandable that the Dutch Catholics, who were with increasing speed and to an ever larger extent taking part in these processes of change, came to force, as it were, the openness of their own traditional bulwark, the Roman Catholic Church. It also occurred just at a moment when among the top leaders of the church there was a growing awareness of the need for structural changes. In addition, the trend towards activation was even stronger among Catholic intellectuals, because they had to overcome a more "closed" type of Catholicism than was to be found in comparable churches in other countries. This put church leaders under heavy pressure. They came to realize that leadership should reflect the reasonable wishes of church members rather than their own autonomous actions. The Dutch Catholics became increasingly sensitive to the legitimacy, the credibility, of ecclesiastical leadership rather than to its legality. Accordingly, the policy of the Dutch bishops was directed towards imposing as few sanctions as possible and avoiding drastic statements via "pastoral letters." They hoped the faithful would follow and obey voluntarily. Through this attitude the trust in the bishops' guidance grew much greater than many an observer from abroad can imagine. But it presupposed that the bishops could maintain a sufficient amount of freedom to practice this kind of leadership.

2. Church and Welfare State

Meanwhile a new tendency was growing which forced the church to engage also in external social criticism. The Netherlands like a number of other western countries, is a "welfare state." The state assumes the responsibility for a minimum of health service, economic security and "civilized living." There are also reasonable opportunities for social and cultural education. This does not mean that everybody is prosperous, and certainly not that everybody is happy. The Netherlands are not a paradise. Careerism, increasing production, the threats to environment, the exhaustion of natural resources, all of these aspects of the modern consumer society are being criticized more and more. The social change, we all eagerly demanded to ensure a good future, all of a sudden no longer appears to be an absolute ideal. The many institutions that have promoted change, often independently or in competition, are now seeking mutual contacts in order to establish cooperation. It seems as if they themselves create the problems they must solve. They feel helpless.

Here the church faces again a new responsibility. There is a flight from the future into the present, an inclination towards reflection and contemplation. A new asceticism, which no ecclesiastical Lenten law could have achieved is arriving (J. van Doorn,

1972). The crisis brought about by the modern "concerned" state causes a kind of confusion without perspective. F. van Heek (1972), who has pointed out the above-mentioned aspects of the modern state, concludes that there is a need for a comprehensive ideology that like Russian or Chinese communism offers an alternative system. Since industrial and technical innovations have proved unable to change man "from within," a certain degree of charismatic inspiration might be of great importance (F. van Heek, 1972; P. ter Hoeven, 1971).

Completely in harmony with this trend the Dutch bishops, after all the internal ecclesiastical strife of recent years, have started looking outward, and have devoted their Lenten Pastoral of 1973 to the consumer society under Gospel criticism. Clearly the church is not adapting itself but is actually taking a critical stand. In other countries as well such socially critical groups are operating within the churches. Sometimes they are rejected by both the church and the establishment. Within the history of the Catholic Church in The Netherlands, this is a clear example of a reform movement, originally fostered by the young and the so-called "critical Catholics", that was later sanctioned in a pastoral letter.

In a study of "The Crisis in Dutch Catholicism" Daniel de Lange, as early as 1966, pointed out this development. The new generation shows little interest in discussions about the essence of the church. They ask what the church can do to change society.

> For this generation being a Catholic has stopped being a social determinant to which one cannot but conform. For this generation being a Christian has become a matter of life and death. They feel constantly compelled to compare customary forms and solutions with the Gospel and concrete historical reality. To them, the church is primarily the church when it leaves the protection of its own atmosphere, its traditions and its climate, to enter, in servility and defenselessness, the big and small realities of the moment. The big realities: the global questions that must be answered today and tomorrow; the small realities: the day-to-day life of the "man in the street" who is in danger of becoming alienated from himself in the historical maelstrom, and who has a right to expect that the Gospel will give him back to himself.

3. Denominational Organizations

It seems that in this way an entirely new motivation or — as van Heek asks for — a new ideology is arriving by which as a practicing

Christian or as a church one is directed toward the problems of society. This development is connected also to the gradual process of transition from a strongly clerical, vertical pluralism towards new forms of "denominationalism," which are typical for the Catholic Church in The Netherlands. It is an area least understandable to foreigners: Catholic newspapers, universities, hospitals, Catholic welfare organizations, trade unions, Catholic broadcasting and television corporations, which historically acted to reinforce the group cohesion of Catholics, are at present becoming sally-ports to society at large. Although since 1954 when the Dutch bishops issued their last socio-ecclesiastical directives, they have exerted no more direct influence on the structure of political, social and cultural organizations, they have kept the name "Catholic." A tendency was growing to deconfessionalize or "de-columnize." To an ever-increasing extent the leaders of those organizations were assuming their own responsibility, without any approval by clergy or hierarchy. Later however the question was discussed anew whether it was really advisable to depart from these institutional and religiously inspired starting points.

Sometimes one finds now the same tensions as were present at the initial stage of the development in church—society relations. During the early years of this century socially engaged priests like Ariëns and Poels were often attacked by conservatives. Nowadays priests are blamed for occupying themselves too much with peace problems, with industry and labour relations, and with the military. It is very likely that here again they are preparing the way for a new sense of responsibility among the laity.

In a comprehensive report on the problems of social organizations on a denominational basis, edited by R. Cornelissen (1973), the section on welfare work is carefully worded. Will a certain vision of man and society always be necessary for welfare activities? Is there not a need for pastoral labor, resting on a scientific and methodical basis, in relation to social care? We quote here two unanswered questions.

> Why, for instance, do some people (in our case Catholics), who have long since become accustomed to the phenomenon of interdenominational or non-denominational organization for welfare care, return to the Catholic group with a yearning that cannot be qualified as mere home-sickness; are they asking "the church" for answers to welfare problems; are they looking for a Catholic ideology? In our opinion this has to do with the fact that secular welfare care, the planning of social and cultural change includ-

ed, misses the motivation behind the contributions of its people. Concern for social justice and professional ethics do not seem to be sufficient. Welfare care is not only a matter of technology or law, nor is it morally indifferent. What view of the world, what view of man do we have? Where is the sacred fire gone which inspires the activities of, e.g. socialists and Maoists? Where is the power that inspires Christians, Catholics?

Another question, connected to the foregoing, is about the value system or systems on which social and cultural change (social and cultural planning included) are to be based. Up till now Christians have failed to present an unambiguous model of society-to-come. Wherever technology and organization, as well as legislation have made progress, we find that the development of society is not tackled fundamentally enough and that the dangers now threatening people's lives cannot be averted. We ascribe this to the people's lack of willingness to work on it, to a motivation that lacks strength, and to our human conscience that lets us down. We should consider if, in the present phase of social and cultural development, a Catholic contribution of values can (already) be dispensed with.

These two unanswered questions offer a snapshot of the actual relation between social change and church renewal in The Netherlands. Dutch Catholicism has been blamed from time to time — among others by the English "Slant" group — for not showing enough social commitment. We were said to keep within the boundaries of the allotted territory of only slowly changing Catholic social organizations, which was not done to this extent elsewhere. We were said to have no priests like Daniel and Philip Berrigan. But we do have Dutch missionaries tortured in Brazilian prisons because of their social protest. There is a Shalom Movement which has crossed the church's threshold and, with a Christian motivation, become an institute for social change. There is a Septuagint Group, with an ecumenical character, which goes on working on social issues. There is a group of priests active in industry and business.

Among the Dutch Catholics there is certainly not a broad consensus about the church's social commitment. There is mutual criticism. We already mentioned that the parish clergy are sometimes blamed for laying too much stress in preaching and liturgical texts on the responsibility of the faithful concerning problems of peace and social justice. Many local communities prove that, living in the world, they are conscious of the duty to serve their fellowmen. This is usually the case in communities that have grown from so-called student parishes (chaplaincies) in university towns. On the other hand, there are also groups that do not take the social developments seriously; they want the church to stick to what they call purely religious things.

4. Church and Management

Modern industrialized and urbanized society has compelled the churches to revise their management. Not very long ago the Catholic Church received high grades for its international management. The *New York Times* of 23 January 1956 reported on a survey made by the American Institute of Management that had studied religious institutions in the U.S.A. The results showed that "...viewed against the background of modern business corporations, the management practices of religious organizations are appallingly archaic." But the Roman Catholic Church was an exception. It was given an A-group qualification for efficient administration. "Its numerical grade was 88, but since 75 is considered excellent and the Standard Oil Company of New Jersey was at the top of the class with 90 plus, the church's mark was well up in the *cum laude* category" (P. Harrison, 1959).

Fifteen years later I received, via its Dutch branch office, a handbook published by the management consultants, Peat, Harwick, Mitchell and Company in collaboration with the American National Conference of Catholic Bishops (NCCB) and devoted to "diocesan accounting and financial reporting." It is an impressive analysis of the entire financial set-up and problems of the richest Catholic church in the world. All pastoral activities are analysed from the point of view of finance. Cardinal Terence Cook, archbishop of New York and chairman of the financial committee, ends his preface as follows: "Finally, we thank God for giving us the members of the Advisory Committee and the Project Team who were not only dedicated but also efficient. The Catholic Church in the United States has benefited indeed by their talents, experience and wisdom."

On 6 April 1972 the archdiocese of New York published the results in a special issue of *The Catholic News*. Here, too, there is a preface, telling the "story" of the financial beneficence of the Catholics in the 408 parishes of the diocese. The preface reports what could not be counted: "The story begins with men and women, who, for love of God, trained themselves to prefer the advantage of others to their own; and it unfolds itself in uncountable acts of virtue. The depth of that goodness is known only to God." The 408 parishes have a total membership of 1.8 million who in the previous year had brought in about 95 million dollars. All parish premises taken together represent a value of 544 million dollars.

On 28 October 1972 W. McCready and A. Greeley, both connected with the National Opinion Research Center in Chicago, wrote that they need not sketch the dramatic development of American Catholicism since 1960. The exodus of priests and religious believers has become massive. An institution which, seen from the outside, shows a "high level of organizational control," apparently suffers from serious internal decay. Bishops and religious journalists, they wrote, appear to know exactly what the faithful are thinking even though their opinions have not been asked.

And now comes the big contrast with the exact knowledge of the financial situation sketched above which the church authorities have relativized as an indication of religious zeal. "Since the American hierarchy has made the alarming discovery that social research frequently discovers unpleasant things, it is most unlikely that there will be any serious attempt on their part to study the changing attitudes and behavior of the laity. An organization with fifty million members will blunder into the future with only the haziest notions about its present condition" (W. McCready and A. Greeley, 1972).

We have paid such extensive attention to this form of management in order to clarify one of the central problems of church management. In point of fact the church is judged to be a corporation in the traditional sense: What are the financial revenues, and how well does the financial administration function? But in modern enterprises research has already been given a much wider purpose. The production process is analysed from the point of view of setting, change, human factors, and management—personnel relations. If at this moment a study with this much broader scope were to be conducted in the Catholic Church, the management score would probably be much lower. Even in the United States where sociological research is so popular, fundamental data about the processes of change in the Catholic Church appear to be wanting. It is understandable that in a paper read to an audience who were quite familiar with the canonical structure of the Roman Catholic Church, namely the Canon Law Society of America, Donald Warwick (1967) remarked that some formal organization and bureaucracy is indispensable for the church to function properly in modern society. But to this he adds: "The root question therefore is how much organization and what types can be used not only to improve the administrative machinery of the Church, but also to promote community and spontaneity."

Only in the latest phase of recent organizational development did the Catholic Church of The Netherlands stimulate a centralized financial policy. The church is not rich, although many a foreigner will be jealous of the subsidy system by which many activities that can be called Catholic, such as education and health care, receive financial aid from civil authorities on the same footing as other religious denominations and sometimes humanistic organizations. On the other hand, since its establishment in 1945 the Katholiek Sociaal-Kerkelijk Instituut (KSKI: Catholic Demographic Society) for statistics, sociography, sociology and planning at the Hague has conducted quite a number of studies and research projects which have been able to describe the situation of the Dutch Catholics. These studies have certainly contributed to the clarification and stimulation of the rapid processes of change in Dutch Catholicism. Various institutes of higher education have also developed research projects, and studies have been made by more commercially interested people such as publishers of periodicals. A complete bibliographical survey would cover dozens of pages.

5. Tensions Between Old and New Church Structures

The Dutch episcopate was put under exceptional pressure because the existing church structure was insufficiently flexible to react to rapid changes. On the one hand they had the duty to adapt to this established and internationally valid church structure. On the other, time and again this structure proved to be a hindrance to flexible management. The territorial principle was discarded because in a small country like The Netherlands isolated diocesan policies are unacceptable and difficult to realize. Numerous instances in the area of religious instruction, catechesis, liturgy and ecumenism had been organized on a national level. The clerical character of the church was strongly relativized by the increasing influence of the laity. The complexity of policy problems required manpower and advisors who were primarily experts. It was then relatively unimportant whether or not they were ordained priests. Episcopal authority was caught in the tension between centralization and decentralization, between the strong autonomy of ecclesiastical authority and the nearly complete delegation of it. The vertical-hierarchical structure was "lowered" more and more by the increasing need for and desirability of a horizontal structure in which command and obedience had to make room for consultation and cooperation. Thus the bishops exercised their authority on the basis of two conflicting concepts of government, sometimes characterized as "having to sit on two chairs at the same time."

The Roman Curia asks that the traditional values be maintained. Modern society asks for new values. If the bishops should not accept these new values, they would irrevocably end in isolation (H. Laan, 1967). Often the Dutch bishops as well could only nominally opt for a reform of church structures. Later on we shall see that they even advocated reform, but at the same time already knew that their call for structural changes or their promises to the faithful could hardly, if at all, be realized in the present system. In point of fact the structures were only resistant because the central ecclesiastical authorities did not allow any changes and via curial interventions continually obstructed attempts in this direction.

What the Dutch bishops wanted was by no means exceptional. The aims had been formulated repeatedly, among others by Karl Rahner (1968) in his study of church strategy and the general principles of centralization and decentralization in the church. He points out that faith is not incompatible with planning. A naive trust in ancient customs can lead to being "downtrodden." "The need for such a general strategy (which, of course, has never been absent in the church and its top leaders, although it was rather implicitly applied) can only be discussed here in very abstract and general terms." The practical elaboration of such a broad strategy of the church and its institutions would have to take account of "the concrete possibilities and a sensible historical continuity with the customary ways of church government." This widely respected and appreciated theologian has put it quite beautifully. But probably again too abstractly, too generally, taking too little account of the urgent need for realization; realizing too little what might happen if the bishops of a certain country, on the basis of their own authentic pastoral responsibility, were to initiate very concrete structural changes. The existing situation required that Dutch bishops make changes which are not allowed in a local church. Again continuity with the past served to halt the implementation of necessary changes. Again an unconvincing defensive attitude was chosen instead of realistic adaptation. How many abstract, nominal and theoretical expositions there may exist about church management, the actual implementation, the decision to effect the necessary changes within the legal framework of the church as a multinational organization, seem nearly impossible.

It was only recently that acting Secretary of State archbishop G. Benelli (1973), who has been working for five years on the laborious reform of the Roman Curia, gave a report on the results gained so far. He did this in a strikingly realistic talk during the third meeting of the European Bishops' Symposium at Augsburg. He admitted that there are still many imperfections. He advocated cultural exchange, more power for the national bishops' conferences, more technical equipment, and an adaptation to the rhythm of the modern world. Very little was said about the position of the papal representatives in the various nunciatures. Nothing at all was said about the way in which episcopal nominations are made. That changes will have to be introduced was made clear in his literal statement: "Nowadays things are changing so quickly that the structures and methods of the (Roman) Curia must also change continuously, if they are really to be of service."

6. Bishops as Managers

In the Dutch Catholic newspaper *De Tijd* of 12 May 1966 the following editorial comment was given on the fact that within one year three young Dutch bishops had died: "We think that in some Dutch dioceses a series of administrative shortcomings can be pointed out which make the necessary 'managerial work' of the bishops unnecessarily burdensome. From the point of view of administration and organization the present church province is badly equipped....The kind of martyrdom to which the bishops are now sentenced is fatal for the faithful, but probably also for heaven. Bishops, too, deserve a humane way of life." Trying to find the background for this remark we discover that in a modern and committed church lacking an adequate management structure the bishops have an extremely difficult task.

There is no official training for bishops, and even in the most recent Vatican documents no concrete directives are given concerning how a bishop in the above-mentioned situation should give guidance. In fact he is forced to look at the orientation of his predecessor or his neighbouring colleague. If he wants to take an independent position, because in fact his colleagues have been repudiated through his appointment, great uncertainty can develop. This applies especially when he feels obliged to dismiss assistants who know the diocese and have experience in the leadership of the diocese. His responsibility is strongly determined by the vertical organizational structure in which he has only to show obedience to Rome, and in which ultimately the decision-making power within his diocese depends only on his personal vision as bishop.

Most church leaders are unable to handle discussions. They get irritated quickly and often consider criticism an attack on their function or person. Bishops who interpret and organize their leadership in this way have little opportunity to relax, have "unprotected" agendas, and have little time to listen patiently. It is often tragic to hear them addressed as absolute monarchs while personally they neither are nor want to be that.

This characterization by no means applies in general to the Dutch bishops, but is based upon a wide international experience. In The Netherlands there have been various auxiliary institutes that have tried to assist the bishops in running diocesan or national affairs. At present much better conditions are available for modern management. Priests and laity in The Netherlands have grown used to a new type of government. Especially since the Second Vatican Council a new view of the church clearly has emerged in which the focus is mainly on fundamentals: the church-believers and -goers. It is a matter of an inspiring rather than a regulating, a consulting rather than an authoritarian church, a church more concerned for the world's needs than for its own survival. A survey among Dutch priests has made it possible to test this shift, from a traditional image of the church to a new conception, which is against a too absolutistic authority, against church-centredness or institutional self-interest, and towards a preference for continual critical reflection on religious beliefs without institutional control. About 75 percent of the Dutch priests under 35 years of age favour this new image of the church. Parish priests scored a percentage of about 55 (JTS, Institute for Applied Sociology, 1969). The total image of the church, and accordingly the management of the church is still very much in flux. Whether church leaders can manoeuver strategically enough within the current opinions about the church as a multinational enterprise will now be studied further.

7. The Church as a Multinational Religious Institute

In a modern society like The Netherlands ecclesiastical leaders, bishops, are compared with managers, and the church's efficiency and planning are readily put on a par with those of big enterprises. When church authorities present some truths and values as "obligatory," they explicitly want to distinguish these from so-called policy or pastoral matters. On the one hand it is said that democracy in the church cannot go so far that the faithful themselves, by majority vote, decide what are central points of doctrine. On the other, it is suggested that when issuing doctrinal statements the college of bishops should keep an eye on what is alive among the faithful, not only and exclusively by registering what the church members think, but also by judging it and then making an official evaluation of it.

In connection with doctrinal questions the church is less easily compared to a modern business enterprise than in connection with policy questions. Concerning the latter, as an institution with structures for giving and receiving information, with a policy program, with selected, trained and paid personnel, with delegated powers and coordinated activities, in all these respects the church is comparable to a business enterprise. In his book *Managing the Church*, W. Beveridge (1971) flatly states, "The Church is an organization just like any other."

There are new socio-religious theories which pay more attention to this very relation between church, religion and faith. They warn against "overchurching," and one might say they plead for "underchurching." They do not mean that the church should not be a good and efficient institution using modern techniques, but rather they want to emphasize the relative, relational value of the church. This occurs also in other sectors of life, in which institutions try to meet general human needs. In a later phase those institutions tend to become independent, to evolve morphologies and from this point of view to regulate and control the needs of the people. The people then become subservient to the institution; the institution no longer serves the people, it is no longer "of" the people. The demand for education, for the free intellectual development of mankind, can lead to the establishment of institutions for higher education. But these institutions should not monopolize education in a way that suggests that outside the schools there are no opportunities to learn. Here the instrumental value of schools must be relativized. Likewise, charity and justice can be institutionalized into social legislation, but charity and justice can also be practised outside this legislative structure, and even more intensely. Thus the love between a man and a woman need not be expressed and fulfilled exclusively in the institute of a publicly recognized marriage.

In the past the church has too often proceeded from needs which the faithful were assumed to have but which were not really there. In some cases more needs were thrust upon the faithful than really existed. There was more control than stimulation. Now that the Christian or Catholic church in many countries has lost its monopoly, it is beginning to legitimate this situation by recognizing religious freedom and defining the church as the "People of God" in which all of the faithful are considered equal. The Spanish sociologist of religion, J. Estruch (1972) has elaborated this line of thought further. Firstly he apologizes for his possible "disrespectful" treatment of the church as a religious institution. As an institution beside so many others, the church must legitimate itself. The church simply has to compete, and the church members are becoming the critical consumers whom the church as an institute must accommodate. "Always using a terminology that does not mean to be 'irreverent' but which offers the advantage of being enormously flexible, we would say that defining the church as the 'People of God' amounts to admitting that the church has become a 'consumers' cooperative.'' This approach provides additional possibilities for comparing the church, even in matters of doctrine, with a modern enterprise which must also reckon with the needs of the critical consumer. Such a scheme of interpretation need not threaten the sacral character of the church as a religious institution.

Application of this to the Roman Catholic Church illuminates the relation between central government and local church, a relation that played such an important role in the recent developments in The Netherlands. The more "local" a church is, the less distance there is between the ministers and the wishes and needs of the faithful. The churches in a country, a diocese, a local parish are best equipped to represent the faithful. At the same time a local pastor must deal with the person at a hierarchically higher level. What Y. Congar said about the priests during the Vatican Council, "the priests are crushed between the laity and the bishops" can, *mutatis mutandis*, be applied here: the bishops of local churches or national episcopates are crushed between the central church government in Rome and their own local congregation. They are not sitting on two chairs. They are falling between two stools. In other words: local enterprises have much better opportunities to see what the public wants than top managers of multinational corporations in a far-off country. But in reality the "national management" has insufficient room for making policy.

How can these two requirements be reconciled? An understanding encounter and compliance with the wishes of the faithful is attractive and furthers community spirit. The centrally-organized imposition of uniform directives promotes the identity and continuity of the church as a multinational organization. Warwick (1967) calls this the central sociological problem:

> In my view the most basic sociological problem facing the Church is that of reconciling the incompatibilities of community and formal organization....Here, then, we see the sociological dilemma in the contemporary Roman Catholic Church. Given its highly centralized structure, the demands for new services arising from the Second Vatican Council, and pressures from all sides for the modernization of its operations, the Vatican will in all likelihood retain most of the elements of formal organization which it now possesses, and add others. This Paulatine modernization process will be justified on the grounds that it will enable the Church to "do more" and do it better. However, a latent effect of increased centralization (and ironically, perhaps, of better services from the Vatican) will be a continued and geometrically progressive decay of the sense of community in the Church, reflected in widespread defections of clergy, religious, and laity.

How can we curtail centralistic control, how can we replace sanction by conviction, how can we avoid giving the faithful the impression that the "real Church" is somewhere far off and directed by foreigners? This theme in its entirety has dominated discussions in The Netherlands over the past years. What is the proper competency of the local bishop; what is his relation with the world episcopate; what is the Pope's competency; are the heads of the Roman congregations in fact the Pope's executors, on a par or even higher than local bishops, or are they staff advisors? Nominally and theoretically these problems have been discussed frequently, among other things at the first symposium of the European Bishops' Conference held at Noordwijkerhout (Netherlands) in 1967. Attempts to bring about changes are often misinterpreted by the top leaders of the church, exactly because of their high positions in Rome which have alienated them from reality. The collection of information on this reality, partly via diplomatic nuncios or newspaper clippings, is very imperfect. Attempts at more decentralization are often interpreted as sacrilegious. Then the central government reacts very drastically, because of its lack of institutional self-confidence. The Catholics in a local church then begin to have less trust in the central government. It is a vicious circle. "We are, so to speak, in a magic circle that can only be broken by an explosion," writes O. Schreuder (1969), adding, "If there were only five cardinals who would unanimously resist the Roman Curia! But where are these five just men to be found in Europe?"

In this description of the relation between central government and local church weak points are easy to see. Dialogue, a definite pressure from below, a tenacity for fundamental starting points, can clarify and change these tensions and obscurities into competency. It might be good now to draw a comparison with secular multinational enterprises and to see how great the tensions are in enterprises such as Shell, Unilever and Philips that spread from the U.S.A., or from The Netherlands or Britain, over the whole world. According to a study by H. Perlmutter (1969) a number of American and European top managers mentioned the following difficulties:

— a mutual distrust between the native and foreign functionaries within the business corporation;
— a resistance to give "foreigners" top functions at the headquarters or other key positions;
— nationalistic tendencies leading to friction among the personnel;
— the immobility of top executives. Many competent collaborators prefer to work where they have been born and bred, and they are not very keen on international transfers;
— communication problems caused by differences in language and cultural background.

Every high Italian Curia executive will immediately recognize these problems. Here is also the source of many communication breakdowns between the nunciatures and local bishops. Perhaps the methods used in Rome to solve these problems are still to one-sided. B. Euser (1972), a Dutch expert in the field of multinational enterprises, says, "Effective organization is a matter of life and death for multinationals. An organization model once chosen is not an unchangeable mass: Modifications in internal and external circumstances will have to find their repercussion in either different or adapted organizational forms." The Catholic Church, the local bishops and the Roman Curia will have to go through a process of learning dialogue and collegiality. This process also includes seeking and experimenting with other forms of relations between central government and local churches. Patience and time play an important role here.

8. Strategic Manoeuvrability

It has already been said often: the Catholic Church is in a difficult period of transition as regards its structure. The more modern the society in which the church lives, as in the case of the Dutch Catholic Church, the more frequently crisis phenomena will crop up, and the more there is a need, also in The Netherlands, to discover how the ship of the church can be steered clear of these dangerous rocks. For businesses a study method is in development which tries to find out how "strategic behaviour" of a company can be systematically prepared, and what consequences this has for the company's organizational set-up.

It is impossible to apply all findings in this new field of study completely to the Roman Catholic Church, and to take stock of how they have already been applied in The Netherlands. But we shall make a few observations, guided by the excellent comprehensive study by J. Klingen on *Strategic Manoeuvrability and Strategic Management* (1973).

Continuous adaptation to the "surroundings" is called strategic behaviour. If this is normative, then the social needs define the systems to be applied. In the preceding section we have already discussed this. The extent to which strategic behaviour is possible is called by Klingen "strategic manoeuvrability." This freedom of movement is limited by, among other things, competition, the time needed for the development of new products, and the appointment of adequate management and personnel. This is a time-consuming affair. We can immediately apply the description here to the church as a multinational institution: competing ideologies, the personnel problem, particularly with a view to functioning in this transition period, and, finally, the time element. "The ability of the top management to shift to other problems than the ones they are daily confronted with is an important element, often underestimated. Top management is not so flexible as is often supposed; it is usually very much bound to experience acquired over the years in a certain branch of industry." It seems from this that people who actually hold managerial functions are often required to meet too high standards, too quickly. There also seem to be limitations to the reformability of the curia or top executives.

Very often top managers act intuitively. This can be caused by lack of time (quick action is necessary), defective information (the inapplicability of information), lack of financial means (collecting information is expensive). One could think here of the cost of research in sociology or psychology of religion. Very often the central government will have only limited information about a local church. They are aware of public events, but very frequently the deeper background and motives are unknown. It is extremely difficult to observe value changes in a society. The basic question is: where is the church, the traditional one and the new one, visible? The answer may require a long period of observing participation. Not only of observing, of studying periodicals and newspapers, but also of real participation: not only a matter of state visits, but also of entering into a realistic dialogue with various social groups, among them the young.

Largely applicable to the church are the following forms of social strategic behaviour:
— "the training of top leaders for the introduction of renewal and its implementation within the organization;
— participation of a workers' council in policy-making;
— the appointment or schooling of managers and specialists who are open to change;
— subsidizing educational and cultural bodies;
— delegation of responsibilities down to the lowest organizational levels;
— production of goods and services that are ethically acceptable" (Klingen, 1973).

How, then, can we tackle certain ecclesiastical problems? How can we react quickly and adequately to change processes? As to the capabilities Klingen puts great emphasis on strategic and operational "styles of thinking." "Brains" are needed to control these strategic styles of thinking. When applying this, we shall hit upon an entire complex of tensions, to be described later on, between church authorities and scholars, particularly theologians, and at the same time between the executives proper, the bishops and their advisors. Much research work in big business companies shows that:
— the importance of "brains" is insufficiently recognized by the management;
— "brains" carry a very great responsibility in professional decision-making
— in spite of this "brains" do not have an equal status with the managers who take the decisions and regulate their implementation;
— this difference in status is an important source of many conflicts between designer and executor;

— conflict situations could be smoothed out considerably and changes could be accepted more readily by executors if there was an equality of status;

— a "brain drain" from the enterprise might be prevented by this;

— managers should also be prepared to have personal experience with styles of thinking in order to understand the "brains."

As we described in the previous chapter, the church as an institution has a "life cycle" and similarly there is a cycle in strategic government. It consists of a number of phases in data processing with feedback of information, these together forming a cycle. For the developing and programming of strategic behaviour this cycle must be passed through completely, because:

— developing and programming is a continuous process; it can be compared with a ship changing course at sea;

— continuity in strategic government enhances the quality of strategic behaviour in an enterprise; one gets a better view of both oneself and the environment;

— this leads to a confrontation with the internal resistances to change that must be broken down;

— passing through each phase of the cycle makes it easier for those people to participate who are in charge of subsequent phase; this is transfer of knowledge.

In order to assess the efficiency of management, account should be taken of the relation between the speed of managerial actions and the internal or external acceleration of developments; of the degree of communication; of the degree of effort to make changes visible; and of the entire problem of centralization and decentralization. One of Klingen's comprehensive conclusions can be applied immediately to the church's top management: "In order to make strategic management function in the best possible way within the structures of the concern, the concern's president should function as a strategic integrator and a strategic educator. He should be the catalyst to the process of generating ideas which lead to renewal of the concern's structure."

Thus strategic management consists of three important elements: the process of decision-making, the process of communication, and the process of learning.

By comparing the church with a business enterprise we have uncovered extremely relevant factors, drawn from the changes in society and from the most up-to-date findings, about the strategic behaviour of an institution. To summarize these factors:

— " the availability of financial resources;

48

— a positive attitude of the top management with regard to continual change;

—collegiality instead of individual striving for power;

— the availability of managerial capabilities;

— the acceptance of business risks;

— systematic and expert-controled decision preparation;

— strategic thinking and acting as a continuous element in top management" (Klingen, 1973).

Each of these factors can be applied to the developments and changes in the Dutch Roman Catholic Church between 1960 and 1970. With the help of these factors we can examine whether or not in this period the church leaders have met the requirements of strategic governing of the church.

CHAPTER IV

Modern Church Renewal (1900-1960)

The analysis of the structural characteristics of the renewal processes in the great christian churches, and the study of the social pressure presently being exerted on the Catholic Church, have set us on the track of several important factors in church renewal. Both internal and external ecclesiastical affairs mutually influence each other, and the central authorities' wish for continuity and the thinkers' creativity have always kept each other in balance. This "survival" of the institution does not mean that the resistance to change and the refusal to take risks have not alienated quite a number of modern Christians from their church. For them the price, either intellectually or socio-politically, was too high.

In this chapter we shall put the relationships between church authority, scholarship, and the public consequences for church renewal as a whole, into historical perspective. What happened in The Netherlands is a continuation of modern church history. We are primarily looking for models and patterns which can clarify the Dutch situation. An analysis of the conflicts concerning modernism and the worker-priests in France will be emphasized.

The first renewal movement started about 1900 and stagnated at the beginning of the First World War. The second and more pastoral renewal began during the Second World War and ended just before the various renewal movements met in The Netherlands. This marked the end of a largely unconscious prelude.

1. Church Authority and Renewal

Only in the post-war years did the Catholic Church in The Netherlands become the estuary where all kinds of new currents in the fields of scholarship and pastorate flowed together. The convocation of Vatican II acted as an integrating factor, a legalization and a catalyst. This renewal movement for the entire church, which started at the end of the period described in this chapter, made Rome during the Council sessions a meeting point of authorities from the local churches, Curia functionaries and both traditional and modern theologians. Just as Rome became an international exponent of the *aggiornamento*, The Netherlands later assumed the same role on the national level. It also became a conflict center, a laboratory, indeed, a hotbed. The various trends, including their confirmation by Vatican II, came together here, but the impulses, like those for the Vatican Council, came mostly from elsewhere. They came particularly from the local renewal movements that had existed from the beginning of the present century, almost entirely outside the ambiance of the Dutch Church. The repercussions were surely felt in The Netherlands, but a real participation did not take place.

Surveying this development as a whole we can say that at the beginning of this century there was a strongly centralistic and authoritarian church government. This was a reaction to the lasting success and the recognition of the large Reformation churches, the "Enlightenment," the rise of modern science outside the ecclesiastical sphere of influence, with its strong criticism of traditional Christian doctrine, the weakening grip of the church on civil governments since the French Revolution, and later liberal movements. Seen from a traditional view point the Catholic Church had "lost" much, and its reaction was reinforced centralism. The ideal of a Christian society under strong hierarchical control gradually had to be given up, and the faithful took their own social initiatives. Within the church itself the increasing popularization of scientific thinking about religion and church gave rise to a relativizing, making it difficult to impose traditional doctrine by means of sanctions. Still, the central authorities retained their corrective function, albeit in different ways, and every renewal trend was followed by its opposite, every progress by regress, and possibly later on again by progress. Official secessions did not occur any more in this century. Change and resistance to change had to be coped with by the church institution itself which is typical of modern church renewal.

But the internal renewal movements of this century did lead to an increasing friction among the faithful themselves, who started charging each other with heresy. Mainly on the basis of a number of studies by E. Poulat (1962, 1969a, 1969b), L. Rogier (1970) has described this struggle between modernists and integralists. This

51

struggle was limited to small groups; the majority of the faithful strongly clung to its conservative convictions. About this entire period Rogier says: "Large must have been in most countries the contingent of those Catholics who swore by each and every papal directive, detesting all novelties, distrusting methods of ecclesiastical study that more or less left the beaten track. This is abundantly testified to by the Catholic press, mostly edited by clergy or ex-seminarists. For most of them however this did not imply any sympathy for the dark corridors of espionage and slander." The central authority in Rome, the person of the Pope was, especially until the First and after the Second World War, constantly at stake in theological or pastoral renewal attempts.

French church historian E. Borne (1971) finds the repeated appeal to papal authority by conservative groups such as integralists and the "Action Française" reprehensible. Looking back at the events of this century he gives the following judgment: "The worst thing about these kinds of adventure is that abuse of authority runs the risk of doing irreparable injustice to authority; consequently, in order to save and enhance its irreplaceable value it must change both its contents and its style." The authorities should not be seduced into underhanded secret dealings with small groups of conservatives as allies. Literally Borne says that modernism was defeated by church authorities "by using really terrorist methods." A church authority which alternately acts repressively and tolerantly only promotes confusion and supports "the effervescence of fanatics."

In the opinion of many authors the church is now paying the price for not solving the problems concerning ecclesiastical authority, scholarship and the pastorate which already came to the fore at the beginning of the present century. The great crisis of modernism and the little crisis of the "Action Française," Borne writes, can explain in retrospective today's crisis but not completely: "The church is now paying the price, and it has risen exceptionally, for past errors." F. Klostermann (1972) from Vienna confirms this viewpoint: Around the turn of the century nearly all questions that now occupy us, had already been raised, but we ignored them, we disavowed them, or surpressed them with violence. Thinking, however, cannot be suppressed in the long run. We have been late in preparing the faithful for changes that were long overdue, we have even presented to them a church ideal that was in every respect static and immobile, so that even the most harmless change made them think the church itself was in jeopardy." In The Netherlands Schillebeeckx (1967) added that the vehement anti-modernist reaction caused a stagnation of at least thirty years in the development of theology in our country. If there had been some preparatory reflection, Dutch theology would not have been obliged, in recent years, to conduct such a rapid and nearly baffling catching-up manoeuver. The quiet and order that prevailed after the postponed modernist "revolution" were, as was to appear at the end of this period, only a sham. "Restored rest and order were only the rest of a cemetery, indeed of a war cemetery....But just as battles cannot solve the real political problems, the integralist campaign did not lead to any real solutions" (J. de Kok, 1971).

In our century modern church renewal in its entirety is indeed assuming the character of a postponed or prolonged revolution. Strictly speaking it is not a real revolution, but an evolution that is daily becoming more pregnant and more urgent. Exactly because the Catholic Church is an international institution and the local churches are in a subordinate position, comparison with a typology of revolution is difficult. Most revolutions still occur on the national level. Besides national revolutions Jean Baechler (1970, 1972) distinguishes military, liberal, fascist and prolonged revolutions. The conclusion is forcing itself upon us, he says, that revolutions of the latter type, prolonged revolutions, are failures. The system that is finally imposed, is the antipode of what was originally intended. This type of revolution, Baechler says, forms "the real social laboratories, where the researcher finds much to his taste, even though the citizen's interest is not without uneasy scepticism." Every revolution can be examined from the following angles: intensity, motives, fall of the government, take-over of power, development, celebration, acting persons, ideology, results.

All comparisons are inadequate. But the government of the Catholic Church has not fallen, and its central powers are at most relativized. Revolution-like events in the church, such as in postwar France, evoked an "euphoria," a sense of celebration. But even in a real revolution the feast is only short-lived. "Soon the illusion of unity is broken by political conflicts between power-thirsty groups; the necessities of everyday life destroy the exaltation." The elite, the most capable people, always play the principal role in a revolutionary movement. And there are three categories of supporters: those who really believe in it and are in the minority; those who use it for personal objectives (ambition, opportunism); and finally the masses which follow and live on conflicting illusions. "The little group of believers is usually pushed aside as soon as the new regime is in power" (J. Baechler, 1972).

2. From Modernism to *Aggiornamento*

The greatest expert on modernism as it appears in France, Emile Poulat, feels obliged to admit he is at a loss. This he has written in an article in *Archives de Sociologie des Religions* (n.27, 1969b), in which he tries to define modernism and integralism as they have appeared up till now. As a historian and sociologist of religion he wants to keep aloof as much as possible from the animosities surrounding modernists and anti-modernists in the Catholic Church. But today, fifty years later, the topic looks as relevant as in the beginning: "omnipresent and elusive." To some it is an institutional weakness leading to the church's undoing, whereas to others this undoing is caused by the methods used to restrain these renewal attempts. To some it is only an endeavour by isolated individuals, not deeply rooted in the church as such. To others it is an unavoidable crisis of growth which the church must undergo — a crucial moment in "a passage to a new cultural cycle." The fact that the positive sciences can freely criticize a domain that was formerly completely closed to criticism, is called by Poulat the revolutionary principle. In his definition of modernism a tension exists between the past and present: "Modernism can be defined as the actual encounter and confrontation of a religious past, long fixed, with a present that has found outside itself the living sources of its inspiration." Thus not an internal "resourcing," but an external one penetrating into the church structure. This process has been going on for decades now, and it has brought the knowledge of the scholars to the simple church members who have also changed their thinking. The public at large, however, Poulat writes, pays only superficial attention to this. Modernism in the past was quite different from the present-day *aggiornamento*. Nowadays there is unabashed talk about the secularization of religion, about demythologization, about the end of conventional Christianity. But then modernism was not on the eve of church renewal, but of disaster!

It is however not only a stagnation of theological science as compared to the secular, positive sciences, that is at stake here. The problem is not only this type of *aggiornamento*, of updating. It is a matter of essential doctrinal discussion. "Within half a century the frontiers of what is *believable* have moved, in accordance with changes in the Catholic world, the idea of what is *knowable* in the various areas of religious and primarily biblical history." Or, as we said in the second chapter, Where is the boundary between obligatory adaptation and obligatory nonadaptation based on religious convictions. Apart from all auxiliary problems that are solved more or less satisfactorily, the question concerns "a balance of the Christian body which is trying to find an identity in a society that impregnates it with its culture." Under the pressure of the environment, of modern urban and industrialized, scientific and technical society, the church is seeking its balance, is trying strategically to plot its course.

Thus the big problem arising now is how to find the laws which do govern the internal structure of the church. Application of the customary principles of Scripture, Tradition and Authority does not completely solve the problem. Poulat, too, confirms that in fact no answer is given, and he uses the following remarkable wording: "It is increasingly impossible to define what is not possible." The phenomenon is spreading that Catholics do not want to renounce their traditional faith, but at the same time no longer have confidence in the prevailing system. For them the choice will be between the uncertainty of anarchy and the defense of the past. That is then the reason why every movement toward modernism conjures up integralism.

Poulat goes on to analyse this integralism and finally adopts the definition that can be found a few months before the twentieth century set in, in the periodical which to this very day supports Vatican opinion, the *Civilta Cattolica* of 15 March 1899. The article is about Leo XIII and Americanism, the overseas forerunner of European modernism. The text runs as follows:

> The Catholic principles do not change, neither with the years, nor by moving from one country to another, nor by new discoveries, nor for reasons of efficiency. They are always the principles preached by Christ, proclaimed by the church, defined by popes and councils, practised by the saints, defended by the scholars. It is fitting to accept these principles as they are, or to leave them as they are. Whoever accepts them in their fullness and power is a Catholic; who weighs them, manipulates them, adapts them to the times, trims them, may call himself whatever he wants, but for God and the church he is a rebel and a traitor."

There are two concepts of orthodoxy, authority and Christianity. The growing distance between them, Poulat says, cannot be bridged sociologically speaking. It is even more difficult to return to the past. Perhaps there is more mutual affinity than we imagine. But, Poulat concludes in this analysis of modern church renewal, "The process is not finished," or, as we said at the end of chapter II, the procession goes on. Progress and regress alternate.

It is extraordinarily interesting to see how around 1970 a conceptual give and take exists concerning the idea of *aggiornamento*. The large *Handbuch der Pastoraltheologie*, published by Herder, has as its last volume a *Lexikon* (F. Klostermann et al., 1972) containing the word *aggiornamento*. For Pope John XXIII this was the key word for reform expectations, not only synonymous with renewal of the church, but also with renewal of the faith. Without a doubt, the lexicon says, this is what Pope John meant by *aggiornamento*. But usage made this word unclear. It was interpreted as referring to external adaptation only. This led to misunderstandings which caused Pope Paul VI to give a more exact definition. From now on *aggiornamento* means only external, structural and institutional adaptation. "This reform of the social structures of the church is distinguished from real renewal (*rinnovamento*), primarily in doctrine and spirituality. With Paul VI this curtailment is very clearly inspired by the concern that a factual identification of reform and adaptation conjures up the danger of a relativizing of church doctrine." This definition expresses the entire tension between church authority and science. How at the beginning of the present century reformers personally reacted to this tension, and how they experienced church authority will now be elaborated.

3. Theologians and Renewal

In the reform movements of this century, particularly in France and Germany, one is very concretely confronted with the structural elements already described above: the decisions of the authorities and the interpretations of scholars. This hierarchical, and especially curial, stand as regards theologians advocating renewal will be studied at closer quarters, among other things with the help of Alec Vidler's book *A Variety of Catholic Modernists* (1970).

In science, with its independent and original thinking, and, as regards the church, mainly in theology lies the source of permanent ecclesiastical renewal and adaptation. "The age-old contrast between left and right in the church came to a head at the end of the nineteenth century when an academic intelligentsia turned away from the church in large numbers because by remaining faithful to it they seemed to be obliged to confess as truth what scientific inquiry had taught them to be error" (L. Rogier, 1970). In Germany H. Schell (1897) had already recommended reforms in ecclesiastical studies. To his mind this included a revision of the concept of obedience which encompassed more than obedience to church authorities. "In order to be a real scientific discipline theological thinking must also be free, that is: be given the opportunity to critically examine the fundamentals. This lays a grave responsibility on science, but it is quite a different thing from putting ecclesiastical studies under tutelage" (J. de Kok, 1971). A whole series of books by Schell were placed on the Index. There was no consensus among the bishops, as was shown in the struggle between conservative Trier and progressive Cologne (nowadays just the other way round!). The Roman Curia hid behind the denouncers, so that a Roman prelate could declare: "The Prussian bishops have handed over Schell to us; they, and not we, are responsible...." The campaign against this theologian of renewal continued. His reputation was injured. He had a heart-attack. J. de Kok writes: "The repeated difficulties of denunciations and interrogations, this entire underhand business, became in 1906 too much for Schell's ailing heart....Schell's fate is illustrative of what was in store for others, especially in France and Italy, the home ports of the prevailing church system."

France was undoubtedly the centre of modernism. The principal figure was Alfred Loisy; his teacher and predecessor was Msgr. Duchesne of the Institut Catholique in Paris. Marcel Hébert and E. LeRoy were more philosophically inclined. The protector was Msgr. Mignot, Archbishop of Albi. Albert Houtin was the publicist and historian of modernism. The following quotation from a letter by Duchesne to Hébert illustrates the situation. It is the year 1900. The reformers have lost courage. Should they resign themselves? Should they leave the church?

> We are at a turning point [he wrote on 18 January 1900]. Religious authority counts on its tradition, and the most devoted members of its personnel, who are also the least intelligent. What can be done? Hope that this will change? Endeavour to reform it? But it will not change and reform will not come about. The only outcome of such attempts would be to throw oneself out of the window, without any advantage to others or to oneself....It may be that, despite all appearances, the old ecclesiastical edifice one day is going to tumble down....Should this happen, no one

will blame us for having supported the old building for as long as possible (A. Vidler, 1970).

Duchesne hoped that the old church edifice would fall down one day and that he and Hébert would not be blamed for having stayed inside so long. Thereafter came the condemnation of modernism in two papal documents: *Lamentabili*, a syllabus of 65 errors (3 July 1907) and *Pascendi*, an encyclical (8 September 1907). Schoof supports Vidler's opinion that the theology of renewal was not given the opportunity to discuss its still-developing ideas seriously within the church. The establishment of secrecy-bound supervisory bodies in every diocese and the imposition of an antimodernist oath on all priests betray a panic unworthy of the Roman Church. "It is equally undignified to see the objectives of the modernists described by the encyclical...as a well-considered hypocrites' plot against the church, inspired by pure curiosity and pride which will lead to the destruction of all religion. The first step was taken by Protestantism, the second has been taken by modernism, the next one will plunge us into atheism" (T. Schoof, 1968). Loisy wanted to protest against the condemnation, but a friend wrote to him on 11 October 1907 that this would only give rise to more turmoil and scandal. He advised him to assume an attitude that is chosen by many theologians when the official church burdens them with guilt feelings: "Silent, persevering, humble work will do more than anything else." Church reformers are often isolated or isolate themselves.

E. LeRoy writes the following about ecclesiastical authority, obedience and scholarship: "No authority can compel me to hold a given argument sound or unsound: above all, no authority can make this or that conception with or without meaning to me. I do not say merely that authority has no right to do this, but that the thing is radically impossible, for ultimately it is I who think, not the authority that thinks for me." Vidler says that, despite everything, LeRoy nevertheless wanted to remain in the church and shows the enormous tension existing between individual thinking and group thinking for church members. "Religious individualism was a contradiction in terms. He realized that identification with the church apparently involved being identified with elements in it which one deplored, but that was not a sufficient reason for breaking away: on the contrary, reform was possible only from within." This is evidently also a viewpoint about the methodology of church reform: according to LeRoy, it can only be successful if done from within. He also thinks it better not to be too aggressive; thereby the opposition becomes too important "when it would be better to view them with indifference" (A. Vidler, 1970).

Less outspoken reformers such as Maurice Blondel and P. Laberthonnière, both philosophers, also had many objections against the practices of church authorities. Blondel almost scrupulously submitted to the church's authority, but in private, Vidler writes, "he deplored many of the ways in which it was exercised." Laberthonnière was more critical. The Pope's authoritarian behaviour he called "Romanism." Authority is indispensable, but it should serve, not dominate. It should not suppress intellectual initiatives but stimulate them, not ignore them but offer guidance; it should encourage personal autonomy and freedom (A. Vidler, 1970).

Loisy did not submit. In 1909 Henri Brémond was suspended solely because he had been so bold as to say the Lord's Prayer at Tyrrell's open grave. When the protector — Bishop Mignot — died in March 1918, the same Brémond wrote about Pius X, who condemned modernism, "The Roman Church has no heart."

Thus this renewal movement lost its impetus by the First World War. The way in which Rome opposed theologians who, for scholarly or pastoral reasons, wanted to update the church and its doctrine, has been clearly exposed. The usual sanctions such as excommunication, the prohibition to say Mass and to wear the clerical cassock would make less of an impression nowadays. Yet defamation and isolation, mysterious counterattacks, and the sowing of division among bishops and theologians remain some of the means still used by high authorities.

Contact with Germany was and had been infrequent. There were hardly any personal relations between French and German renewal theologians. Between the two World Wars there was a revival in Germany, lead by people like Romano Guardini, Karl Adam, Josef Jungmann and Pius Parsch, who where also widely read in The Netherlands until postwar times, the influence of Hugo and especially Karl Rahner lasted longer. The latter became a celebrated theologian in The Netherlands. During the thirties, Schoof says, three anonymous books were published in Germany in which the demands of Schell's reformation of Catholicism were reiterated. At the German universities the introduction of the antimodernist oath had been refused. Rome clearly assumed different approaches with different countries. The anonymous authors objected to a Romanization of the church in Germany, to the lack of freedom for scholarship, to the externalization and alienation of the liturgy and church life, and to the dictatorship of canon law. They asked for the abrogation of the Index and obligatory priestly celibacy (T. Schoof, 1968) — interesting omens for the renewal movement in our country.

4. Regress in the Renewal Movement

After the Second World War an outspokenly pastorate-oriented renewal of theology started in France. In 1947 and 1948 the famous pastoral letters of Cardinal Suhard, *Essor ou déclin de l'Eglise* and *Le sens de Dieu* were published. Pastoral congresses were held. There was a growing feeling that a good diagnosis of the actual situation by means of sociographical studies could be an important contribution to the directing of church renewal. Those who have not lived through those years, Congar was to say later on, have missed one of the church's most beautiful moments. Congar, Chenu, de Lubac, Danielou were the most outstanding theologians. It was a feast of renewal.

On 30 May 1949 Cardinal Suhard dies. The death of this Paris cardinal has important consequences. From that moment on Rome begins to listen more and more to the conservative voices. A month later the Holy Office forbids cooperation with communists. On 13 August 1950 the encyclical *Humani Generis*, an evident check on the theology of renewal, is published. On 5 April 1951 there is, for the first time since 1906, a meeting of the complete French episcopate. The renewal movement is coming to an end. H. Marrau writes that *Essor ou déclin de l'Eglise* is the last papal or episcopal document with which he could identify. For him it was the "last spring." *Humani Generis* he typifies as: "The church became repressive." All kinds of initiatives are curtailed. He distinguishes three phases since the war: "The church and the fatherland, the church you care about, the church as an obstacle." The bishops are no longer prophets but prefects (H. Marrau, 1971).

On 23 September 1953 nuncio Msgr. Marella calls together in Paris 26 bishops, prelates and religious superiors. He announces the decision of the Roman Curia that the experiment with worker-priests must be stopped. Cardinals Liénart and Feltin are completely baffled by this news. All over the country there are protests. On 4 November three cardinals pay a visit to Rome. They are treated cooly and there is no outlook for a solution. On 18 November Vatican Radio announces that the French bishops have agreed to Rome's demands. In fact, the bishops are divided. On 28 November the Jesuits recall their worker-priests. On 27 January 1954 Cardinal Feltin declares: "Professing one's faith means obeying the church." Before 1 March all worker-priests are to submit to the following new directives: only three hours a day of manual labour, prohibition of any kind of engagement in "worldly" matters, return to presbyteries or convents; prohibition to form an interdiocesan or national group. On 9 February the superior general of the Dominicans arrives in Paris. Without ado three provincials are dismissed. Well-known theologians like Congar and Chenu are forbidden to live in Paris. Jesuit de Lubac had already been advised to stop lecturing.

Large sections of the press go on supporting the worker-priests. Factory workers hold protest meetings. Catholic intellectuals issue manifestos. On 20 February the worker-priests meet for the last time in "Café de la Paix" at Villejuif. On 27 October Cardinal Feltin lets it be known that about half of the worker-priests (40 to 50) have refused to obey. On 10 November this group of priests publishes a White Paper. It is condemned by Cardinal Feltin.

Without notifying the French bishops the Roman Curia bans the leftist Catholic periodical *La Quinzaine*. The bishops and the editors concerned have to read this in the *Osservatore Romano* of 5 February 1955. The editors acquiesce and say farewell to the readers: "If we decide to stop, we know we bear a grave responsibility. We are not sure if the church will be able to assimilate the values of a new civilization that are opposed to the old values by which the church still seems to be emprisoned. But our faith in Christ obliges us not to doubt of his church and to preserve the certainty that, behind a sometimes forbidding outward appearance, it possesses the powers necessary for renewal and that it can produce the new forms its universal mission requires...." (*Le Monde*, 23 February 1955).

The conservative circles are glad this "communist Trojan Horse in the church" has disappeared. They consider the entire avantgarde of the Catholic press and of the Catholic Church in France to be communist. Conservative papers are *La Revue Catholique*, *Artaban*, *Aspects de la France*, *L'Homme Nouveau* and *Paternité*. In these periodicals and in Jean Madiran's pamphlets "They do not Know What They are Doing" and "They do not Know What They are Saying" the bishops are so severely attacked that, on 29 June

1955, six cardinals have to defend themselves against it (*Le Monde*, 30 June 1955).

In the fall of 1957 the Catechetical Institute of Paris is condemned by Rome. A so-called progressive catechism can, with a number of changes, continue to be used. Interventions by Cardinals Lienart and Gerlier saves the Institute's director J. Colomb from being suspended by Rome and his publications from being placed on the Index. But a cooperator is victimized: Abbé Coudreau, Colomb's righthand man, must leave the Catechetical Institute. In the fall of 1958 Rome forbids the paper *Témoignage Chrétien* to be sold at church doors. Editor-in-chief George Suffert is fired. Two Jesuit editors also have to leave.

On 9 October 1958 Pope Pius XII dies.

On 1 July 1959 the worker-priests are definitely forbidden. Cardinal Pizzardo's letter about this remains, however, a secret for a long time. Not until 15 September is the letter printed in *Le Monde* (G. Siefer, 1960).

In October 1965 the French bishops announce that, with Rome's consent, they will resume their appointments of worker-priests.

In a talk with R. Auwerda, in October 1968, Prof. R. Schillebeeckx said that until shortly before the Vatican Council France set the trend. "But the suppression of the worker-priests was a tremendous blow from which the French have never completely recovered. To be sure, the council has mainly been given shape by the French: The documents on the church, on the church in the modern world, and on the priesthood. The ponderous kind of German thinking did not appeal to the council's bishops. And the French, of course, captured the bishops' fancy more because of their lucidity. Although the collegiality idea entered the council mainly via the German and Dutch theologians, the French joined forces with them too" (R. Auwerda, 1969).

In 1969 Pope Paul VI appointed a French cardinal, Jean Villot, as his Secretary of State. France had fought its battle. It was confirmed. It was accepted into the Roman top management. When together with Dr. R. Huysmans, I met Cardinal Villot at the end of 1969, for the first time in his high function, he told me: "Father, twenty years ago France carried the banner of church renewal. Now The Netherlands is carrying it. Think of your great responsibility!."

5. Social Renewal

The picture of modern church renewal is not complete without a description of the way in which the Catholic Church took part in socio-political life. A year after the 1954 Mandement of the Dutch bishops, in which Catholics were urgently requested to keep their own Catholic organizations in the political and social field, *La Quinzaine*, the left-wing political periodical in France, was forbidden by Rome. By 1960 the Dutch bishops published another pastoral letter about "Catholic Organizations in Our Time," offering only their "good services" and leaving it to "the present day leaders and scholars in Catholic organizational life" to carry the full professional responsibility. Every country has had its own developments, but the ideal of a Christian society under hierachical control was for the most part abandoned.

At the beginning of the present century we find an interesting counterpart to this development. The laity at the time started breaking away from hierarchical custody because they wanted to bear social and political responsibility themselves, outside organizations recognized by the bishops. We refer to the "Le Sillon" movement of layman Marc Sangnier (1875—1940) who broke off his army officer training and began to lead a Christian-democratic movement, which was forbidden on 25 August 1910 in a letter sent from Rome to the French bishops. Alec Vidler calls this movement a "sociological modernism." Information about it can be found in Jeanne Caron's Sorbonne thesis "Le Sillon et la démocratie chrétienne" (1967), and in studies by A. Dansette (1957) and J. de Kok (1971).

Sangnier was supported by priests, periodicals, training institutes and national congresses. The movement was strongly Christocentric and found its inspiration in devotion to the Eucharist. There were discussion groups on social and ethical problems, and there was quite a network of personal relations. Dansette calls it one of the finest youth organizations France has ever known. As "Le Sillon" took ever more independent positions, the bishops became divided. Sangnier's supporters were against a Catholic political party and in favour of a party "of Catholics." According to Vidler rightist groups of the "Action Française" accused them of "...wanting to democratize the Church, of weakening the spirit of absolute submission to the hierarchy, and of flirting with Protestantism...." In the long run forty bishop became opponents of this "Sillon" movement.

On 25 August 1910 the bishops received the letter *Notre charge apostolique* in which both the movement and the periodical of the same name were forbidden by Rome. The letter ends, "for the true friends of the people are neither revolutionaries nor innovators, but traditionalists." Msgr. Mignot, advocate of "Le Sillon," wrote to Loisy after the prohibition had been made public that Pius X's letter meant a victory for the "Action Française." Seldom has there been such dismay among Catholic lay people who thought that as Christians they carried a social responsibility. In his *Histoire du catholicisme sociale en France, 1871—1931*, G. Hoog describes the reaction: "Our first impression was that of a thunderbolt which struck and destroyed our entire dream. In one single moment it seemed our youth was completely collapsing. Our faces showed only complete bafflement, and on many faces there were tears." Vidler points to an important consequence of this Roman prohibition, which may also apply to the disintegration of Catholic political organizations in other countries: "It might be argued that, though this was not exactly his intention, Pius X served the cause of French Catholicism well by dispersing the Sillonists in so many directions."

6. Typology of Progress and Regress

In the cycle of renewal movements since the beginning of this century we have found many points of recognition. Progress and regress occur again and again. The movements seem to be enclosed by a wall which prevents them from spreading to other countries. But the quickly developing means of mass communication, and particularly television, will promote internationalization. Vatican II itself is a case in point.

A typology can be made on the basis of what has happened in the church during the present century. Local initiatives for church reform might be better understood then. It could be a model, a paradigm for progress and regress. Renewers gain influence; there are climaxes of solidarity and enthusiasm. Good relations are sought with the hierarchy or attempts are made to find favour with individual bishops. Bishops sometimes give their support, in some cases approving by remaining silent or by a personal hint not to ask for formal approval. Then the central ecclesiastical authorities, wanting to curb the renewal movements in local churches, step in and order corrections. As a rule this is preceded by secret

64

collaboration with certain local groups that oppose renewal. Mass media which support renewal come under attack. Sometimes they disappear or take a different approach. A search is made for the people who most be eliminated. Their reputations are attacked. They become hereby notorious as opponents of the Roman measures. If these measures become public, the defamation of individuals, of theologians or bishops, is continued. Sometimes local church leaders are disavowed, if not formally, then at least factually. Visits are paid to Rome. The struggle, which was already latent, starts between supporters and critics of the Roman attitude. The hierarchy is no longer dependable. The faithful and the priests begin to "drop out". Professors and literary people protest. Letters to the editor, pro and con, are sent in. The conflict between Rome and the local church becomes a conflict *within* the local church. Internal polarization paralyzes and leads to regress. On one side there is embitterment and resignation, on the other silent triumph. The losers publish a White Paper. Religious orders and congregations, less bound to the hierarchy, take sides. Rome may or may not put pressure upon them, and they may or may not submit to it. Then silence sets in. The final phase has begun.

This typology may sound too negative because the continuation of church renewal, either later on or elsewhere, is not mentioned. Every fall is followed by winter and spring! The expression "Spring is over" is often heard. Kurt Lewin (1947) has distinguished three phases in this process of renewal: unfreezing, moving, and refreezing. In the unfreezing phase established opinions are stirred. This causes uncertainty and resistance to change. The second phase, "moving," already offers perspectives for solutions, and renewal experiments are carried out. The third phase, "refreezing," stabilizes what has been renewed, and then the process starts again.

Without these partial renewals Vatican II would not have been possible. It became the first renewal movement to be called by the highest ecclesiastical authority itself. The renewal process is a learning process. How are we to handle the relative autonomy of the bishops, the coming of age of theologians, national bishops' conferences, and modern mass media? How can we regulate these in such a way that they contribute to permanent renewal? The principle of leadership is always being stressed; the actual practice of authority is criticized: there are still more individual displays of power than collegial authority; there is still no openness to change; the position of the church alongside other equivalent social institutions is still something unfamiliar; there is still a lack of expert advice; there is still too much fear of taking risks.

When I trained for the priesthood, during the war, I had a colleague who was studying at the Institute Catholique in Paris. He brought with him books by Godin, Michonneau, Daniel, de Montcheuil and others. Later on at Louvain I studied all the issues of *Jeunesse de l'Eglise*, the subsequently forbidden books by Emmanuel Mounier; I subscribed to *Témoignage Chrétien*. I read the publications on *Economie et Humanisme* by Dominicans Lebret and Loew, the first dockworker-priest of Marseille. Much of this I have forgotten, but not the expression, "when it rains in France, it drizzles in The Netherlands." This weather forecast is over thirty years old. We shall now try to analyse and explain the local renewal movement in Dutch Catholicism. It is already drizzling in The Netherlands. I see the clouds gathering.

CHAPTER V

Church Renewal in The Netherlands

Instead of a threatening thundercloud hanging over The Netherlands, we can better talk about a storm of renewal gathering slowly and, when it is over, leaving us in a remarkable and almost unreal calm.

The analysis of internal church reforms, of the influence of social change and of the continuity with church renewal in other countries, particularly in France, already has given us many intimations of what has been happening in Dutch Catholicism over the past ten years. From an international and historical viewpoint this means a relativizing and an attempt at objectivity. The applicability of the typology of progress and regress on the Dutch situation will certainly become more evident when the facts are described in more detail. All the same, there were in The Netherlands very special conditions explaining the unexpectedness and the deep-going dynamism of this church renewal. As will be seen, these are closely linked with the way authority is exercised, the strategy of ecclesiastical policy and the influence which a certain theological view, as well as the view of other sciences, has on the renewal process. The publicity surrounding these changes was caused by the great and nearly fervent interest of the mass media, attracted by this "something special" in Dutch church renewal. In the present chapter the emphasis is on analysis of renewal.

1. The Particulars of the Dutch Situation

Many authors have already racked their brains about the elements which made the developments in the Dutch Catholic Church after Vatican II so fascinating for foreign observers. The Dutch Catholics are almost equal in number to their fellow Catholics in the United Kingdom, sociologist P.G. McCaffery writes in his doctoral thesis (May 1971), but their influence in the world at large is much greater. "This is chiefly because a section of them has displayed a readiness to put forward and implement innovations even at the cost of incurring the displeasure of the church's Roman authorities — a readiness which scarcely exists at all in English Catholic circles, though in the last two or three years it has begun to show itself here." These rapid changes in The Netherlands also provoked well-organized resistance, "an exceptionally self-conscious and well-organized body of traditionalist opinion, vociferously expressing disapproval of the more startling innovations." Tensions between Rome and the local church exist in many countries, as do tensions within the local church as an accompanying phenomenon. Perhaps the tempo in The Netherlands makes it something special. What in France cost fifty years, with less result than in The Netherlands, took place here in twenty-five years, the zenith being reached after the closure of the Second Vatican Council in 1965. All this in spite of the adage ascribed to Heinrich Heine that in Holland everything always happens fifty years later.

Another author, R. Auwerda, wonders if the relations between progressivism and traditionalism in The Netherlands are different from those elsewhere. No comparative studies are available, but could a small difference in the left—right percentages be decisive? Something quite different is going on here. "Without wanting to reject or exclude anybody the bishops have clearly given their blessing to innovation, also in their contacts with the church universal." Auwerda wrote this in 1969, that is before Bishops Simonis and Gijsen were nominated as colleagues. He thinks it of specific interest that the Dutch bishops firmly refuse to be isolated from their congregations for the sake of a central Roman policy which, with unconvincing arguments and without consulting the membership, takes decisions which oppress evangelical freedom and Christian conscience. After 1960 the Dutch bishops were clearly looking for ways more to accompany than to direct, more to contribute to the discussion than to speak the last word, more to seek their authority in the weight of their words than in the importance of their office. "In a later stage they themselves created possibilities for specialists to influence policy on the basis of their expertise, and for the laity to do the same on the basis of their convictions and uncertainties. The founding of the Pastoral Institute of the Dutch Church Province (1963) and the convocation of the Dutch Pastoral Council (1965) are the consequences" (R. Auwerda, 1969).

Schillebeeckx considers the peculiarity of Dutch Catholicism to be a mystery, but he does not hesitate to explain it, and points to the elements also mentioned by Auwerda. They can be summarized as a special way of exercising authority, inspired by Vatican II's new conception of the church. Frequently the Dutch bishops are blamed for not intervening often enough. This cannot be attributed to fear or weakness, but "it is a new manner of exercising authority. The tactics of the Dutch bishops is not to pronounce any laws, rules or directives without first having discussed the matters concerned with theologians, psychologists, sociologists, management experts and representatives of the faithful. In addition, the bishops only approve notes or improve documents which are the result of the free initiative of theologians and the faithful themselves. Thus a real, living, local church arises. I believe this, and only this, is the secret of the Dutch Church. After all, Vatican II has confirmed that the church universal *hic et nunc* is actualized in the local community" (E. Schillebeeckx, 1972). This prominent theological advisor to Cardinal Alfrink also thinks it of special interest that the Dutch Pastoral Council has very courageously formulated viewpoints. "A constructive dialogue with other local churches and with Rome is impossible without first taking decisions. It is not necessary that local churches be silent as long as Rome has not spoken decisively. The speaking-out of local churches is necessary for dialogue, although there is no doubt that this outspokenness can create great tensions within the local communities."

The peculiar thing indeed is the exercise of authority by means of dialogue between the bishops, experts and representatives of the faithful in an open and public local church community. The relative autonomy of scholarship has a special place here, as was also noticed by L. Bright (1968). This Dominican, a member of the British critical group "Slant," visited our country in the spring of 1968 with a delegation from the Newman Association. According to him, the revolution was over, because a partnership of bishops and church members had been found. Like Auwerda and Schillebeeckx he then points to the institute which organized the dialogue between bishops, specialists and the faithful, and to the Pastoral Council! Bright writes, "One of the important factors in the development of the Dutch Church is certainly the Pastoral Institute, paid for by the hierarchy though independent of it. Here all the different movements in the church are coordinated and the necessary information spread." The tension between central policy and independent or even unasked-for advice was well noticed by Bright.

The realization, the actualization of a local church in a modern fashion, using modern scholarship and the information channels of press, radio and television are, in my opinion, the most striking characteristics of Dutch Catholicism after 1965. That this was done in an atmosphere of freedom was a relief for many foreign journalists. This atmosphere was (still) unknown in their own countries. Discussion in The Netherlands was not about the essence of this or that detail. In this respect people here may have been slightly too pragmatic and slightly too antispeculative. The many years of the Vatican Council had yielded enough directives: people wanted to get on the move. This was called "The Dutch Experiment" or "Laboratory for Church Renewal," a test-track where new church models were tried out (W. Goddijn, 1969). The question now is how did this special development in the previously so unknown Netherlands with such a traditional, Roman church model, come about?

2. Identity Crisis and New Self-confidence

The crisis which the Catholic group in The Netherlands has undergone in the last decades has sometimes been unfriendly dubbed a puberty crisis. Local churches with a longer history, especially in predominantly Catholic countries, therefore looked on with a kind of benevolence, expecting "they will get over that." "Compared with French, Italian, Spanish and to a large extent German Catholicism, the Dutch Church province might be called a 'late-blossomer,' optimistically heading for the future in a time when its elder brothers are already tired and frustrated by all the misery they have had to face" (L. Alting von Geusau, 1968). After all, it was only in 1853 that The Netherlands received its own bishops, and in 1908 that the patronage of the Roman Congregation for Missions was abolished. Our Catholicism had been clandestine, a discriminated minority, emancipated in the Batavian Revolution of 1795, and then needing first the liberals and subsequently the Protestants to find its own identity. Within the Catholic group a kind of middle-class Catholicism dominated for a long time, with the clergy providing the leadership. There were not

70

many Catholic noblemen, army officers or scientists. Not until 1923 was the Catholic University of Nijmegen founded, staffed by many priest-professors; there were 189 students, 26 professors, 5 readers and 2 assistants. For a very long time the initiatives for all kinds of Catholic activities were in clerical hands. The Catholic upbringing itself did not really call forth mature attitudes.

Rogier (1958) said that nowhere in the world did Catholicism look so much like a play-pen or a hothouse plant. At the end of his famous 1958 speech on "The Phenomenon of Cultural Inertia among Dutch Catholics" he spoke the following prophetic words, suggesting he wanted to put into Dutch hands the banner of renewal raised by France. To us and our children is charged the task defined by French church historian A. Dansette as the duty "to give the eternal message a form adapted to the present day world": "Shouldering this task requires self-denial, a little bit of courage and perhaps also thick-skinnedness; carrying it out may cost blood and tears. In our childhood years, how easy and peaceful the conversion of the world seemed to be, how uncomplicated....Of course, the impossible will prove possible, albeit through a series of miracles. But shouldn't we cooperate?" The church organization which The Netherlands after Vatican II is going to create for adult and self-confident priests and laity will indeed cost blood and tears, just like the new Cathechism which will be for adults. To expect that it is a simple and uncomplicated matter to be a modern church would seem naive in 1973, too. Stamina and thick-skinnedness also belong to the elements of a growing self-confidence.

For many authors the Second World War was the decisive turning-point for Dutch Catholics. Many bridges were blown up then in order to prevent the Germans from drawing neutral and poorly-armed Holland into a war, but the resistance to the Germans lowered the bridges among the many isolated religious groups. The Dutch Catholics broke out of their group context, they left the fortress they had built to safeguard their own identity against heretical and liberal influences in the environment. Catholic politicians had united nearly all their fellow-Catholics into a political party that had the greatest number of parliamentary seats. The traditional and clerical allegiance to authority, the denominational educational system paid for by the government, social care for the large Catholic families, Catholic newspapers and radio broadcasts, were important means to guarantee a stable religious community.

The war brought the separate religious groups together in common solidarity against the German occupiers. As in every war, people learned the meaning of anomie. Laws had to be made and carried out according to the consciences of the people themselves, without passive obedience to the authorities. The most noble and constant features of the Dutch national character came to the fore: love of freedom, hate of injustice, a deep respect for human dignity, faithfulness to tradition and the pride of being an independent and hard-working people. Through cooperation with the so-mistrusted non-Catholics in the resistance during the war the national consciousness of the Catholics also began to grow. At a given moment during the war the Archbishop of Utrecht J. de Jong, later ordained as a cardinal, could, as the only remaining authority of Dutch Catholicism, pronounce a prophetic "no" against the Nazi occupying forces and the injuries perpetrated by them. "That the church in The Netherlands, however tumultuous it may often seem to be, has in any case remained a living church and not become a dull routine institution which, according to some, it still ought to be, is mainly a result of the stand taken by that church in those times and those circumstances when practically all others had failed or retired into passive expectation. The attending circumstances were, of course, highly exceptional, particularly for The Netherlands that since the Napoleonic period had not known a real state of war" (C. de Groot, 1973).

It is even longer ago that Dutch Catholicism was "at war" with Rome. That was in 1723. Then, too, resistance from Utrecht played a role, just as it does today. At the time the Utrecht Vicariat independently chose Cornelis Steenoven as archbishop, which one year later led to a schism and the creation of the Old Catholic Church. In this context one should also see the comparisons to the German occupation drawn after the completely unexpected appointment, in the beginning of 1972, of Bishop Gijsen to the See of Roermond (Limburg). Since the war Catholic Dutchmen have been highly allergic to authoritarian behaviour, also in the church; and certainly when, as appeared shortly before Bishop Gijsen's nomination, German prelates tried to influence ecclesiastical procedures in Limburg (a diocese which borders on Germany) (G. Adams, 1973).

At any rate, Dutch Catholicism awoke in those war years from some kind of inferiority complex. In concentration camps talks were started with "the others." In a certain sense the new church was born at St. Michielsgestel and Haaren, where many intellectuals and political leaders of all denominations were held as hostages as if in permanent conclave. There the dialogue started, the dialogue with Protestant Christians, with humanists, with socialists. The Nederlands Gesprekscentrum has promoted and continued this dialogue to this very day. The Pastoral Council organized an internal dialogue among Catholics in which Protestants and humanists took part as observers. It is remarkable, for that matter, that, according to C. de Groot, the Italian priest Balducci, referring to the Second Vatican Council, once wrote, "The Council was born in the concentration camps."

Perhaps the ecumenical movement as well received a strong push during those war years. There was cooperation between the Archbishop of Utrecht and Protestant church leaders. The Netherlands with its large Christian minority groups (in 1947: 38.5% Roman Catholics, 31.3% Dutch Reformed and 9.7% Reformed) was eminently suited to ecumenical discussion. Amsterdam was elected as the meeting place for the first General Assembly of the World Council of Churches in 1948. Catholics had to remain aloof, but this event had a great influence on the ecumenical movement in The Netherlands. A Dutchman was appointed secretary general — W. Visser 't Hooft. And there was *one* Catholic observer "smuggled in" as a journalist — J. Willebrands — chaplain in Amsterdam, now cardinal-prefect of the Catholic Secretariat for Christian Unity in Rome (H. Divendal, 1972).

Finally, Dutch Catholicism was also challenged by the rapidly increasing prosperity. After the First World War there started an internal migration of Catholics from the south to the more Protestant northern provinces. Around 1950 this migration was stimulated by developing industrial areas, a project of Catholic government minister Van den Brink. Government workshops were set up to train unskilled labour for factory work in the western regions of the country, where most of the big cities are situated. Because the Catholics had always been overrepresented in the lower working classes, they now made stronger economic progress. Migration and urbanization had their main impact on the Catholic population. This entire process more or less stabilized around 1970 and could be said to be governed by the trends observable everywhere in western Europe. Through its strong structural basis, its educational system, its trade unions, its publicity media and its adequate forms of spiritual care The Netherlands was saved from what, in spite of all pastoral exertions, happened in countries such as France.

3. Socio-ecclesiastical Research and Reflection

Every ten years in The Netherlands the government organizes a national census in which adults are asked also which religious denomination they wish to be considered a member of. Dutch church leaders have to contend with much ignorance about the religious situation, but to a certain extent they know more about the feelings of their congregations than many colleagues abroad. Moreover, the Dutch Catholics had at their disposal the first ecclesiastical research institute of the whole church, already set up in 1946 through a joined effort of priests and laity (W. Goddijn and C. Thoen, 1956). This institute counted everything countable in Catholic Holland with its many organizations. It knew exactly how many Catholics were living in the province of Friesland, down to the smallest village, but it also calculated the number of "Roman Catholic beds" in hospitals: this proved to be more than 50% in a province with only 7% Catholics. Publications of this kind did not further ecumenism. It was known that 37.5% of all members of football clubs were united in the Dutch Catholic Sports League. For gymnastics the percentage was 25. But this was already a branch of sports less favoured by the Roman tradition because of the danger of mixed marriages. Where moral dangers were most serious the lowest percentage of "organized Catholics" were found, namely in swimming; there the percentage was between 10 and 20! Of the cycle-racers, a typically southern sport, nearly 90% were Roman Catholics (*Kath. Archief*, 1962, p. 1071). In 1951 the 35,000 Catholics of Friesland, as was shown by a census, had produced no fewer than 221 priests then living, only fourteen of them doing pastoral work in Friesland itself. They had 772 Catholic organizations, that is one Catholic organization per 45 church members. In the provincial capital of Leeuwarden there were 1440 Catholic families, of whom 47% read a Catholic newspaper, 55% were members of a Catholic organization, and 66% were members of the Catholic Broadcasting Corporation (W. Goddijn, 1961).

The findings of this research work, often officially commissioned and paid for by the bishops, helped guide church policy between 1960 and 1970. In 1960 after fifteen years of work, French sociologist of religion Boulard came to the conclusion that, in spite of all efforts of the preceding years, a far-reaching de-Christianization had occurred in the big cities of France. In the countryside he observed the growth of a modern atheism. He blamed this mainly on the increasing contact with the big cities. These conclusions were not based on much exact knowledge. Therefore he then states: "A long-lasting labour of documentation and exchange of ideas with specialists in the social, theological and pastoral fields must continuously support spiritual care and organizational life: such a work can only be done under the responsibility and guidance of the entire episcopate" (*Kath. Archief*, 1969, pp. 571—573). Boulard's wish became a reality in The Netherlands.

In 1960 the Dutch bishops knew the situation in their dioceses and parishes. There were three averages for the country: in that year people on an average received Holy Communion 43 times, 12.2% of the faithful did not observe Easter duties, and 8.9% of the marriages were mixed. In a KSKI (= Catholic Demographic Society) comment on the 1960 census a relatively strong decline of the Catholic birth-rate was pointed out. "This example was also chosen because it can emphasize again the serious personal conflicts of conscience ensuing from deliberate birth control. It can be assumed that this tension was for a number of Catholics one of the causes of a weakening of their religious and ecclesiastical allegiance."

Membership in the big Catholic political party is called "political orthodoxy." This is seen to decline mainly in the big cities in the western area, but in the predominantly Catholic provinces of Brabant and Limburg in 1962, 75 and 82 percent of the vote still went to the Catholic People's Party (KVP). In general, the KSKI establishes indications of an increasingly marginal church allegiance. Ecclesiastical and social patterns of behaviour can no longer be taken for granted. If no new directions are given, then "there is a fair chance that a number of people will start disregarding all those acts that qualify them as Catholics. That many people do not have the personal possibilities at their disposal to respond to the appeal for a personal experiencing of their Catholicism is, in other words, no wonder." In this transition period the religious mentality of the overall majority has not been attacked, "but the neglect of, the uncertainty about and the tensions around its external forms, especially in the field of religious activities, have strongly increased" (KSKI, 1963). We emphasize here those observations showing that a decline of intensive ecclesiastical allegiance had already set in during the 'fifties and 'sixties.

To take a quick look at the year 1971, the decline in church attendance was sometimes very off-handedly ascribed to the renewal movement and the conflicts with Rome. The KSKI comment on the 1971 census findings points out that the Catholic percentage of the Dutch population had grown, since 1920, to 40.4 in 1960, and that now for the first time it had decreased to 39.4%. But this stagnation of growth proved to be a national phenomenon. There seems to be a kind of return to normal proportions, after a period of exceptional development. In fact this drop is ascribed to the declining birth-rate and the increasing number of Catholics declaring that they no longer belong to a religious denomination. It is estimated that over 300,000 people, who still declared themselves Catholics in 1960, did not do so in 1971. Especially the younger generation seems be to taking its distance (KSKI, 1972).

When at the beginning of 1973 the KSKI was asked to give a survey of the actual position of the Dutch Catholics the following data were presented:

In The Netherlands there are 5.3 million Catholics; there are 1350 chapels, 2200 churches and other places for worship, in total visited more or less regularly by about half of the Catholics; there are 1835 parishes, 1030 of which have parish councils in which 9700 men and 4900 women are involved in discussion and decision-making; 2050 parish boards of governors in which 10,000 men and 1500 women bear administrative responsibilities; 1100 workgroups with 9800 members who prepare the celebration of the liturgy; 68,500 people have direct liturgical tasks as acolytes, servers, readers and collectors; there are 4900 choirs with 3700 directors and musicians and 135,800 members adding lustre to liturgical services; 1200 people are in charge of the preparation of the church itself; 2000 people assist in presbytery housekeeping; on the parish level only 22,800 people engage in activities like catechesis, fund-raising, charity, ecumenism; the 3830 orientation and reflection groups have 40,800 members. There are 7 bishops; 3600 priests belonging to 7 dioceses; 8300 religious priests belonging to 36 orders and congregations, 4150 of whom are working abroad; 23,400 nuns are working in the country and 3200 abroad; there are 4100 male religious, non-priests, in The Netherlands and 1500 elswhere; 350 deacons and lay pastoral workers assist on behalf of the pastorate in the parish; 750 theology students are training for full- or part-time functions in the church's service to mankind.

4. The Exercise of Authority

In every modern and free society the processes of democracy are developing, characterized by public control of authority and the possibility of having a say in the appointment of officials.

Especially after 1960 all forms of authority were severely questioned in The Netherlands. Mass media strongly promoted this by starting discussions on all kinds of established opinions and taboos. This process spread to family life, business life, the legal system and even the military organization. Among the Catholic population of The Netherlands, always particularly law-abiding, there were sporadic changes before the Second World War, and the first resistance to episcopal directives occurred outside the political and social organizations.

Rogier (1969) thinks that "Romanist triumphalism" hung itself mainly by its political activities. " 'Political Catholicism,' which more and more hid the faith behind the uninviting facade of party politics, became an annoyance to the non-Catholics and paralyzed all 'missionary zeal,' but besides it became something distasteful to the Catholic youth who ran amock in periodicals such as *Roeping* and *De Gemeenschap*, loudly crying for 'heart and ardour,' but who among themselves were divided, on the one hand, into extreme right-wing, anti-democratic, pro-fascist groups, and on the other were leftist-oriented." Rogier, professor of church history at Nijmegen University, has repeatedly reproached the strong fealty of the Dutch Catholics. Apart from being a residual of historical oppression and discrimination, this attitude is a factor also found among Catholics abroad: an overemphasis on the duty to be docile.

> Docility is not a virtue; it is the instinct of sheep; it is subhuman and even lacking in little children. It has to be taught to us. This may have its use like the many things we must learn in self-discipline, its use for a community that cannot function with the unbridled individualism of its members, its use for ourselves, provided it is the outcome of a voluntary decision to obey....Obedience is a conscious self-denial; it is a *virtus*, that is, an exertion of the human will. Docility is nothing of the kind; it is the undoing of all societies: it not only cuts off the excesses of stubbornness, but also kills initiative and the sense of personal responsibility (L. Rogier, 1958).

His speech, a classic text for this period of modern Dutch church renewal, confirmed the reactions four years earlier of a number of Catholic intellectuals to the bishops' published directives urging them to remain united as much as possible in Catholic social and political organizations. Then for the first time a group of practising Catholics had formed a workgroup within the socialist party. The bishops were surprised at the reactions in Holland. It was their last rather authoritarian and clerical attempt to close the ranks. This "Mandement" was originally planned for 1953, the centenary year of the restoration of the hierarchy. A draft text, written by people from "St. Adelbert," an organization of Catholic intellectuals, and from the St. Willibrord Society for ecumenical work, was rejected by the bishops. Ultimately auxiliary bishop Hansen of Roermond became its principal author. It was especially the Limburg diocese that requested this "Mandement," as a help to slow down the increasing marginalization of the faith. The later Cardinal Alfrink, then auxiliary bishop of Utrecht and the only still active member of the episcopal college of those days, did not favour this way of exercising authority, but as the youngest of the bishops he acquiesced to the majority's decision. A. Manning (1971), professor for twentieth century world history at Nijmegen, concludes: "The Mandement was an old-fashioned attempt to synthesize an organized and prescribed kind of Catholicism, while all kinds of different indications were becoming visible. It was somewhere between old and new, but it leaned more towards the former."

A separate study could be written about the development of attitudes towards ecclesiastical authority in The Netherlands during the last decades. This movement had already started before the Second World War, got better chances to expand during the war, and was then adopted by authors and pastors who defended a more critical attitude towards church authority.

One could start with articles by Father N. Perquin S.J. on "Constraint in Religious Education" and "Authority and Freedom" (Dux, 1947) and the many bible-inspired publications of Nijmegen's prof. Grossouw. This approach was continued by the activities of the Catholic Central Bureau for the Promotion of Mental Health. There, authors like Terruwe and Duynstee, who were aware of the interrelationship between compulsory behaviour and religious experience, were protected against disqualifications by the Roman Curia. Later on both of them were rehabilitated through the intervention of Cardinal Alfrink. The director of the then-still Catholic bureau suggested a more prudent policy. "Gradually some members felt the time was ripe for offering some resistance to authoritarian interference by the central church authorities. For some, the indignation about this infringement on the laboriously gained human and scientific insights was stronger than the age-old timid dependence on the Roman Curia" (H. Suèr, 1969). A fundamental and lasting contribution to the relations between the pastorate and mental health care in The Netherlands was given by Han Fortmann, who died in 1971. He fought against neurosis

78

scrupulous formalism, dogmatism and authoritarianism openly and expertly. His work at Nijmegen University is continued by pastoral psychologist Dr. W. Berger.

Pastoral practice was much influenced by the methods developed by army chaplains. Their philosophy and approach had close links with the aforementioned Bureau for Mental Health at Utrecht. In the Catholic military training centers two-day courses were offered to groups of about two hundred Catholic soldiers. Discussions and the search for a personal and authentic position in relation to the existing ideas of church, of faith and morality, were the main issues. Their own periodical with a circulation of about 35,000 in 1960 often spread radical ideas. Later on the courses assumed a different character but via the participation of thousands of Catholic army people and pastors they have had a very great influence on making religion an individual and private experience.

It is an interesting question whether the disappearance of social apartheid and of the strong allegiance to ecclesiastical authority, as well as the increased possibilities of personal choice and individual religious practice, have also deepened the faith. J. Auping (1972) asked this question. He points out that in recent years very large printings of prayer-books have been sold. "In summary, we can say that many did not and few did respond to the invitation to a freer and deeper faith as implied in the weakening of social connections between church and society.... We are waiting for the church historian who, with an adequate biblical knowledge, will write this history with all the biblical themes that characterize it: oppression, exodus, settling in the promised land, prophetic announcement of possible freedom of belief, false prophets and exile, renewal and restoration." The typology of progression and regression can be expressed in biblical terms.

5. The Bishops

In 1956 two new episcopal sees were established in The Netherlands, namely at Groningen and Rotterdam, respectively branches from Utrecht and Haarlem; The Netherlands then had seven dioceses. The chairman of the bishop's conference, Msgr. B. Alfrink, had been an aide to the rebellious Cardinal J. de Jong since 1951; he became Archbishop of Utrecht in 1955 and a cardinal in 1960. As chairman he has no other power over his colleagues except that of a capable chairman. Still it is enough to enable us to say that there has been a strong continuity in Dutch episcopal leadership because Bernard Alfrink has been a member of the episcopal college from 1951 to this day. The composition of this college shows a wide variety of personal qualities. The number of bishops is not large, but in comparison to other countries a few things can be said. Just before Vatican II, where the number of bishops entitled to vote was to weigh so heavily, a study showed that Belgium, Germany, Austria and The Netherlands, in this order, had the relatively highest number of Catholics per European diocese. Italy ranked eleventh. Although the Italian Catholics only formed 27.5% of all European Catholics, Italy contained half of all European dioceses. Half of the Italian dioceses had fewer than 100,000 Catholics, and were comparable with an average deanery in the rest of Europe. If the Italian "diocesan density" would be taken as the norm, The Netherlands should not have 7 but 28 dioceses (L. Grond, 1960). And according to Roman-Italian standards its influence would have been that much heavier.

For internal-organizational reasons the new diocese-division of 1956 was not looked upon very positively. There was a tendency to large-scale operations. There was a growing number of national bodies for liturgy, catechesis, ecumenism, etc. Generally speaking they were advisory commissions, composed of priests and lay people. In other countries auxiliary bishops are sometimes nominated for these tasks. In The Netherlands they are not found nowadays. Even the cardinal has no auxiliary at this moment. This means we lack the group of priests from whom Rome usually chooses people for the episcopacy. The diocesan governing bodies however have been enlarged since 1960. The number of vicars rose from 8 to 22. Formerly, these vicars had only incidental social contacts; presently they participate in national ecclesiastical bodies that perform the preparatory work in order to lighten the Bishops' governmental tasks. The small number of bishops and these national councils provide good opportunities for communication. This communication especially developed during the Vatican Council.

Because of their living and working together for months in the hospitable house of Msgr. J. Damen in Rome, the Dutch bishops began to know each other quite well. Back home after Vatican II they met every month or even more frequently.

They believed that together they were able and allowed to accomplish a lot for church renewal, more so because they could no longer retire to a phantasy world outside of reality. Such frequent meetings, such mutual solidarity is more difficult to form in other countries, if only for geographical and quantitative reasons: dissension tends to be greater and the chances for discussion more limited. The degree to which the bishops are then aware of developments in their country may be less extensive, and the possibilities for real action smaller. Their policy with regard to renewal may be more hesitant, slower, more restricted dogmatically and canonically; there is less room for experimentation available" (R. Huysmans, 1972).

Many countries have an episcopal presidium that meets more often; big numbers, like in Italy with its about 240 dioceses, make plenary meetings cumbersome. Only in November 1967 was the Dutch episcopal college given the formal status of a bishops' conference. Up till then, the cardinal's auxiliary was in charge of the secretariat. He retired in 1970. In 1968 a secretary to the bishops' conference was appointed; in 1970 a second secretary was added. In 1972 a new central secretariat was set up, in which various national institutes, such as the aforementioned advisory bureau (the Pastoral Institute), were centralized under the direction of a board almost entirely composed of episcopal vicars.

Cardinal Alfrink has always been careful in formulating the powers of the national bishops' conference, Wherever necessary and useful for the benefit of the faithful and the prestige of the bishops and the church, he would try to promote an identical policy in the seven separate dioceses. In The Netherlands only unanimous decisions were accepted, and if this unanimity was lacking, each bishop kept his autonomy. The authority of such unanimous decisions was not more than the sum total of the bishops' local authority. The chairman of the bishops' conference has the special duty of "assessing all motives and decisions as to their conformity with the unanimous faith of the church and the bishops of the whole world" (J. Groot, 1964).

Alfrink was a well-known scriptural scholar who continued to publish until 1959. Having taught for barely ten years — he was professor at Nijmegen — he was nominated consultant to the Pontifical Bible Commission. In 1964 Cardinal Bea said that Cardinal Alfrink was one of the "most quoted" personalities in the Vatican Council. Not only because he was a member of the preparatory committee and of the presidium, but especially because of his proposals to reorganize the church's central government on the basis of the collegial character of the apostolic ministry. At a very early date he launched the idea that the Pope be assisted by a kind of episcopal council, as a visible token of the collegial government of the church universal. Then already Cardinal Bea (1964) said of his former pupil at the Biblical Institute: "Everybody knows — or should know — how difficult it is becoming for the average person to keep a happy medium. Whoever tries to do this, runs the risk of being accused by leftists or rightists of sometimes completely opposite opinions, or to be blamed for a lack of sincerity or a weakness for comprises."

Cardinal Alfrink immediately considers anybody who offers arguments as a serious discussion partner. At the Pastoral Council, itself a very special form of modern authority practices he not only defended the dialogue structure, but was also the one who applied it best. The frank and trustful contacts with priests and laity made the Council able to succeed without incurring great conflicts. Utrecht church historian G. Abbink (1970) best describes the permanent field of tension during the Pastoral Council, in which Cardinal Alfrink moved about sometimes quite at ease and then again with almost no prospect of succeeding:

> There was a special desire to preserve the personal responsibility of the bishops. But how hierarchical government and government by dialogue can really be combined was only answered in practice, not in theory. The delegations were a democratic representation, but theologically speaking the bishops belong to a nondemocratic church structure. The two seem irreconcilable. The term used to bridge the gap is dialogue. But dialogue cannot be described in juridical terms. A number of representatives at the council see dialogue as democracy and think therefore that the bishop ought to conform to the viewpoints of the delegation from his diocese; but the bishops are convinced that they will indeed often conform to those points of view, but that this will not necessarily be the case. Hierarchical government in dialogue remains hierarchical government and is not transformed into democracy through dialogue. Democracy is something fundamentally different.

To the bishops of Den Bosch and Breda, W. Bekkers and G. de Vet, a doctoral thesis has already been devoted (L. Groothuis, 1971). Bishop Bekkers died 9 May 1966. He had very personal views about his ministry and became especially known through his television broadcasts. Particularly the broadcast on 21 March 1963, about the primacy of conscience in marriage ethics, was completely in line with the changing conceptions of authority in The Netherlands.

> If Bishop Bekkers has created a new episcopal image, an image that has made the episcopal function acceptable even to non-episcopalian Protestant Christians and to non-believers, this is owing to the natural courage and nerve he had never to hide behind his office. This courage can indeed compromise a minister, in whatever function. Bishop Bekkers knew this.

But the person who does not look for cover himself will in the long run, albeit through pain and sorrow, really become invulnerable — and the people will worship him (E. Schillebeeckx. *Kath. Archief* 1966, p. 638).

"His was a spiritual freedom which appeared among us as something unique" was Father J. van Kilsdonk's judgment. In the preparatory years of Vatican II Bekkers had been worried about the "unworldly" draft reports that were circulated and that had only to be approved of by the bishops. In the first council days of October 1962, the bishops in Rome were snowed under with 4000 reports in Latin, English and French, criticizing these council drafts. Bishop Bekkers spread these notes, composed by experts, theological and otherwise, under his own name and thus had a very strong influence on the first council session.

If Msgr. Bekkers was the pastor in the episcopal college with a strong feeling for pastoral assignments, Bishop G. de Vet was the pastor with a deep organizational knowledge and feeling for management. It was especially he who managed to convince his colleagues of the necessity of the Pastoral Institute and the Pastoral Council. Both Bekkers and De Vet did everything to establish a meaningful unity of church and world, of faith and life, by really taking seriously the actual experiences of their actual fellowmen and by remaining consistently faithful to them. They turned a hierarchical church into one of invitation and sympathy, open to everybody and respecting everybody. This is Groothuis' conclusion in his thesis for the Theological Faculty of Münster (Westphalia).

Bishop Th. Zwartkruis of Haarlem did not attend the Vatican Council. His toughest problems have been with the radical students in the parish of Huub Oosterhuis and his colleagues in Amsterdam and with Jan Ruyter's critical parish in Beverwijk. He is quite well-known in the English-speaking world and has a "feeling" for publicity abroad. His predecessor Dr. J. van Dodewaard unfortunately did not take a good holiday after Vatican II — he was the first bishop to draft a postconciliar plan for his diocese. After its publication he toured his entire diocese. This was ended by his sudden death.

Bishop P. Nierman of the new diocese of Groningen was present during the whole council. In the episcopacy he was the representative of the part of The Netherlands where the ecumenical pastorate was of the oldest standing. A few years after Vatican II he was succeeded by B. Möller, a sharp-witted philosopher with outspokenly spiritual interests. When Bishops Bekkers and De Vet were succeeded by J. Bluyssen and H. Ernst respectively, some kind of consultation was conducted among the priests and laity, in order to alleviate the responsible task of the diocesan chapter which, as is customary in The Netherlands, submits three candidates to Rome. The Dutch bishops' conference advises Rome of the chapter's suggestions. Later on, following the procedures in the diocese of Den Bosch, more forms of consultation were implemented for the appointments in Groningen, Breda, Rotterdam and Roermond.

Concerning the exercise of authority Bishop Bluyssen made a few characterizing remarks. In an interview with *De Nieuwe Linie* of 26 November 1966 he said: "When ideas are changing, authority runs the risk of sticking too long to the old structures, and this leads to an authority crisis. Especially in periods of growth and change the authority should have the flexibility to think and grow with the times. Then the tension can be happily solved, because there is enough room for an exchange of ideas and consultation." In 1967, after a series of pastoral talks in his diocese were completed, Bishop Bluyssen said: "Personally I live with the conviction that my authority as a bishop finds its origin both in the Lord and in the community of God's people, and this both at the same time and inseparably; and also that the exercise of my authority should have its effect through both the Lord and the community of God's people." Then he pointed out how this new climate of leadership should be effectuated in various consultation structures, already being prepared on the diocesan and national level in the form of diocesan councils and the national Pastoral Council (G. Dukker et al., 1966; H. Verbeek, 1967).

On 17 December 1967 H. Ernst was ordained Bishop of Breda as successor to Msgr. G. de Vet. In preparation for his appointment the diocesan pastoral council received a letter from the diocesan chapter with, among other things, the following: "You may have some personal ideas or wishes which may help decide the composition of our presentation." Here again we have an attempt to realize some kind of consultation for the nomination of a diocesan bishop. Rome however always kept the formal right to ignore both the chapter's presentation and the advice of the residing bishops. In such cases the information supplied by the nunciature becomes decisive.

At the end of May 1967 Msgr. G. Beltrami left The Netherlands where he had been Apostolic Internuncio since 31 January 1959. He was succeeded by Msgr. A. Felici, who received the title Pronuncio, and who previously had filled a high post at the State Secretariat in Rome.

Bishop M. Jansen was the first bishop of the new diocese of Rotterdam. He also attended the entire Vatican Council. This former seminary professor had a great pastoral interest, was always very straightforward, and possessed a good sense of humour. Health reasons forced him to hand in his resignation in 1970. The chapter held extensive consultations and gave the faithful themselves the opportunity, via an opinion poll, to sketch a "profile" of the bishop they wanted. The new papal representative at The Hague, Msgr. Felici, objected to the names of the candidates being made public. The diocesan pastoral council agreed and was, after all these well-managed preparations, convinced that Rome would take into account the wishes of the diocese. When, on 30 December 1970, Msgr. A. Simonis was nominated, the widest public discussion ever held in The Netherlands about church renewal burst forth. For the first time there was a feeling that the Vatican was very deliberately and very fundamentally interfering with the policy of the Dutch bishops. For Bishop-elect Simonis had, during the Pastoral Council always been the competent and eloquent spokesman and defender of Roman theology and Roman directives. He called himself the mouthpiece of the "precise," a term from the history of Protestant Christianity when modernists and fundamentalists opposed each other.

The day after Bishop Simonis's nomination the Vatican announced that the Pope had accepted the resignation of Bishop P. Moors of Roermond in the province of Limburg. He, too, had attended the Vatican Council, and at the college of bishops he was the administrator who refused to make rash decisions but who very carefully handled the Roman documents, always comparing them with earlier, carefully registered decisions of the college of bishops. Roermond was "to do better" than Rotterdam where many priests and lay people had been frustrated by the fact that Rome had completely ignored the preparations made for the bishop's nomination. Again Rome disregarded the chapter's presentation and the advice of the Dutch bishops. Even more than in the case of Simonis the appointment of J. Gijsen on 22 January 1972 meant a disavowal of the policy of the Dutch bishops. Against the advice of the bishops Pope Paul VI himself ordained Bishop Gijsen. And in spite of his objections, Cardinal Alfrink went to Rome to assist at the ordination as co-consecrator. It was difficult for him to refuse.

6. Scholarship and Pastoral Practice

Characteristic for the special development of church renewal in The Netherlands is the open relation between the bishops and the practitioners in the various fields of scholarly disciplines such as theology, sociology, psychology and philosophy. The bishops exercised their authority realistically and in good communication with pastors and the faithful. The scholars stimulated this candor theologically, and offered suggestions for an ever better concretization of this communication in the practices of the pastorate, its preachings and catechesis. Theology in The Netherlands was clearly concerned with society and wanted to remain understandable to the people. Besides intelligibility and the willingness to listen, personal involvement, joint responsibility and the ensuing joint decision-making function were also stimulated. Concrete attempts in this direction were not only made by organizations such as the Pastoral Institute which formulated advice for the bishops with the help of hundreds of experts. Nor was this only done by the Pastoral Council which tried to concretize the joint responsibility of experts and representatives of the faithful, in dialogue with the bishops. Various other institutions, in particular the faculties of theology, the Higher Catechetical Institute, and the KSKI also advised the pastoral leaders on many levels. The give and take of personal advice continued.

It took a long time before the Dutch bishops allowed scholars to function outside the so-called seminaries or educational institutes for priests. At the beginning of the century The Netherlands had no Cardinal-Archbishop Mercier as Belgium had. He prepared the way for neo-scholasticism, for the study of psychology and for the ecumenical movement. Not until the 'thirties was a university graduate found among the Dutch bishops and at that time in the diocese of Haarlem seminary students were forbidden to mix with the university students of Amsterdam and Leyden. Cardinal de Jong told L. Rogier in 1953 that in the seminaries you lost your faculty of critical thinking. This same J. de Jong, Archbishop of Utrecht and a well-known church historian, wrote home in a letter from Rome where he was studying: "When you are a Roman doctor of theology or philosophy you are like a man from the Middle Ages looking wonderingly at the twentieth century" (L. Rogier, 1970; H. Aukes, 1956).

In his book *The Power of the Catholic Church* German theologian M. Becker (1967) wonders how criticism is possible in the church when the authorities are not open to it, as is usually the case. "It should have a place where it can be formed and a road along which it develops." According to Becker the origins of criticism lie in theology, and its course of development is mainly set by sociology and psychology. The problem is to continually view theology critically, as an ecclesiastical science, in its relation to the pastoral practices of the faithful. The bishops are usually afraid that knowledge may endanger their authoritative position. But the number of theologians wanting to become bishop is as small as the number of philosophers wanting to become government ministers. There are only conflicts between church ministers and theologians when, contrary to new theological insights, the bishops stick to outdated pastoral practices (M. Becker, 1967).

In contrast to Becker's opinion, the origin of the renewal movement in The Netherlands is not found with the professional theologians. According to Schillebeeckx, who in 1958 came from Flanders to Nijmegen University as professor of dogmatics and the history of theology, The Netherlands was the first country in which priests and laity interested in religion studied religious problems from the viewpoint of the social sciences. "The contribution of sociology and psychology, and of the social sciences in general, started the breakthrough in this country" (R. Auwerda, 1969). In the then-existing theological periodicals Schillebeeckx found little instigation to renewal. Abroad, there were surely good sociologists, but they lacked any connection with theology. This connection did exist in The Netherlands, because the attitude here was decidedly pragmatic.

We shall now try to indicate a number of social characteristics of theology or of theological practices in The Netherlands. Church renewal is directly linked to the renewal of theology and to the possible openness of church leaders to new theological insights. Already before and even more after Vatican II theologians knew they had the support of several fundamental opinions of Cardinal Alfrink. He was an advocate of a collegial form of teaching authority and doing pastoral work. This implies more emphasis on the local churches, an acceptance of a certain pluralism, a preference for belief based on personal reflection about the faith, and for a mature experiencing of the faith. Feeling oneself being appealed to arouses the wish for mutual responsibility and partnership on all church levels. This goes together with a respect for the continuity of the church and its doctrine, and with the recognition that the authority of bishops and Pope cannot be reduced to an authorization by the church community.

How Cardinal Alfrink's views on this matter were appreciated can be seen in an assessment by Cardinal A. Bea. It is quite uncustomary for a cardinal to evaluate thus the ideas of a colleague. It means both an appreciation of the starting-points for Dutch ecclesiastical policy and of the methodology of this policy. Being the judgment of one who is simultaneously a "foreign observer" and a Roman insider, this assessment is particularly valuable. "When discussing the collegial character of the apostolic ministry, and consequently also the collegial character of the ministry of the followers of the apostles, the bishops, he (i.e. Cardinal Alfrink) remarked that the expression 'Peter and the Apostles' was misleading. It did not say clearly enough that Peter was also a member of the apostolic college; to be sure, he was the first of the apostles, but he should always be seen in combination with the others, as a member of the college." Therefore the cardinal suggested speaking of "Peter together with the other apostles." Later on, during the discussions on the various aspects of the episcopal ministry and particularly on the problem of the concrete implementation of the collegial character of the apostolic ministry, he suggested the establishment of a bishops' council to assist the Pope. It is striking how the cardinal warned against misunderstanding and elaborated further on the proposal of a bishops' council. This bishops' council, he argued, is not representative of an episcopal college in the sense of parliamentary representation. Rather the council suggested was a visible sign of the collegial government of the church universal, and would help to create a balance between the central government and regional authorities, both of them equally necessary. On another occasion he went even deeper into the matter and elucidated the relations between the bishops' council and the local bishops' conferences, and the relation of both of them to the Pope.

This demonstrates one of the cardinal's characteristics which so far has hardly been mentioned: his down-to-earth equilibrium. His openness towards new problems goes hand in hand with his constant faithfulness to traditional beliefs and the church's magisterium. Cardinal Alfrink is not a blindfolded "party man." Parties shouldn't exist at all in the council, because every council bishop, guided by the Holy Spirit, must follow "his own conscience and his own convictions gained through an earnest study of the subject under discussion. Nor has the cardinal's openmindedness become fetish-for-renewal; even new things that are good are only accepted after thorough study, and only in as far as they have passed close scrutiny" (A. Bea, 1964).

In a letter to the faithful (24 December 1960) the Dutch bishops had, even before the opening of the Vatican Council, developed a theology about the distinction between priests and laity, and in particular about doctrine. In this letter the personal views of authority held by the central government were first relativized, and reference was made to the collective ideas about faith of the whole church community. "When we really sustain a collective opinion of the church community as a whole, it is not only by right, but also in actual fact infallible....Because of the premature ending of the First Vatican Council the isolated dogma of papal infallibility seems to be a completely independent thing. In point of fact this personal infallibility is incorporated into the ministerial infallibility of the entire bishops' college, which in its turn is borne by the infallible faith of the whole church community" (*Kath. Archief*, 1961, p. 369). The reference to the links between church authority and the entire religious community is of fundamental importance here, and it was not only to stimulate theology but also the interdisciplinary cooperation of theology and the social sciences. From that moment on theology started to contribute to church renewal.

Vatican II started the real dialogue between the bishops and the experts on a world level. This official permission and promotion of dialogue, and the spreading of information about the differences of opinion among prominent church leaders by publicity media to all corners of the church universal, already worked toward a relativism. This new relativity made renewal and change possible. Here, clear possibilities grew to check the new theology against the pastoral practice of the bishops. They studied the memoranda written by the theologians for their council hall interventions, they attended study meetings and dozens of conferences. It was a process of mutual brushing-up and possible recognition. This learning process through meetings between bishops and experts, often attended also by professional journalists, had a great influence on Dutch church renewal.

In his opening address to Vatican II Pope John XXIII said the council's objective was not to reiterate existing doctrine, but to apply such methods of expounding doctrine as would be best suited to the teaching ministry "which indeed is mainly pastoral in character." The safe and unchangeable items of doctrine would have to be studied and explained in such a way that they were "adapted to our times." This is how Schillebeeckx formulates this openness of theology to renewal: God's salvatory message is directed to all men and should again and again be placed in perspective with the actual spiritual situation of mankind. "It is exactly this ever-renewed assimilation of the faith, prepared by the growth of theology, which stimulates a growth in faith and helps to effect the development of dogma. Running away from the duty to develop and renew theology is therefore *ipso facto* an offence against the life of faith itself" (*Catholica*, 2, 1968). This is a strong affirmation of the influence the modern life of the church, actually founded in Christian communities such as in The Netherlands, can and must have on the renewal of the faith and the wording of doctrine. In this way faith is also experienced as a personal responsibility. I remember quite well how these starting points were discussed at Doorn, at the training center of the Catholic Labour Organization, where bishops and experts met to prepare for the Pastoral Council. Even after the promulgation of the documents of Vatican II, the question is not only how to apply these to the local Christian community, but also how to adapt them to the characteristic "mental climate" of The Netherlands. There is not only a movement from above, but also from below. Many meetings of the bishops, experts and publicists, at Doorn and Noordwijkerhout, dealt with this theme.

Much more difficult was finding, after Vatican II, the forms in which these conversations between bishops and experts, between theology and pastoral practice, could be continued. Characteristic for The Netherlands is that the situation was judged suitable to venture an experiment in the Pastoral Council. In the U.S.A. the courage to do this was lacking, as is shown in the report of the "Interdisciplinary Consultation," held in Chicago from 28 to 30 August 1970, on a "National Pastoral Council" after the Dutch model. Switzerland only started it after long years of preparation. Western Germany gave it a very strict canonical structure.

In The Netherlands the position of the experts first had to be clarified. Initially they wanted to participate in great numbers in the decision-making of the plenary sessions of the Pastoral Council. But gradually it became clear that, however difficult this might be, the faithful should be reasonably represented at the plenary sessions, and that the specialists were only to advise, among other things through the preparation of draft reports. The suppositions on which this entire post-Vatican experiment with the Dutch Pastoral Council was based also indicate how theology was studied and functioned.

Professor P. Smulders (1970), one of the "ideologists" of the Pastoral Council, formulated the following suppositions:

> The objective of a church leader should not be to hand out the directives that are best from an abstract point of view, but those directives that are recognized by the religious feeling of the faithful and can be comprehended by their Christian conscience.
> — For it is not the task of a governor to make obedience as difficult and heroic as possible, but rather to facilitate a spontaneous and convinced acceptance of the law.
> — Basically, the bishops and the faithful are guided by one and the same source of faith and the same ideals. The bishops may have more experience, they may have better insight into the complexity of the problems, they may have more theological knowledge and a higher degree of sanctity; but they have no source different from the faithful. Therefore the faithful can understand the bishops' basic insights and understand their motives.
> — This conception presupposes maturity in the faithful and a willingness to be guided by the Holy Ghost. Every bishop must suppose this good will to be present in his community; otherwise he destroys the community. After centuries of tutelage, spiritual adulthood is not always present. But one should remember, first of all that a person is only helped toward maturity if he is treated as an adult; and secondly that the time is near that in the western world only an adult faith will be able to survive.
> We should recall our initial statement: the bishops have an authority that cannot be reduced to a faculty conferred upon them by the church community; they have it as Christ's deputies. Accordingly the theoretical ideas developed here should be completed by the practical question: can common consultation and common decision-making in a church province be organized in such a way that the specific authority of the bishops receives its full due? I think the Working Formula of the Pastoral Council has managed to do so and that, with all its shortcomings, the Pastoral Council's development has not impaired the bishops' authority, but in fact strengthened it. For it gave birth to a new confidence between bishops, clergy and laity, and to a new understanding of each other's ideas, intentions and motives.

Another important experiment bringing out the theological activity in The Netherlands, and simultaneously a feature of church renewal, was the book, *New Catechism*. Its subtitle ran "Preaching the Faith to Adults." As the bishops wrote in their Preface, it wanted: "nothing but to proclaim the message brought by Jesus of Nazareth into this world," and it tried "to reflect the renewal given a voice by the council" (*New Catechism*, 1966). The entire preparatory period of this New Catechism again shows the interplay of scholarship and pastoral practice. The bishops ordered a new catechism for schools to be composed as early as 1956. When, at a European catechetical congress in London (1961), it appeared that one of the "schemata" for the already announced Vatican Council was to deal with the catechesis for adults, the bishops approved a project for such a catechesis. Under the chairmanship of Father W. Bless many specialists started working. In 1961 a two-hundred-page draft was sent to 150 psychologists, sociologists and theologians, but also to a great number of "fathers and mothers" as representatives of the local community with its permanent task of handing down the faith in the family. More than 10,000 reactions were sent in. Jesuit Fathers P. Schoonenberg (the wellknown Nijmegen theologian), G. Mulders, W. Bless and G. van Hemert (the final editor) played the central roles. On 9 October 1966 Cardinal Alfrink publicly presented the book, published under the responsibility of the Dutch bishops' conference. It is not an optional text, Cardinal Alfrink said, neither is everything the "infallible Gospel," but it is a "safe guide" for the Dutch Catholic community.

Typical of the catechism was its didactical structure, its direction towards the adult, in the cultural sense of the word. In contrast to earlier times, and particularly in The Netherlands, modern man is on a different cultural and intellectual level, and is using a manner of expression that is quite different from that of earlier generations. An enormous amount of hard labour had been required to adapt this preaching of the faith to modern man. Through this catechism theologians were again getting into contact with modern man via some kind of feedback. The text starts with a description of man in search of God and it ends, via the history of Christ's coming, with God in search of man (L. Alting von Geusau, Utrecht, 1969).

On 10 October 1967 the first translation, in English, was published by Burns and Oates, London, and Herder and Herder, New York. The latter publisher received in the United States an award for the best Catholic book of 1967. In June 1968 the German edition appeared, in July the Italian and French ones. The Dutch catechism was becoming a world catechism. Translations were made into Spanish, Catalonian, Danish, Japanese, Croatian, Basque, Bengali, Slovene. Not long ago the third printing of the Korean edition was published.

In the meantime, in November 1966, it had become known that a number of Dutch Catholics had, over the heads of the bishops, denounced the *New Catechism* in Rome. Discussions about it lasted till the end of 1968. The yearbook of the Catholic Documentation Center at Nijmegen gives in its 1972 issue eighteen pages of bibliography in all the world's languages about the *New Catechism* (W. Bless and J. Roes, 1972). When describing the stagnation in church renewal we shall again take up this subject.

We have to limit ourselves to these few illustrations of renewal. They had international repercussions and became the main examples of the tension between doctrinal authority and freedom, between central government and the local church community. In their answer to questions asked by Cardinal A. Ottaviani, then Prefect of the Congregation for the Doctrine of the Faith, and sent to all bishops' conferences in the world, the Dutch bishops replied:

> Our serious theologians by no means have reduced the normal doctrinal authority of the Pope of Rome to the level of merely personal opinions. But it is known that in The Netherlands there is a very frank and open discussion of theological problems, in which, moreover, many nontheologians also take part. In this country theology is no longer the exclusive domain of professional theologians. This unavoidably entails the airing of a number of rash and one-sided opinions. But this frankness, openness and general interest are of great benefit to the church. For they make it impossible for our theologians, as they used to do, to study theology in seclusion, and they are obliged to take part frankly and openly in those discussions in order to guide and orientate them. If the faith of the church is to be renewed, it is necessary that modern theologians are involved in what is happening in the world. It goes without saying that this creates problems and entails risks, because theology today is much less self-confident and safe than it used to be (*De Volkskrant*, 29 December 1967).

Schillebeeckx, who for this and various other texts acted as the bishops' principal advisor, was impeached by the Roman Congregation for the Doctrine of the Faith. *Le Monde* of 24 September 1968 gave the first information, which was basically correct. The nunciature in the United States where Schillebeeckx was doing a lecture tour (November and December 1967; 42 conferences in six weeks) was said to have put in a complaint against him.

Very recently, in a conference for the Theological Faculty of Tilburg, Prof. G. Kerkhofs of Louvain called the Dutch church province a *locus theologicus* for inner-church freedom." For this freedom the Second Vatican Council supplied the "ideology" in *Lumen Gentium* regarding the theology of the local church; in *Gaudium et Spes* regarding the autonomy of human behaviour (including culture, science and sexuality); in the Decree on Ecumenism for Christian cooperation and intercommunion; and in the

Decree on Religious Freedom for, among other things, new ideas about missionary work.

The freedom required for church renewal also creates the danger of confusion. The Dutch bishops were well aware of these concomitant phenomena. Being a church in modern times in this way is risky. In their pastoral letter "Renewal and Confusion" (1968) the Dutch bishops say: "The treasure of the faith is not a dead capital we can preserve safely by burying it, albeit in a reconstructed church. In other words: faith is first of all an attitude to be cultivated, a venture asking for courage, but also an invitation to happiness and freedom. It is the courage to admit that, wherever God sends his Spirit, the recreation and innovation we need are being brought about."

7. Publicity and Communication

The small size of Holland, the small number of bishops, the existing Catholic media of press, radio and television made possible an intensive communication among the bishops themselves, between the bishops and experts, among the experts themselves, and among the professional publicists, all these groups and the Dutch public. Thus an important condition was fulfilled for public dialogue, for the creation of trustful relations and for a greater involvement of the community of the faithful in church renewal. This also applies to scientific periodicals such as *Tijdschrift voor Theologie*, founded in 1961, and to books like the New Catechism. In this context we should also point to the discussion groups as a form of communication. During the Pastoral Council period there were thousands of groups, on the parish level or otherwise, discussing the faith. The weekly publication *Katholiek Archief* (later *Archief der Kerken*) offered good documentation on all important events and studies in the entire church: it was read in every presbytery and convent; experts were regularly given the opportunity, in the so-called *capita selecta*, to discuss current theological subjects, offering full bibliographic information from all over the world (*Kath. Archief*, 1961, p. 771). A book like Bishop J. Robinson's *Honest to God* sold, in Dutch translation, 70,000 copies within four months.

The flow of communication from abroad to The Netherlands was very strong. In the post-war years the diocesan and regular seminaries performed a large number of ordinations. Many new priests did not start working in the pastorate straightaway, but continued their studies at universities abroad, particularly in Paris, Munich, Münster, Tübingen, Innsbruck, Rome and, last but not least, Louvain. Returning home they introduced the "new theology," now developing everywhere, into the seminaries. The limited size of the Dutch linguistic area caused an accelerated interpretation and processing of the new ideas, not only desired by the priests but also by the faithful.

The many Catholic organizations in The Netherlands, for all areas of cultural and social life, also had the opportunities to make contact with experts abroad, particularly in Europe. Thus the St. Willibrord Society stimulated the contacts with ecumenical theologians abroad; J. Willebrands, who later became cardinal, played an important role here. He was succeeded by theologian J. Groot, who was given the special position of episcopal delegate for ecumenical matters. There were international organizations, to which much support was given by Dutch experts, in the fields of catechesis, sociology of religion, Catholic education, missionary work, charity, migration problems, the industrial pastorate, Christian-democratic politics, Catholic employers and workers. Later on The Netherlands contributed towards the foundation of "Pax Romana," an organization of Catholic intellectuals, and "Pax Christi," an international peace movement of which Cardinal Alfrink is now president. On all these subjects international congresses were held, attended by Catholic Dutch experts.

Two international periodicals were founded in The Netherlands: the post-Vatican theological periodical *Concilium* and *Social Compass*, the periodical for sociologists of religion. In The Netherlands Msgr. R. Etchegary's plans to set up a European Bishops' Conference were worked out, and in 1967, at Noordwijkerhout, this country was host to the first meeting. Our country also took the initiative for the European workgroup on synodal problems, and also strongly supported the contacts among parish pastors and, later on, among the representatives of European priests' councils. An important but rarely noted factor is the large number of regular priests both in the country itself and in missionary areas — there is one secular priest to two regulars, a proportion that is usually just the opposite in the other western European churches. Their activities, too, strongly influenced communication, because regular priests have a much more elaborate international communication network than diocesan priests.

The communication flow from this country to other language

areas was made exceptionally difficult by the linguistic isolation of The Netherlands. As early as 8 September 1967 H. Divendal of the Pastoral Council's press center at Heemstede published an extensive memorandum on this problem. The high costs of interpreters and translators hindered effective performance. All the same, even then much publicity work directed toward foreign countries was carried out. Reports and studies, episcopal letters and documents were translated for the Vatican and personally explained.

Before the Pastoral Council even held its first session H. Fesquet had already written about it in *Le Monde*, R. Laurentin in *Le Figaro*, P. Gallay in *La Croix*, J. Horgan in *Irish Times*, M. Alcala in *A.B.C.* (Spain), D. Fischer in *The Tablet*, and J. Farnworth in *The New York Times*. Many articles, among others by E. Kleine, were to be found in newspapers and periodicals in German-speaking countries. Even in Hungary reports were published by B. Szanad. The six sessions of the Pastoral Council, from January 1968 till April 1970 were attended respectively by 27, 30, 47, 58, 88, and 70 foreign journalists. Dutch publicists and radio and television reporters raised the total number to 172. Thus it is absolutely incorrect to suggest today that the recently established (1973) press secretariat of the Dutch Episcopacy is starting in a complete vacuum.

An important problem was the fact that other groups, not in contact with the bishops, were directing information toward and finding audience by authorities abroad who considered the renewal movement in The Netherlands to be chaotic and who wanted to hold the Dutch bishops liable. Only recently the press chief of the Dutch episcopacy experienced this, when an excellent religious editor of a famous foreign newspaper thought that in the Netherlands about half of the priests had married, but were nevertheless allowed to remain in the priesthood (*Utrechts Nieuwsblad*, 7 May 1973). In a talk at the beginning of 1970 with Cardinal Marty of Paris he seemed to think that there were about two hundred "underground parishes" in The Netherlands, whereas I couldn't mention a single one.

The relation between bishops and the international mass media is a delicate thing. The press asks for complete openness, whereas on certain subjects the authorities do not yet want this openness, for example in order not to disturb negotiations or dialogue. These conflicts are also found in nonecclesiastical circles. Sometimes the press feels years in advance what situation is going to develop.

Thus in 1965 there was a rumour in The Netherlands that Rome was going to send an apostolic visitator; an official inquiry into church renewal in The Netherlands was said to be impending. In an address on "Church and Mass Media" Cardinal Alfrink responded:

> I would have wished, for example, that the publicity media which paid so much attention — in some cases several columns — to the rumours circulating abroad about an impending apostolic visitation of The Netherlands, had paid the same attention to the most explicit official *dementi* which I either did not find mention of in the press or only in one single line in an obscure corner. Giving prominence to this *dementi* would also have been a service to the church. And it would have been of great importance if the international press had put matters straight (*Kath. Archief*, 1965, p. 661).

Gradually the relationship between the press and the bishops improved. But the willingness to provide direct information remained poor, so that journalists tried to get "scoops" and in sometimes mysterious ways managed to have a look at secret documents, which they then made public. For years on end television has covered the entire renewal process in The Netherlands, particularly through interviews with Cardinal Alfrink. The Catholic Broadcasting Corporation (KRO) remained the medium with the greatest Catholic membership, and television broadcasts provided opportunities to reach a large number of non-Catholic viewers as well. The "writing press" was sometimes annoyed by the preference church leaders showed for KRO-television, but this preference is easy to understand.

8. The Dutch Catholics and the Renewal Movement

Nijmegen psychologist J. Weima has studied the relationship between authoritarian behaviour and religious conservatism. The characteristics he describes in his hypothesis are clearly the opposite of those active in the renewal movement in The Netherlands.

Voices can be heard in this country declaring that the policy of the "great majority" of the bishops has failed. And indeed everybody has the right to their personal opinion about this. A prominent scholar like prof. C. de Vogel (1973), a convert from Protestantism when she was less than forty years of age, calls herself a "young Catholic" because she has been a church member for about thirty years. She is opposed to the policy of the Dutch bishops, except for Bishops A. Simonis and J. Gijsen. She applauds

Rome's "interference" through episcopal nominations. These nominations, she says, are not arbitrary. "They are made on the basis of sound information from the country itself, in such cases collected with much care because numerous complaints about the goings-on and urgent appeals for help in what is experienced as an emergency situation, have been coming in from the country for a long time.... Policy must serve the faith. Where the faith has been deeply affected, the policy has failed." It is tragic that a convert sees the church of her youth changed, becoming modernist, or, as she puts it, "being Protestantized." To be sure, among the faithful of The Netherlands there exists a group which feels unhappy about the renewal movement. Despite their competence they have often not been enlisted in any activities, for example in the Pastoral Council. In other cases they have a great need for certainty or longing for the past. As a rule this also applies to the nonreligious aspects of life. Besides a "massive" disbelief they also see a "massive" anomie in society. There is a rigidity in their thinking and an adherence to traditional ideals and usages. Ethical norms are considered unchangeable and as such independent of actual situations. Implicitly or explicitly there is a preference for objective ecclesiastical rulings as opposed to the subjective criteria of individual consciences. The outward forms of religion are emphasized. There is an antipathy to psychological and sociological explanations and a leaning towards religious and moral judgments. Finally, there is a refusal to admit that one's own group or church has shortcomings or faults. (J. Weima, 1965). By formulating the opposite of these traits the characteristics of a positive attitude towards church renewal in The Netherlands become apparent.

In The Netherlands strictly speaking only one significant survey has been conducted about the attitude of Catholics towards renewal. It was done by the Dutch Institute for Public Opinion Research (NIPO), at the request of *Elseviers Weekblad* (5 April 1969). We want to conclude this chapter by reporting what the faithful think of their own bishops. In this representative opinion poll 88% of the Catholics interviewed had a general confidence in the Dutch bishops; 9% lacked this confidence; and 3% had no opinion. Concerning their own bishop in their own diocese, 86% of the interviewees expressed confidence, 10% did not, and 4% had no opinion.

Yet eight months later the central church government in Rome was to inform Dutch Catholics that the Roman Curia had no confidence in the Dutch episcopacy.

CHAPTER VI

Stagnation in Church Renewal

Everybody is agreed that the episcopal nominations made by Rome at the end of 1970 and the beginning of 1972 indicated a disapproval of the pastoral policy adopted up till then. Things had to be changed. In their first interviews the two new bishops immediately made this known. In various respects they took their distance from their colleagues. Solidarity within the college of bishops had been broken. Now that it had become more difficult to take unanimous decisions people retreated behind the boundaries of diocesan autonomy. The stagnation of church renewal had begun. Experts and publicists who had experienced the meetings of the Pastoral Council as a feast of renewal withdrew or were seldom seen or heard again. Institutes and persons who formerly had lent their names and energy to bring about renewal disappeared noiselessly, on their own account or forced by moral or financial pressures. Others stayed and resigned themselves to the limited possibilities. They had no alternative. The wind had reversed. This quiet has also been called the stillness of a cemetery where the tombstones are made of Roman marble.

Surveying the situation one clearly sees parallels with the typology of progression and regression, so characteristic of the renewal movement in France which had just preceded the Dutch one. In this country however we had no experience and little sense of history. It would not happen here. Just like pacifists saying "there will be no war," until the unimaginable does happen and occupying forces flood the country. Attributing the change from progress to stagnation to Roman interference alone however would be incomplete. Regress elements were already present for a long time in the Dutch Catholic community. And on the international level the process of stagnation had begun at an even earlier date — already during the sessions of Vatican II. In its blessed innocence The Netherlands had remained outside this regression for a considerable time — until its role as the vanguard changed into one of international scapegoat. A schism did not occur. Many had feared a breach with Rome, others had hoped for it. Staying inside the international church community makes it possible to convert the stagnation in renewal into an institutionalizing of the results already achieved. One can learn from the past. Can the distrust between bishops, experts, publicists and faithful again become a trustful dialogue? Or has the price been too high and the frustations so immense that the elite and especially the younger generation are lost?

1. Evaluation

If the specialty of the renewal movement in The Netherlands was continually being able to find its impulses in the trustful consultation of bishops, experts and representatives of the faithful, critically followed by the news media, then this process of change itself can also be evaluated, completely apart from possible Roman corrections.

A serviceable exponent for this evaluation is the organization of the Pastoral Council, with the six three-day general assemblies between January 1968 and April 1970 as its public zenith. It should be noticed, however, that the renewal movement cannot be identified with the Pastoral Council, and that the Pastoral Council as a change process cannot be identified with the general assemblies either.

In the evaluation of the Pastoral Council "experiment" two elements prove to have been decisive. First of all, there is the orientation toward the Second Vatican Council that ended in December 1965. The entire construction of the Pastoral Council could not but give the impression that The Netherlands were going to "re-do" the Vatican Council, albeit for a local church. This gave rise to many misunderstandings which, in spite of repeated statements to the contrary, lived on and had a stagnating effect. The timing of the Pastoral Council aimed at profiting from the appeal for renewal launched by Rome. Accordingly, there should not be too long a lapse between the end of Vatican II and the convocation of the Pastoral Council. The experts who had advised the Dutch bishops in Rome were given preference in this national continuation. But, as compared with the model of Vatican II, the new element was to be a real participation of priests and laity in the consultations. The term "council" — and not "synod" which was used later on in other countries — suggested a certain equivalence on a local level with the Roman world council, which in fact did not exist. The Pastoral Council was meant to be a consultation, in which the voting procedure aimed only at getting more exact assessments of the various opinions and not, in case of overall majorities, at converting these into policy decisions. The entire structure, with its parliament-like character, as well as the associations with the Vatican Council, which could indeed make decisions, even about doctrinal formulas, led to an ambivalent idea of what was happening in the Leeuwenhorst building at Noordwijkerhout. Cardinal Ottaviani is reported to have said, "That is no council, it is a congress." In saying this he minimalized the fact that this Pastoral Council was an expression of a new manner of exercising ecclestiastical authority, with all the limitations inherent in this experiment.

The second factor hindering the Pastoral Council was related to its failure to convene until more than two years after the Vatican Council had closed. At that moment the organisation of the Pastoral Council could no longer derive any prestige from Vatican II. It was rather the opposite, because Rome had made it quite clear that Vatican II's model of exercising authority was to be considered as something temporary. When the Pastoral Council was officially announced in March 1966, the restraining of the renewal movement, which Vatican II had called forth, had already started, and in the year in which the first plenary sessions were held the regress became most manifest in the encyclical *Humanae Vitae* (July 1968). The manner in which this encyclical was prepared and published was the exact opposite of the dialogue form of the Pastoral Council: without foregoing consultation of the world episcopacy, against a majority advice of the experts, and at variance with the developing pastoral practice. In their 31 July 1968 letter to the priests, the Dutch bishops clearly expressed their concern: "In this critical hour we realize that many Catholics are feeling uneasy.... It is understandable that only after thorough discussion, with theological and other experts as well, will your bishops be able to offer the guidance you so badly need.... It is to be hoped that the discussions around this encyclical may contribute to a better appreciation and functioning of ecclesiastical authority. In these days, let us pray for our Holy Father and for each other." All essential elements of the Pastoral Council as a new way of practising authority are mentioned in this letter. Its wording expresses deep concern. It looked as if alongside the banner of renewal a storm-signal was raised.

The letter of support sent to the bishops on 7 August 1968, by 117 people lecturing in theology and philosophy, struck the same note: "It is especially your wish for 'a better functioning of ecclesiastical authority' that expresses our innermost thoughts: we are grateful that, as pastors in Christ's Church, you have not bound the faithful on an argument of authority, but have pointed to the fundamental human values that are at stake here. For in our opinion the manner of exercising authority which this encyclical *Humanae Vitae* seems to symbolize is detrimental to the evangelical task of the pastor, to guide the People of God" (*Kath. Archief*, 1968, 850—851). The fundamental contrast between the centralistic and autonomous Vatican policy-making that revived after Vatican II and the Dutch bishops' way of exercising authority increasingly exposed the already latent antagonism between the Dutch Church and Rome. However there were already groups of Catholics in our country who wanted to follow the Roman directives without any more ado and who did not at all appreciate the critical attitude of the bishops.

2. The Slow Learning Process

In addition to these two influential factors, the orientation toward the model of Vatican II and the contrast between the regress already begun in Rome and the still ongoing progress in The Netherlands, we shall, for our evaluation, mention several other observations.

It is said that at the Pastoral Council the position of the bishops, however much protected, remained unclear. Here the comment of protestant religious psychologist H. Faber that the church is one of the places where awakening is slow should be called to mind. Modern ideas and movements are very keenly followed, but the reaction to them is as a rule very hesitant. "The extreme reactions of blunt rejection and radical enthusiasm are both clearly represented; the Pastoral Council of the Dutch Catholic Church Province is one of the rare attempts to take account of the changing situation in a realistic and responsible way" (H. Faber, 1970). Without relinquishing the inherent character of the ecclesiastical hierarchy, the bishops have admitted the fundamental democratization process. German jurist H. Dombois (1971) who, as a Protestant scholar, is very much interested in the structure of the Catholic Church, wrote a study of hierarchy examining the limits of this contested structure. The established and traditional church order is becoming a process (as was developed in the Working Formula of the Pastoral Council) coordinating the dialectic between authority and freedom, and between bishops and the members of the congregation who want influence and shared responsibility. This process can only develop and be carried through if both partners are willing not to push each other aside by a majority vote or manipulation. In this independence of both partners, both critical of each other, the hierarchy and the ministry as well unavoidably get into a fundamentally different position without losing their significance. The objective prestige, and the conviction that there must be a hierarchy, will rather increase, even if the formal competency seems to decrease." Dombois calls this a relation of critical solidarity, a historic step from the bureaucratic sealing of the *depositum fidei* towards a communal process in which the treasure of the faith is, as it were, acquired and tested anew. As a motto for this process he offers a quotation from a report on the Pastoral Council in the then still-existing German weekly *Publik*: "In this open dialogue in which the ministry and the laity united as the one, learning church, to listen together to the Gospel, the spiritual authority of the bishops gained a new and up til then unheard-of credibility" (H. Dombois, 1971; *Publik*, 14 March 1970; R. Huysmans, 1970). At any rate, the process described by Dombois was actually tried out over a number of years in The Netherlands, without leading to damage or internal conflict, and with increasing respect for the hierarchy.

Such a process entail risks. The discussions, which in an incidental case were also marked by insufficient information or a lack of eloquence, sometimes seemed to deal a little too carelessly with the tenets of belief. Alongside the dialectic of authority and freedom there was an attitude lying between the more empirical and more transcendental approach to the church, between the more practical-pastoral and more fundamentally theological ideas. The approaches are equally legitimate, but they were too much seen as opposing each other, and their advocates were given too few opportunities to hold a dialogue with each other. Because of this the report on authority, even in its second version, was not accepted by the assembly, and the discussions about the status of the ministry and of the faithful remained unsatisfactory.

During the council meetings the experience, and sometimes the exasperation and impatience, grew about the bonds with the church universal and with Rome. It became increasingly clear that the bishops of a local church have only limited room from manoeuvering. And also that "Rome" was a complicated thing and that a visit to the Pope by a delegation of council members would not have much effect. Here, too, there was a learning process going on. Cardinal Alfrink objected to this dialogue with Rome and the world episcopacy being labeled as "diplomacy." The entire church had still to grow familar with the idea of collegiality. "We shall not master it in one or two years. I mean to say, not only that Rome has not yet learnt it, but that we, too, are sometimes still unfamiliar with it. It may take some time, but we are under way, and of course some experiences disappoint us; on the other hand, there are sometimes particularly gratifying experiences." Groningen psychologist J. Snijders, the council's first chairman, was a committee member at the fourth plenary assembly (April 1969) and he remarked: "To have a 2500-strong college function like the first twelve apostles, is a romantic but impracticable ideal. In point of fact in such a big group the center unavoidably rules the roost. Therefore collegiality must of necessity be accompanied by decentralization. The smaller episcopal colleges must be given real decisive powers in this decentralization" (Pastoraal Concilie, 5, pp. 247—248).

During and after the Pastoral Council one often heard people sigh: "If only we had had more time." Because of its striving for the greatest possible involvement of the faithful in conciliar events, the entire construction of the council model became a public happening. A group of specialists could have been delegated for some years for the intricate job of drawing up a watertight council procedure. This alternative was deliberately rejected. The council was to be a leisure activity. No new institutions were set up. For all functionaries the council was an extra dimension alongside their everyday business. This free form of cooperation slowed down the work pace and created the impression of amateurism. There was too little time for the processing of the draft reports, which could be commented upon by individuals (via "mail boxes"), by discussion groups or by major Catholic organizations. Sometimes the draft reports were too "learned" and a "translation" into more comprehensible wording was requested. Parish priests had no time, or desire, to hold extensive discussions with the faithful about the reports. Preaching could hardly keep up with the new themes. Adequate training of the parish priests for the role of "change agents" would have taken years. Thus the faithful could not sufficiently identify themselves with the council's change processes. Even those participating in the general assemblies found the programmes overloaded. Till the very end a discussion went on about the correct division between inner-church themes and those of a socio-political nature.

3. Criticism Concerning the Representation of the Faithful

For our critical evaluation the representativeness of the committees and the delegates is of great importance. At the Vatican Council the bishops represented their church communities, and they had intended to give priests and laity a say; but the laity were not consulted at all and the very few "pastors" who were permitted to attend the meetings felt more like silent pastoral tourists than ministers who, after the council, must perform the actual pastoral work. In spite of all good intentions the representation of over 5 million church members at the Pastoral Council through about a hundred delegates remained an awkward business. Nationally matters depended on the composition of the delegations from the seven dioceses. These delegations were representative in so far as the diocesan council was felt to be representative of a diocese. This differed from one diocese to the other. In the smallest dioceses, Groningen and Breda, the delegates felt themselves more representative and often acted as a united group. The other council members (15 seats) were appointed by the episcopacy on the advice of the Central Committee. Usually younger people, marginal Catholics and representatives of conservative trends were sought, although the diocesan delegations could by no means be called predominantly progressive. Repeatedly people that were known as conservatives refused to remain members of committees of experts, or to be put on the advisory list for the additional seats. This was the case with J. Asberg and J. Bongaarts of *Confrontatie* and Father J. van Rijn of *Waarheid en Leven*.

At this point I must insert a personal intermezzo in order to describe the serious attempts made by the council secretariat to establish closer contacts with the principal group of "the alarmed," in some measure united around the periodical *Confrontatie*. Leaders J. Asberg and J. Bongaarts paid an informative visit to our bureau in Rotterdam. Among other things Mr. Bongaarts said that he had checked my "credentials" and that he had found that there were no objections concerning my orthodoxy. Further contacts were mutually promised. On 24 January 1968 I had a long talk with J. Asberg at Bloemendaal. On 17 March he informed me that *Confrontatie* would like to be represented at the forthcoming general assembly. In the same month's issue of *Confrontatie*, the movement's periodical, it was said that Cardinal Alfrink had commissioned me to establish these contacts. On 28 April Dr. A. Simonis from The Hague urgently requested to be allowed to attend the meeting with *Confrontatie* that was in preparation. On 30 April Prof. Granpré Molière offered a few suggestions for this meeting. On 1 May he wrote a letter about this subject. On 6 May Mr. Bongaarts sent a note about the conflict with the Credogroup in Rotterdam. "The alarmed" group was now composed of this Credogroup, *Confrontatie*, and the Michaellegion. Prof. van de Ploeg and Dr. den Ottolander gave an interview, in a newspaper in the Brabant province, about this coming talk with *Confrontatie*. On 13 May I received a long letter from Prof. van de Ploeg, in which he explained why after all he did not want to take part in the *Confrontatie* dialogue. On 16 May Mr. Asberg rang up and asked if Dean Joosten could also attend the *Confrontatie* meeting. Finally, the discussion with the people assigned by *Confrontatie* took place, at Doorn on 20 May. A report approved by Mr. Bongaarts was published in *Katholiek Archief* (1968, p. 1102). On 24 May Dr. A. Simonis expressed his thanks for the good meeting with *Confrontatie*. In the July and August issues of the periodical *Confrontatie* there were several negative articles on the Doorn talks. On 4 September a letter was sent out in preparation for a second meeting with *Confrontatie*. This had been decided upon by unanimous vote. On 10 September J. Asberg and J. Bongaarts wrote on *Confrontatie* stationery that they considered a repetition of the Doorn meeting of little use. Other suggestions for a dialogue with "the alarmed," which were requested, they did not give. Thus this dialogue was then broken off one-sidedly. The paradox of all this is that those who repeatedly criticized the representativeness of the Pastoral Council were themselves sometimes the cause that this representative character could not be established fully (H. Goddijn, 1970).

4. Publicity

The publicity factor also deserves an extensive evaluation. Just like the bishops, the publicists attending the general meetings had a home front: the viewing and reading public. The plenary meetings were the public highlights of the change process. The journalists not only reported on these meetings, but they also furthered a very critical and public learning process. Frequently television had to select and boil down into ten or fifteen minutes what had been recorded over many hours. The television-viewers of Holland could not but get a one-sided idea of Noordwijkerhout. It looked like an argument-center rather than like a consultation-center. More than once the short t.v.-broadcasts summarized the only rarely occurring conflicts, so that the real atmosphere of consultation was not conveyed to the millions of viewers and stay-at-homes at a distance. The press reports were much more balanced. In a opinion poll after the council had ended, one of the respondents very aptly expressed the distance between the council's participants and the faithful they publicly represented:

> In my opinion there is a (necessary) short-circuit between Noordwijkerhout and the man in the street. What is done at Noordwijkerhout is theoretically correct and probably necessary with a view to the future. But in fact it (still) has no roots in the life experience and the real ideas of the average church member. Accepting something by means of study and voting (e.g. ecumenism, celibacy, etc.) is still far from living it out and acting upon it. People who were not at Noordwijkerhout feel they are on the side of life that has not got that far yet; those who intensely participated at Noordwijkerhout have the feeling they no longer belong to the home front.

Of both Vatican II and the Pastoral Council the principal legacy is the documents published. The most important Pastoral Council documents, the recommendations that were passed — some of them with the proviso of later textual re-editing — have so far not been published as a collection. Careful reading of them shows how much account was taken of the minority voice and with how much respect attention was paid to the solidarity with Rome and the church universal. It is a pity that the council reports have not been reworked and published in a systematic pastoral handbook, as was always Bishop de Vet's ideal. In such a handbook the documents of both Vatican II and the Pastoral Council were to have been incorporated. This synthesis was never begun.

5. Results of the Pastoral Council

Consultation with Rome could have led to the decision to hold a formal canonical synod at which a number of policy decisions could have been made. This possibility, already suggested at the beginning of the council by canon lawyers, was not adopted as a means to establish the policy-making character of the Pastoral Council. In this way diocesan officials, such as vicars-general, might have been given a more active role in the council's conclusion. Instead they felt a little outside this national event. In Cardinal Alfrink's closing address on 8 April 1970, called by Hans Küng "one of the few great signs of hope in these post-conciliar days," it was announced the Pastoral Council was to have a follow-up in a permanent consultation structure. The "follow-up" was as inadequate as the continuation of Vatican II in the bishops' synods.

The results of this Pastoral Council experiment with its new form of exercising authority can be summed up as follows:
—Experts (priests and lay people) from all disciplines worked together on reports, which in their turn can become parts of a pastoral program. Important current topics were studied and published in a modern way.
—The laity were challenged to great creativity based on their own responsibility.
—Scholars cooperated with experienced practitioners who knew the actual possibilities and obstacles to the translation of "ideas" into practical work.
—Vatican II's documents did not remain abstract, but were applied to the local situation of the church which developed an awareness of its own cultural identity.
—Possibilities were opened up for a learning process regarding the new authority relations. As church members the bishops took part in discussions guided by rules that applied equally to everybody.
—Dialogue was practised without mutual prejudice. The participation of representatives from other denominations and philosophies was a very enriching element.
—The inherent moral character of church authority was strengthened.
—The worldwide tensions between centralization and decentralization in the church were made public and became a subject of discussion. This counteracted the isolation of the central government in the church at large.

It is now possible to weigh this actual, tested experiment of the Pastoral Council against the objections raised in the U.S.A. towards a possible "National Pastoral Council." Quite a number of organizational objections could be brought forward, which do not apply in the little area of The Netherlands. The "ideological" objections were very strongly formulated by the "Parents for Orthodoxy in Parochial Education" movement, in their letter of September 1970 to the American National Catholic Bishops' Conference. It was a petition not to hold a "National Pastoral Council." The text runs as follows:

> The national Pastoral Council is imprudent and dangerous. It would:
> *Undermine* your authority and that of the Holy Father.
> *Establish* a counter hierarchy (as in the Dutch N.P.C. disaster)
> *Pit* the "American Catholic Church" against the Church Universal.
> *Reject* the principle of subsidiarity.
> *Be Manipulated* by the mass media.
> *Minimize* the authority of Bishops in communion with Rome.
> *Erode* the spiritual life of the faithful.
> *Stamp* with official approval the "American Catholic Church."
> *Separate* the pastor from his flock.
> *Destroy* parishes.
> *Concentrate* unlimited power in the hands of an elite.
> *Establish* another bureau for proliferation of propaganda. (J.P. O'Connor, 1971).

6. Cultural Contrasts between The Netherlands and Rome

In the renewal process of the Dutch Catholic Church the indistinctnesses and organizational mistakes inherent in every big experiment occurred. The evaluation of these shortcomings should be seen with leniency, because bishops, priests and the faithful, who from their early youth on had been accustomed to a centralistic type of church, were just begun with this new learning process. There were, however, in The Netherlands little groups of priests and laity who preferred a more self-confident and authoritarian-guided church. It has rightly been pointed out that the desire for certainty regarding life's ultimate questions should not be confused with conservatism. There is no objection to bishops speaking in unmistakable terms about these, and they in fact did so. On the other hand the conservatives have no right to claim a monopoly over authentic religiosity and prayer life in terms such as, "We shall now turn the talking church into a praying church." as if, e.g. the Pastoral Council was not a first-rate expression of religiosity (H. Goddijn, 1970).

In fact the shortcomings brought to light by the evaluation did cause a certain amount of stagnation of renewal. The tensions between "the alarmed" and the extremist minorities who thought the bishops did not go far enough provided another hindrance to the renewal movement. These contrasts were reinforced by the antagonism between Holland and Rome, an antagonism at first latent, but gradually less so, and in time developing into an open conflict.

Antagonism between religious groups is usually marked by nontheological factors, as well. This is indeed the case in the Holland—Rome antagonism. There are striking cultural differences between Dutch and Italian Catholicism. Prof. L. van Holk, well-known Dutch observer at the Vatican Council and, at the Pastoral Council, representative of the Remonstrant Confraternity, is of the opinion that The Netherlands have been a little naive in their great reform zeal. From the very beginning stagnation was a threat. Miscalculations have been made regarding a large number of elements which were as opposed to the "Dutch spring" as the Russians to the "Prague spring." Van Holk mentions: the Roman leaning to imperialim and the Roman Curia's thirst for power; the typically Mediterranean and strongly folkloristic religiosity; the deep-rooted aversion to novelties; the same Mediterranean mind's feeling for the connection between celibacy, the inferior role of women, and transsubstantiation; the Italian aversion for everything "northern"; the tendency to intimate one's real wishes quite indirectly, "diplomatically" and with Byzantine formality; and finally "the influence of that supreme Catholic value: the preservation of the unity of the church which always favours obedience above independent thinking and personal conviction — it is this influence which the Dutch Catholics have terribly underestimated both internally and within the context of the church universal" (L. van Holk, 1972).

Apart from criticism of the Roman Curia, which is often exaggerated, there is an Italian cultural pattern which is in opposition to deep-rooted convictions in our country. The emphasis on obedience is, by the way, also to be found in other countries. A striking example, in my opinion, is to be found at the end of the pastoral renewal movement in France. Progress had been halted by Rome, and the task of "selling" the Roman measures to the priests fell upon the bishop who had most suffered from them. When Msgr. Ancel had to submit to the Roman prohibition of worker-priests, he wrote a letter to those remaining worker-priests. At the end of this letter he referred to a priest who in earlier days had been a supporter of the conservative "Action française" also condemned by Rome. "Very many times I have told you how carefully and with what fidelity we must submit to the Holy See. I remember a sentence, spoken long ago by a priest who had given his name to the 'Action française,' and who wholeheartedly submitted himself the moment it was prohibited. He said: 'One is not twice in one's lifetime given the opportunity to show the Pope that one loves him' (*Kath. Archief*, 1960, p. 68).

How much the Italian ideas about the position of the layman are at variance with those in The Netherlands is shown by a joint pastoral letter, sent by the Italian bishops to their priests on 25 March 1960. The letter deals with the dangers of laicism. The following are mentioned as the principal causes of the many "temptations" to which the laity can fall victim: the lack of theological training, the influence of the press, the influence of certain progressive religious literature "in particular from across the Alps, where an unremitting perturbance goes together with the most dangerous boldness in thinking, and which gives unconditional approval to every experiment in the apostolate which ignores traditional methods, convinced that it is only in this way that the road is prepared for appropriate methods to ensure the re-establishment of the contacts with the world." Moreover, mention is made of the influence of Protestantism, the influence of democratic ideas, the overestimation of the layman's task as compared with the priest's, the shortcomings of some members of the clergy, the lack of solid spiritual training, combined with the "day-to-day rugged contacts with the world." Finally, the Italian bishops say these are only possible temptations, but they cannot but be afraid that the Catholic lay people of The Netherlands have already succumbed to all these temptations (*Kath. Archief*, 1960, pp. 598—599).

The *Osservatore Romano* of 20 April 1961 has the following quotation from Msgr. P. Felici, secretary general of the Vatican Council, about the mass media. "The journalists and the public must have patience; and although it is highly desirable — as was repeatedly said by the Pope — that all church members show a lively interest in this great event, one should not forget that the council is a solemn meeting of the highest doctrinal authority and the supreme governing body of the Apostles' successors with the successor of St. Peter as their head. In reverent silence we should look at them and pray to the Holy Spirit that he may illuminate and comfort them for the benefit of the Holy Church. The menbers of the study committees are bound by deep professional secrecy which should be respected by all people interested, as is the explicit wish of the Pope" (*Kath. Archief* 1961, p. 541). Silence, and especially reverent silence and patience were not exactly the characteristics of Dutch Catholics and journalists.

How differently the Dutch bishops and the Pope approached the Dutch Catholics appears from a comparison between the letter Pope Paul wrote for the opening of the Pastoral Council (Rome, 23 November 1966) and the letter the bishops read from the pulpits (Utrecht, 27 November 1966). Pope Paul calls the Pastoral Council "a demanding and delicate enterprise" and, further on, "something quite new and unique." Particularly remarkable was the Pope's wish that the council's consultations would lead to a "clear and unwavering profession of the faith, counteracting certain unripe and incorrect opinions which, as is known, have of late obscured the purity of faith in certain points, and have disturbed the steadfastness and the balance of many Catholics." The fruit of this consultation, it was hoped, would be a solid forming of consciences "showing itself in an inner and spontaneous adherence to the church and in a filial, active and joyful obedience" (Pastoraal Concilie, I, pp. 38—40).

In the bishops' letter there is a similar concern, but the tone is different.

We hope we shall be able to make the face of Christ better recognizable in the church, and that we and our separated brethren will mutually rediscover Christ's features ever more clearly. But we also know, in advance, that we shall only be partially successful. New life, in the church too, can in the last analysis not be forced, but it is the fruit of hard labour, often with sorrow and pain. Neither should we be too optimistic as to the results of our consultation. We are living in hope, but we also know that, despite this hope, human disappointment will also be our share, for the differences of tempo in the large world church — which are self-evident — the slow budding and blooming of the governmental principles that were stated by the Second Vatican Council, are aspects of the church that are sometimes difficult to accept. Our wish to remain in touch, to remain in close touch with the interests of the world church is a love which often entails pain, but which we want in spite of that pain (Pastoraal Concilie, I, pp. 45—46).

The two letters were written and approved independently. Therefore they offer good possibilities for comparison. Very clearly two different models are discernible. Rome favours preservation, more authority-bound relations, a restoration of balance and unity around the teaching ministry; it calls for joyful filial obedience, and shows no openness to or even mentions other churches. Utrecht lays stress on the new life, on change, on the attitude of

112

"new life cannot be forced," on hard labour, sorrow and pain, the difficult aspects of the duty to remain in touch with the world church; it points to differences in tempo and culture, and wants to find unity among the separated brethren.

The Dutch Catholics gradually realized these contrasts between Italian culture and Dutch ideas, but in attempts to gain more understanding and more room for church renewal in The Netherlands, these contrasts were insufficiently considered. Dutch people tend to keep harping on matters of principle. They ask whether something is or is not allowed. Italians accept more easily living at two levels, and they are less "precise." In public they praise certain Roman directives, but in practice they have a keen eye for the loopholes. "You are too earnest," Cardinal Garonne once told me in Rome. This latent antagonism helped feed the growing conflict between Holland and Rome.

7. The Beginning of the Conflict

The beginning of the conflict was marked not only by the latent antagonism and the already incipient international slowing-down of post-conciliar renewal, but also by the following events. Catholic Holland, always faithful and docile with regard to Roman directives, took some initiatives ahead of the Roman Curia, thus interfering with Vatican plans. It must have been extraordinarily irritating that in the beginning of 1961 the Dutch bishops published a letter which not only offered detailed proposals for the organization of a Vatican Council, but in which also certain views on the Pope's personal infallibility were relativized. The Roman Curia was, with a great number of committees, still quite busy working out Pope John's daring initiative, when the Dutch already offered a blueprint which, in 1961, was translated into French, German and English. The Italian translation (1962) caused the first conflict. The Salesian Fathers had prepared the publication in their Turin printing office, but the congregation's superior general stopped its distribution, and the booksellers had to return their copies. Cardinal Alfrink discussed this first conflict with Pope John, for it was clear that a "superior authority" had interfered. A few months later Cardinal Alfrink was made a member of the council's presidium. The first conflict had been settled.

Following the example of Father Lombardi S.J. who, to the

great annoyance of the *Osservatore Romano* had published a book criticizing the Roman Curia and the Italian clergy (11 January 1962), Dutch Jesuit Father J. van Kilsdonk gave an address to the St. Adelbert Society severely criticizing the Curia (1962). Cardinal Alfrink reacted a month later, five days before the opening of Vatican II. He specifically mentioned Lombardi, and about student chaplain van Kilsdonk's words he only remarked that it is incorrect to allege that "the Roman Curia is entirely on the wrong track and is the only or principal cause of the silent defection from the faith of young intellectuals." Furthermore he said that the central governing body is not a homogeneous block, that every judgment must be based upon experience, and that he hoped for openness between the center and the periphery. "Public and unqualified cries of despair, even if prompted by love of the church, tend to create an unfavourable atmosphere but do not open many perspectives for improvement. Rather, they evoke new resistance and a seemingly justified tenacity" (*Kath. Archief*, 1962, pp. 995–996).

During the Vatican Council there was, in Rome, an evident lack of free and expert information for the council fathers, the scholars and the mass media. A group of Dutch people took the initiative to establish the "Documentation Center for the Council" and were put in charge of it. Later on, another communication center was opened, just opposite St. Peter's, especially for journalists. This as well was for a long time managed by a Dutchman. The DOC, later given its international form of IDOC, was led by L. Alting von Geusau. The CCC was run by L. Grond. Through these centers numerous commentaries on the council documents were spread, and dozens of conferences were organized. The IDOC was in frequent conflict with the Roman Curia, and the very fact of its existence must have irritated the Vatican press office.

8. Stagnation in The Netherlands

The first major comment on the renewal movement in The Netherlands was published by Father E. Schoenmaeckers S.J. (1964) in *Orientierung*, a Jesuit-edited Swiss periodical. He pointed out the positive and negative aspects of the crisis in Dutch Catholicism, and he was, as far as I can ascertain, the first Dutchman to air critical views in a publication abroad. This article became known in The Netherlands in two ways. First of all, there was an apparently censored version in the special issue of *De Heraut* on occasion of Cardinal Alfrink's golden jubilee (July-August 1964). The following fragment had been omitted: "Church life in The Netherlands nowadays looks like modern art: shapeless and chaotic. Good things are mixed with the very bad, the holy with the unholy, superstition and unbelief are unrecognizably disguised in the garb of religiosity." The article was also printed in a different version in the British periodical *The Month*. It is this version which the Italian newspapers had at their disposal when agitating against The Netherlands after the publication of Pope Paul's encyclical on the Eucharist (dated 3 September 1965). They had a preference for quoting the passage saying the Dutch church was going through its worst crisis since the Reformation and the phrase: "Dutch Catholicism is the most anti-Roman, anti-clerical and progressive of all progressive trends in West European Catholicism." Bishop G. de Vet of Breda issued a public protest against "the scandalous, not to say slanderous article by Father Schoenmaeckers, which has led to the most bizarre stories in the foreign press about Dutch Catholicism and the Dutch bishops and theologians" (*Kath. Archief*, 1965, pp. 1019—1020).

It should not be forgotten that the first publication of Schoenmaeckers's article in 1964 coincided with the founding of the periodical *Confrontatie*, the first regular publication of an "alarmed" group. According to Rome informants the secretariat of state received full Italian translations of the *Confrontatie* issues. In the Apostolic Constitution on the Roman Curia of 15 August 1967 it states that the bureau of the secretariat of state is in charge of "collecting information and periodicals, newspapers and similar publications, and also of the gathering and ordering of data" (*Kath. Archief*, 1967, p. 979). The ordering of data, that is, the collection of the original clippings of articles from Dutch periodicals on the left, and on the right short summaries in Italian, was for a long time the task of a Curia official who came from Strasbourg and who was known for his anti-Dutch feelings. The literal Italian translations of all articles in *Confrontatie* were not the charge of this Curia official. Some months later, sixteen prominent Catholics, among them a few professors and noblemen, addressed themselves to the Dutch bishops in order to declare their concern about "some expressions of the fermentation process that religious and ecclesiastical life in The Netherland is experiencing." The crucial passage read, "Because of the unlimited experimenting in liturgy, the premature airing of new opinions or the minimalizing of truth, and the lack of good catechetical instruction, thousands of people are brought into the greatest possible confusion as regards their religious convictions, their forms of worship and their moral lives." Among the signatories were Prof. Granpré Molière, already mentioned above, and H. de Goey, a very influential man in publicity circles. Another subscriber was L. Knuvelder of Amsterdam. In 1964, he started the meetings of the St. Michael Legion, a group even more right-wing than *Confrontatie*. In February 1968 the Michael Legion was formally organized. *Confrontatie* refused to publish appeals to attend meetings of the St. Michael Legion. The *Waarheid en Leven* group, established at the end of 1968, was an initiative of a number of priests in the province of Limburg.

It is clear that the movement of "the alarmed" starting in 1964, had as its center The Hague. There the nunciature is situated, and via foreign embassies and the Foreign Office (until 1971 Mr. J. Luns, now secretary-general of the NATO, was foreign minister) many international contacts are possible. The Hague also is the provincialate of the Jesuits. Other centers were Groningen, Tilburg and southern Limburg. It was only at a later date that the ultra-conservative Father W. Kotte of Utrecht came to the fore. In Cardinal Alfrink's residential city he rented a church for a group of adherents. At the solemn opening service J. Luns was very demonstratively present. Father Kotte has been accused of previous contacts with anti-Pope Clemens XV who lives in the north of France.

In a talk before the Dutch Documentation Center in Rome (15 September 1965) Cardinal Alfrink was unusually vehement in his defense against the insinuations in the Italian press. He protested against the "one-sided, negative, distorted manner in which, for a few months, the international press has almost defamatorily been talking about our Dutch Catholic community." He does not want to cut off a public and open discussion. "But the press reports — generalizing, half-truthful, one-sided, often incorrect and accusing the entire community, focusing on a danger, or rather a certainty, of imminent schism, — present a picture of the Dutch Catholic community which is no less than a caricature" The *Osservatore Romano* printed part of this address. Henry Fesquet of *Le Monde*, who was to attend all sessions of the Pastoral Council, praised the cardinal. "The first Dutch bishop, who saw his church being defamed, has taken up the gauntlet. He has done this with a complete frankness which is the opposite of the palliative manner of most

episcopal corrections. In this respect this statement is exemplary"
(*Le Monde*, 16 September 1965).

Within the context of this growing Holland—Rome conflict the
first signs of a stagnation in Dutch church renewal had now become visible. To the degree that Rome was to give more support
to right-wing minorities, were these to become more successful also
in the country itself, with their endeavours to discredit the bishops
and to suggest that a breach with Rome was in the offing.

9. Development of the Conflict

The next conflict was sparked off by the publication of the
New Catechism. After its publication on 5 October 1966, it was
reported on 22 November that a group of Dutch Catholics had
sent a letter to Pope Paul VI, listing seven objections against the
catechism and saying these entailed a danger to the souls. The
entire letter was written in the exact tone and style of the Roman
Curia. The very first sentence already strikes this note: "Prostrate
at the feet of Your Holiness we, the undersigned, write the following with great sorrow and sadness." The letter is outstanding in its
conciseness and its references to Vatican documents. For the first
time the Dutch bishops were passed over by a mysteriously operating right-wing group which was, without any consultation with
Utrecht, immediately taken seriously by Rome. Generally speaking the bishops only indirectly learned what Rome had "decided"
about them. In the previously mentioned White Paper about this
conflict the failure of the Holland—Rome dialogue is described.
The struggle was to last till the end of 1968. A relatively small
group in Rome was trying to attack Dutch Catholicism by condemning a number of passages from the catechism. A formal condemnation was never published. Catholic Holland had again irritated Rome, for the catechism was internationally distributed as
described above. The motivation to compose a catechism for
adults came from a Roman rumour that the Curia was planning
such a document for the Vatican Council. Again The Netherlands
was first.

It was gradually becoming clear that the action against the bishops had been started by *Confrontatie*. Schillebeeckx writes: "They
complain about the lack of obedience to the Pope, and in the
meantime they do everything they can to sap the Dutch bishops'
authority thus reinforcing the uncertainty in the Netherlands." He

thinks this kind of integralism even worse because it keeps up the appearance of pious submissiveness and the defense of orthodoxy (*De Volkskrant*, 23 November 1966). A repetition of this catechism story was to follow later, and at this moment it has not yet come to an end, It concerns an experimental catechetical course ordered by the Brabant foundation "Ons Middelbaar Onderwijs"; in a letter of 30 September 1971 Rome took steps against it.

In July 1968 *Humanae Vitae* appeared. The critical reaction of the Dutch bishops has already been mentioned. On 24 September 1968 *Le Monde* reported on a suit being prepared against Schillebeeckx by the Congregation for the Doctrine of the Faith. A wave of protest against the Roman Curia swept over the country. To this affair, too, a complete White Paper was devoted (R. Auwerda, 1969). A letter of protest, prepared by the theology students of Nijmegen and addressed to Cardinal Seper, head of the Congregation concerned, ends as follows: "We regret that the faith should have to be safeguarded in such a cunning and anonymous way. We therefore press for full information and, with a view to the future, for guarantees for an honest dialogue."

On 16 December 1968 the periodical *Concilium* sent a letter to Rome about the freedom and the function of theologians in the church. Among the 38 signatories there were several from The Netherlands. In the *Osservatore Romano* there appeared an anonymous protest against this statement (4 January 1969). The Vatican was particularly irritated by the public character of the letter, "a form of publicity that is assuming the character of opposition and pressure." Dutch editorial secretary J. Micklinghoff sent a letter to the *Osservatore*, but it was not printed. But a protest by French theologian Daniélou against the *Concilium* letter did get a place in the *Osservatore* (4 March 1969). In the same month he was ordained a cardinal.

The Dutch Church remained one of conflicts. After describing the Schillebeeckx affair R. Auwerda also pays attention to the conflicts around Bishop J. Bluyssen of Den Bosch who was turned out of the Council for Liturgy, a move the Roman Curia later rescinded. The conflicts with Rome about liturgical matters deserve an extensive study by themselves, from the earlier introduced custom of "Communion on the hand" to the special penitential services which were to replace sacramental absolution. Bishops in the neighbouring countries of Germany and Belgium lodged vehement protests against similar practices in their own dioceses. Fur-

118

thermore, there were differences of opinion as to pastoral guidance for divorced people and homosexuals, pastoral tasks for priests who had left the ministry, intercommunion with members from other churches, and, at a later date, concerning the continuation of the Pastoral Council. In October 1971 Cardinal Alfrink had already discussed this last item in Rome. In the beginning of January 1972 he sent an additional note to Rome about the new structure of this consultation. On 13 July Cardinals Wright, Seper and Confalonieri wrote a letter to the Dutch bishops asking them to postpone the start of this national council because the position of the bishops had not been stated correctly. The first meeting was put off till the beginning of 1973. The escalation of the Holland—Rome conflict had, however, already reached its high-water mark a few years earlier.

10. The Culminating Point of the Conflict

The culminating point of the Holland—Rome conflict lies no doubt around the January 1970 assembly of the Pastoral Council, which dealt with the ministry of the priesthood. After this fifth plenary meeting, the bishops issued a press communiqué on January 19. In it they declared that they were of the opinion that it would be beneficial to their congregation if "next to a clearly voluntary celibate priesthood the Latin Church could also admit married priest, married men could be ordained priests and, in special cases and under certain conditions, priests who had married could be restored to the priestly ministry." This statement caused an unprecedented explosion in the world press. Rome had done everything to prevent the Pastoral Council from openly discussing the problem of celibacy. Personal intervention from the Dutch side in December 1969, to have special Roman representatives attend the January session had failed. Even the pronuncio stayed away, although he had asked a priest living in Rome to make special notes and then to report to The Hague. In his opening address Cardinal Alfrink assured that in the preceding days he had done his utmost to clear up the misunderstandings that still existed in Rome. Above his house in Utrecht, and later at Noordwijkerhout, there circled that day a little advertising airplane bearing on its train the words "Unity with Rome."

Against all diplomatic customs Pope Paul took a personal public stand against the happenings in The Netherlands. In his Sunday address before the Angelus on 1 February he called sacred celibacy a fundamental church law which should be neither given up nor discussed. The Netherlands are mentioned in a letter of 2 February, sent by the Pope to his secretary of state Cardinal J. Villot. The Pope only leaves open the possibility to admit to the priesthood, in a situation of extreme shortage, mature married men. In March 1970 Cardinal Alfrink had a talk with Cardinal Villot in Paris, offering extensive documentation that the question of the priesthood in The Netherlands would become very urgent. On 8 July he went to Rome. A prospect that the problems of the priesthood would be discussed at the 1971 bishops' synod was the only result.

For a number of years the priesthood had been the subject of studies and research in The Netherlands (R. Bunnik, 1967). A real dialogue did not develop. The number of ordinations in The Netherlands dropped from 301 in 1963 to 269 in 1964, 237 in 1965, 227 in 1966, 193 in 1967, 145 in 1968, 110 in 1969, 47 in 1970. In 1972 the unbelievable number of 26 ordinations was to be reached.

In the meantime Bishops Simonis and Gijsen were appointed. That was Rome's way of solving conflicts, by accepting the law of might over right.

On the day of Bishop Gijsen's ordination in Rome, Cardinal Alfrink told his latest biographer, "Someone made the following comparison regarding the problems between Rome and us: When you think a ship is off its course, you can try to correct this by means of radar contact. A more drastic method is to fire a shot before the bow. But what they are doing now is immediately hitting amidship. I think it a good comparison, although, of course, the Pope did not want to hit amidship. That it is actually happening is rather the result of certain Curia measures" (T. Oostveen, 1972).

11. Reactions Abroad

The conflict around the bishops' statement on celibacy of 19 January 1970 and the immediately preceding plenary session of the Pastoral Council, 5—7 January, provides a good opportunity to assess the reactions abroad.

We first mention some comments, given by foreign journalists, in a television broadcast on 20 January 1970 for the Catholic Broadcasting Corporation (KRO).

G. Zizola (Rome): I see no solution for the Holland—Rome conflict. If there were two ways out, if there were time for reflection, it might appear that both virginity and human love promote the Kingdom of God. I do not see how this inflexible Pope will learn that imposed decisions have been out since the last century, that free discussion must be possible, that a crisis is not solved by a kind of pity intended to save principles, that the study of this problem, to be undertaken by the bishops' synod, cannot bear fruit without courageous experimenting: only through living does one discover what is needed for it. On the other hand there will be no solution if The Netherlands does not have much patience. This is always an evangelical virtue. The Dutch know about the Gospel and about agriculture, so they also know that a seed needs a long period of germination if it is to bear good fruit.

L. Walterman (Cologne): In the German Federal Republic, too, there is discussion about celibacy, and not only by priests and students of theology. All the same, I do not expect this statement to have an immediate and strong influence in Western Germany. The statement will become an important element in the discussion, but nothing more for the time being. The Noordwijkerhout decisions are the results of a process that has been going on in The Netherlands for several years. Such a process has not taken place so far in the Federal Republic. There is no basis for it. I suppose this process, this conflict situation, is still to come, later on, and with more theory, as is the case with so many things in our country. The groups that oppose celibacy are in the minority, but they are an active and reasoning minority, although they are little heeded by the Catholic press. Although opinion polls have shown that a majority — of both priests and laity — are against celibacy, the German bishops, with one exception, want to maintain it. The discussion is taking place outside the episcopal studies. Even though a number of pronouncements and demands in the matter of celibacy displease the bishops, still they have till now a firm grip on the developments, among other reasons because no serious group wants to risk a breach.

A. Cambier (Brussels): Exceptional I consider the decision of the Dutch bishops, and very realistic. They have not disappointed the very dynamic majority of Dutch Catholics. Had they done this, it would have meant great damage to their church. It is also a courageous decision, because they have chosen the most difficult course. As a matter of fact the reactions in Flanders, and in Belgium as a whole, are divergent. On the one hand Cardinal Suenens said it is not a problem that can be solved by one church province, and he referred to the third bishops' synod. The Walloon bishops have refrained from giving any comment, but they have declared that they support the Pope's views. The other Belgian bishops have refused to make statements. As to the various groups in our country, the progressives have expressed their satisfaction with the decision and they have congratulated the Pastoral Council on its recommendations and the bishops for having given a policy orientation. There are also conservative groups who think the bishops are beating a retreat and are finally shaking off particularism in order to appeal to Rome and the church universal.

A. Savard (Paris): The Dutch bishops' communiqué on priestly celibacy has captured the interest of the French Catholics. The press has underlined the spectacular character of this decision. But an attentive observer at the Pastoral Council at Noordwijkerhout knows that the bishops could not have done anything less. They did not make a decision, but they listened to the wishes of their people. And they made it known that they want talks with Rome. We are interested in this dialogue, the more so because a movement exists among the clergy to allow priests to choose between marriage and celibacy. Last year a contesting movement already formulated its demands; they are now being voiced publicly. The French bishops are still adhering to celibacy. As late as this past November the episcopate told us they were only going to ordain people who took both the priestly and the celibate oaths. But now a number of bishops think the two oaths can be separated from each other so that, whilst priests are not allowed to marry, young people can be ordained who want to marry before their ordination.

R. Nowell (London): If the Dutch Church's view of celibacy leads to a breach, the bishops will say it is not their fault. They followed the principal recommendations of the Pastoral Council, but they insist on consulting with Rome on a matter which is going to have many consequences. Everything depends on the reactions of other dioceses and of the Pope. Generally speaking the English bishops are not opposed to married men becoming priests. But they will object to priests marrying and continuing their ministry. If this is the general opinion of other European clergy groups, the Dutch bishops are threatened by a situation the council especially warned them against: allowing married men to be ordained, but denying those who are already priests or who are going to become priests before long a choice. Furthermore, the question is in how far the church accepts the principle of subsidiarity recommended by the Roman synod. The problem is that only in The Netherlands have the celibacy issue and other urgent problems been discussed so thoroughly that they have led to conclusions that are valid for the entire Dutch Church. Other churches in Europe are lagging behind in the realization of ecclesiastical consultation. As long as they have not come that far, there wille be difficulties, because the churches are moving at different paces. This problem will remain with us, and we must accept differences of approach. I hope the Dutch Church will be allowed to find its own way.

Auxiliary Bishop K. Jacoby of Trier attended the famous council session. A frank interview in the diocesan newspaper *Paulinus* of 18 January 1970 provides a sharp insight into the impression the new manner of exercising authority in the Dutch Catholic community made on an unprejudiced outsider. The bishop is referring to the activities displayed by two radical action-groups during the council meeting: the "Septuagint" group, originated in 1968 around the celibacy problem, and the "4/7" group which, inspired by the German group "Kritischer Katholizismus," called the Pastoral Council a "fake democracy," set up to adapt the church.

Question: Your excellency, by order of the German Bishops' Conference you attended, as a guest, the fifth plenary assembly of the Dutch Pastoral Council at Noordwijkerhout, from 4 to 7 January. What impression does an observer from abroad have of this meeting? How did you find the atmosphere;

Answer: I was strongly impressed by the *openness* reigning at the Dutch Pastoral Council. In actual fact this council is composed of three groups: the delegates from the various dioceses, the bishops, and the representatives of the religious orders. A layman holds the chair. According to the statutes all participants have equal rights. Among other things this means that everybody must abide by the ten-minute speaking-time. But it also means that all interventions are considered. For the sake of this democratic principle it is accepted into the bargain that, occasionally, the debates will take a rather long time. But this has of course also to do with the openness I just mentioned. All arguments should come forward. And I can assure you the participants spoke with great frankness.

Question: Did this frankness ever lead to strife?

Answer: By no means. Perhaps the atmosphere was often tense, but the suggestion that kind of fronts formed and that there were hard disputes — that suggestion is false.

In am thinking, for example, of a "conservative" dean, who was not a member of the council. The assembly agreed to the proposal to let him speak to the entire assembly. He was speaking, he said, in behalf of a thousand priests and many lay people, against the proposals concerning the priestly ministry. One could feel, during his talk, that the meeting disagreed with him, but no one thought of attacking him through interruptions.

Things were the same when a spokesman for the radical groups "Septuagint" and "4/7" was given the floor to present his stand.

Question: And what about the bishops? Were they sitting in dock?

Answer: No, this wasn't the case either. In so far as I could see, the Pastoral Council had no intentions of settling accounts with anybody or anything. One could feel that it was with a great sense of responsibility that this meeting was tackling the problems. *Involved responsibility*, that is how I would describe the second characteristic, next to its openness, of the Dutch Council.

Question: Now there was this sensational decision of the Dutch Pastoral Council to recommend that in the future priests should no longer be obliged to be celibate. Of the 106 voting members — including the bishops — a total of 90 voted for, and 6 against the recommendation; two delegates abstained. Did not this result at Noordwijkerhout have the impact of a bomb?

Answer No, there was no explosion, if that is what you mean. The voting result as such was not surprising. For much preliminary work had been done and many preliminary talks had been held on this theme. I believe that even the bishops themselves were not so much surprised. They were aware of the trend that had shown itself long before. Surprise there may have been about the unanimity of the voting result, at any rate with some. But please allow me to correct here something which, in the press reports on the Pastoral Council, was presented incorrectly or was misunderstood. The eight Dutch bishops present have not abstained from voting — they had said beforehand, we shall not take part in the voting. I think this is an essential distinction.

Question: Now the results of this voting are at clear variance with what Pope Paul VI repeatedly has said about celibacy. As late as in his Christmas address of 1969 to the Roman Curia he stressed his intention "as the supreme shepherd to maintain the legal obligation of priestly celibacy in the Latin Church." Is there not a serious conflict announcing itself here?

Answer: That is possible. But at this moment it cannot be said with certainty. There is one thing we must clearly realize: the Dutch Pastoral Council does not want a breach with Rome. In many talks I was told this repeatedly. To be sure, the recommendation of the Dutch Council runs contrary to what the Pope has said. But at Noordwijkerhout there was no intentional siding against the Pope. The delegates should like — to put it quite simply — the Pope to consider their proposals. They hope he will lend an ear to their earnest concern about the church and the clergy in The Netherlands, and will agree to their view of this problem.

Question: But is it realistic to hope to persuade the Pope, who in this matter has so unambiguously committed himself?

Answer: That is what I, of course, am also wondering about. On the other hand, one should not forget that the Dutch tend to think more pragmatically, and not so fundamentally as, perhaps, we Germans do. This makes it easier to understand that they do not think of their stand against the Pope as an insult to him.

Question: In its wording the Noordwijkerhout vote is a recommendation. Is this also its intention? Or is there an ultimatum element in the whole thing?

Answer: The plenary assembly has discussed whether the bishops should set a deadline within which what is allegedly a recommendation should be realized. The meeting rejected this. But it would seem to me that behind the council's recommendation there is a firm *determination*. I already mentioned openness and responsibility as special characteristics of this assembly. As a third characteristic one should add the determination. The Dutch Pastoral Council wants its resolutions to be implemented.

Question: But has the Dutch Council not got its own bishops into trouble by commissioning them to work for a change of the celibacy law in Rome and for the whole church to see?

Answer: The Dutch bishops are certainly in a difficult position. They have declared that they are first of all going to discuss the Noordwijkerhout resolution with the religious superiors. It is only then that they will make the next move.

Question: What immediate effects could the Noordwijkerhout results have on the neighbours, for example on us in Germany?

Answer: I believe there will be no immediate special effects. Basically Noordwijkerhout has not brought anything new into the celibacy discussion. The really new thing was that a body of chosen representatives of the

Dutch Catholics have clearly, openly and officially pronounced this recommendation, which should be passed on.

Question: The German dioceses are going to hold a communal synod. Have you had, during the Dutch Pastoral Council, specific experiences that could be useful at the German synod?

Answer: Two things seem to me of great importance for our synod. First of all it is desirable that at an early date fundamental and broad information about the questions to be discussed be gathered. Without this information, without detailed knowledge, there is no competence. And where competence is lacking, few results can be expected. And secondly, if the questions on the agenda are to be given good and solid treatment, a limitation to essentials is necessary, maybe in the manner shown by the Dutch Pastoral Council. (Pastoraal Concilie in de Publiciteit, 1970).

Our last quotation is from the American periodical *Newsweek* of 9 February 1970. Here the influence of German Prelate G. Fittkau is already described. He was not present at Noordwijkerhout, but he attended previous sessions and regularly informed the regional bishops' conference of Westphalia. Later on he was to launch, in a German advertizing magazine, personal insinuations against the Roermond chapter's candidates for the episcopal nomination, whose names had become public.

When the Dutch Roman Catholic bishops announced their support of a married priesthood last month, they took two calculated risks. First, they chose to accept the conclusions of their Pastoral Council against the written directives of Pope Paul VI to uphold mandatory clerical celibacy. Second, they gambled that their liberal colleagues in other countries would second their request for "deliberation by the whole church" on the subject of optional celibacy. On both counts, they assumed that the doctrine of collegiality in church government permits one Catholic province to propose issues for debate for the entire church.

So far, only Leo Josef Cardinal Suenens and a handful of other bishops from Belgium, Canada, South Africa, The Philippines, Brazil and Norway have individually indicated support of the Dutch position. The Pope has refused to see Holland's primate, Bernard Cardinal Alfrink, and has used the Vatican Newspaper *L'Osservatore Romano* to criticize the Dutch bishops for bowing to "little pressure groups." Rome seems convinced that a recent papal letter to bishops, demanding support of mandatory celibacy, will effectively isolate the Dutch episcopate.

Last week, Dutch church leaders used the hiatus to drum up support among neighboring bishops. Franciscan sociologist Father Walter Goddijn, secretary-general of the Pastoral Council, took the Dutch case to several bishops in Germany and Austria. Appearing on Austrian television from Salzburg, he denied that the Dutch were moving toward schism with Rome. But, he admitted, "despite the constant flow of information from The Netherlands to Rome, there are many, many misunderstandings between us."

Attack: Even as Goddijn spoke, German conservatives were mounting an attack on the Dutch Pastoral Council and on Goddijn himself. Berlin's Alfred Cardinal Bengsch publicly accused the Dutch hierarchy of weakening "the ties of loyalty and obedience which bind every bishop and every priest to the Holy Father" by yielding to the pressure from "opinion groups" inside the Dutch church. The cardinal was quickly supported by theologian Gerhard Fittkau of Essen, who has been an observer for several German bishops at the sessions of the Dutch Council. In a letter widely circulated to the German press, Fittkau charged that the Dutch position on clerical celibacy "is clearly no longer Catholic and barely Christian." A minority led by Goddijn, he said, "has dishonestly manipulated" the Pastoral Council and even the Dutch bishops.

Fittkau's charges suggest that much more is at stake in Holland's challenge to Rome than the question of clerical celibacy. The Dutch Pastoral Council is the only experiment in representational government in the entire Catholic church. Though the Dutch bishops are not bound to accept council recommendations, they must respond to them. Only by denying the representational character of the council, conservatives feel, can they nip such experiments in the bud — and preserve the Roman system of "collegial" government from the Pope down.

Despite all Dutch attempts to establish a good dialogue with the world episcopate the Catholic church in The Netherlands has remained the only local church that clearly spoke its mind. Later on, it received support from cardinals in Canada and Spain. In an interview with Henri Fesquet in *Le Monde* of 12 May 1970 Cardinal Suenens defended the Dutch bishops very efficiently, emphasizing the right of joint responsibility and dialogue. Publicly or confidentially several individual bishops expressed their approval. A number of Austrian bishops even paid a visit to The Netherlands. Still The Netherlands seems to be somewhat isolated, but there are ever louder voices saying the ministry crisis in the church has come to a head. The *via facti* disapproved by Rome with regard to the local churches and never followed by the entire church community of The Netherlands, now seems to be practised by Rome itself. They are just waiting till the personnel shortage in the western world and in the developing countries becomes untenable. Any solution will come too late. Even in The Netherlands with their many priests one out of three parish ministers is over 55 years of age (KSKI, 1972).

CHAPTER VII

Church Renewal: An Interpretation

The preceding chapters, it is hoped, have contributed towards interpreting the so-unexpected institutional changes in the Dutch Church. The continuity with attempts at church renewal elsewhere, after 1900 and in particular after 1945 is clearly visible. Relations between the local church in The Netherlands and the central government in Rome proved to be continuously tense, without leading to a schism. How could the needs of modern society be met to the benefit of the community, and at the same time the bonds with Rome and the world church be preserved? How could solidarity with Rome be respected without running the risk of isolation, as a large sect, from the ever-changing outside world?

The central problem remains this: how can the Catholic church survive as an institute and simultaneously continue to participate in a process of change? Or is this change only a sham? Is there, in fact, no gradual progress at all, but only a zigzagging, a marking time? Are there no real reforms and must we rather speak of what was called by an American priest "moving the deckchairs on the Titanic" (*Time*, 26 December 1969)? Is no real change of course possible any more in the Catholic church, and is a shipwreck imminent?

By way of postscript we want to offer an interpretation scheme which tries to explain why in one case progress occurs whereas in another there is regress. Strictly speaking these terms only insufficiently characterize the movement in its entirety. The problem is not only one of linear movements forward or backward, but of synchronous and asynchronous processes of, on the one hand, creativity and renewal, and, on the other, the institutionalizing and stabilizing of change. This interpretation scheme may serve as a "blueprint for survival," helping not only Dutch Catholicism but also other local churches to assess their own place within the periodic processes of change.

1. Three Relevant Factors

In our analysis of the renewal process again and again three relevant factors cropped up, with their progressive and regressive variations. Those three factors are: the exercise of authority, scholarly study, and publicity. All of them have intermediary connections with the public at large or, in a stricter sense, with church members. Authority, scholarship and information are always conditioned by the amount of freedom they allow each other in their actual interrelations. Put into functional terms we find: the bishops, the scholars, especially the theologians, and the publicists or journalists.

Bringing together those three elements, dimensions, unities or factors within one system, we can point out various relations. Especially through indicating those relations are the elements formed into a coherent pattern, which thus becomes a conceptual model, a paradigm, or an interpretation scheme. As an hypothesis it may explain many of the changes in the Roman Catholic church.

In recent Dutch church history there were bishops with a modern style of exercising authority, in good communication and interaction with priests and laity. Experts from various disciplines, in particular theologians, made their studies in close touch with pastoral praxis and the actual local church community. There were competent radio, press and television reporters, financially independent of the church and having a certain affinity with what was happening in the church community. Their reports and comments stimulated a free and critical development of opinion. Moreover, there was actually good communication and cooperation *within* the episcopal college, between theologians and other experts, and also between the mass media, although with the usual competitive atmosphere especially as relates to "scoops."

Alongside this communication with the diocesan faithful (bishops), with the pastoral praxis in the church community (theologians) and with the public (journalists), and alongside the internal cooperation of the groups (bishops' conference, committees of experts, press conferences, journalists' club), there was also intensive interaction between those three groups. Authority was exercised with the help of expert advice, and the mass media spread this among the public at large.

2. Application to The Netherlands

This interplay, concretized in the Pastoral Council where bishops, experts, delegates from the priesthood and the faithful, and publicists met in the same building for days at a stretch, was an excellent source of and a stimulus for church renewal. It was the concretization of this "something special" in Dutch church renewal. There was great mutual openness and trust, and a critical solidarity, directed at a great commitment of capacities and energies in order to strive, with great freedom and as Christians of equal status, for a better functioning of the church as an institute.

This renewal process can be characterized as a gradual growing together of bishops, theologians and publicists who did not lose touch with the Christian community. They were not palace or audience bishops, not armchair theologians locked away from modern reality in their studies, not publicists shying away from political viewpoints. It was exactly in their common subservience to the same religious community that they met in their functional qualities. With respect for each other's position: the irreducible responsibility of the bishops, the free scientific statute of the experts, the publicists' freedom of opinion, they sought through consultation a certain balance in their mutual relations. This process was not without tensions and conflicts. It was a dialogue process, a training in communication, with all the risks inherent to it. But it proved to be, in fact, a source of continuous renewal, tested in its provisional institutionalization against similar processes on the international level, defined as to its content and tempo by relatively superior authorities.

In The Netherlands this interaction at grassroots level took the form of pastoral group discussion. It was "a dynamic process, bringing out and formulating much that was latent, that caused irritation, that caused concern, enabling members of the group to deepen mutual insights, to enrich and inform each other, in the last analysis to make each other more of a person and of a believer....This means that the discussion group is groping its way towards a form of religious experience that is more in harmony with actual life, towards discovering the actual values and meaning of the Gospel for modern man." Government by decree, and central and authoritarian ways of exercising authority are relativized through the public interaction of authorities, experts and the faithful. There is an obvious connection with tendencies towards democratization and co-responsibility. Therefore the church, too, is going through a communications revolution, leading to an ecclesiastical communications structure that increasingly shows dialogue features." On all levels these new forms of communication have practical and organizational aspects; attention must be paid to dialogue techniques, to themes and contents, to reporting. It is a learning process: experiences and criticism contribute to it (H. Hoekstra, 1967). In later years a certain fatigue set in, and social problems became more and more the issues. Alongside the discussion groups there are now action groups, "contesting" either a fixed issue or sometimes more institutionalized like J. Ruyter's parish at Beverwijk. "From a distance" the authorities keep in touch with those groups which, mainly through publicity, put pressure upon those authorities (J. van Dijk, 1973). Comparisons could also be made with experimental groups, mainly found in The Netherlands among the religious. Their common features show much similarity with the interaction phenomena of church renewal (W. Simpfendörfer, 1963-64).

The higher the ecclesiastical structural levels and the wider the geographical boundaries, the more difficult it is to align and coordinate bishops' conferences, experts and the free mass media. But foreign observers affirm this interpretation scheme is basically correct. Thus G. Zizola (1970), the well-known Italian religious journalist, calls the models of pastoral councils tried out so far "such as the Dutch one," convincing proofs of a real democratic experience. Louvain professor J. Remy (1971) points out that in this dialogue authorities, scholars and the public must have equal status. Therefore mass media should circulate information about renewal movements, free from control by the authorities. Mass communication here means public communication, i.e. the possibility for church members to express nearly as many opinions as they listen to.

Nijmegen pastoral theologian F. Haarsma (1969) summarizes the actual Dutch situation regarding the interaction of the elements mentioned:

> A revolutionary reorientation of the present structure towards a democratic one is alluring, because time is pressing. But because at this moment large parts of the church are not mentally ready for democratic relations, such a revolution would lead to a schism. So the only possibility

seems to lie in the introduction of those elements of democracy which are by principle recognized or at least allowed by the present church order. First of all this entails the further development of collegiality into a synodal "opposite" of the ministry on all levels: the parish council; pastoral councils in deaneries, dioceses and countries; episcopal synods; provincial, regional and ecumenical councils. This will have to be accompanied by the greatest possible openness in every policy stage. Without extensive information these new organisms cannot function effectively. If they are to remain interested and avoid quickly becoming frustated, it is also indispensable to have the implementation of decisions, on all levels, accounted for.

The search for a permanent form of exercising authority in a dialogue with experts and publicists was given a new start in the Dutch National Pastoral Consultation. The fact that, after a first meeting in the beginning of 1973, a second one is scheduled for as late as the end of 1974 indicates a certain malaise. In the suggestions offered by the committee chaired by Prof. P. Steenkamp, who was the Pastoral Council's chairman during the second period, a more permanent structure had been suggested, in which a continuous process of communication and coordination with regard to authority, expertise and publicity was envisaged.

3. Application to Vatican II and the Church Universal

The Vatican Council in Rome was an international meeting of bishops and theologians, closely covered by the mass media. There a process of learning to know each other, of mutual criticism, and of mutual help in the study of draft reports and the preparation of interventions was begun which was at the same time a process of renewal. There the same three relevant factors were found in a pattern of interrelations. Theoretically there was freedom of interaction among the three groups of functionaries, and also among the council bishops, the experts — who were only in part official council *periti* — and the publicists.

In practice, there were organizational limitations. During the second session (1963) 2676 bishops were on the official list of council fathers, wheras an average of 2135 attended the meetings in the council hall. Only ten percent of them had real influence through their interventions. The others contributed to the communications process as listeners and as voters on documents. American council sociologist E. Caporale says that after the meetings he found many bishops unable to formulate their opinions and needing an explanation by experts. But within and without the council hall the bishops talked with each other: people from various cultures, continents, linguistic areas, bishops with a big escort of experts, authoritarian and nonauthoritarian bishops, pastoral bishops and learned ones, very old prelates and newly-appointed pastors. The strain was great. There were daily meetings in St. Peter's, followed by many committee consultations. Some countries had good internal communication because the bishops were residing in the same homes. Others lived as far as thirty miles from the Vatican or were spread over nearly a hundred buildings in Rome. The same practical limitations also existed for the experts and the journalists who wanted to contact the bishops.

Here, too, the interesting question arises whether such a gigantic discussion among bishops, experts and publicists, each of them representing the community of the faithful in his own way, could be made into something permanent. Is it always necessary to wait till the international problems have reached such a pitch that a Vatican Council, lasting for years, must be convoked? Is not it possible to have permanent information, an exact inventory of changes, initiatives and experiments? Could not the same thing be asked regarding scientific evaluation? And could not this information and evaluation be assessed in a permanent communication of representatives of the bishops? This time, Caporale says, mutual information was an incidental and unexpected by-product of Vatican II. The Brazilian bishops lived in one house, the "Domus Mariae." Their experts were on hand, there was an excellent library and even an information bulletin. The three relevant factors were present in an ideal combination. But could the same be possible for the entire church? This is possible, a French bishop said, according to Caporale, but not in Rome. You had better look for a different place with adequate facilities (R. Caporale, 1965). One could add that the Roman Curia is not only in charge of the executive tasks of international church government, but is also to a large extent involved in a number of the pastoral and political problems of Italy. If, besides all this, this Curia would also have to provide administrative and organizational services to a permanent governing body chosen from among the world's bishops, it would be overburdened. Or one would have to resign oneself to the fact that fostering church renewal is a kind of periodical leisure activity on the amateur level.

It is strange that comparisons with the structure of the United Nations Organization in New York are seldom made. The representation of national governments is also criticized there. Very small

132

sovereign states have the same voting rights as the Soviet Union or the U.S.A. Regional representation on the intermediate level is considered a good alternative. In any case, this is a permanent organization structure, and United Nations officials certainly refrain from interfering with the U.S.A. governmental center in Washington, D.C. In addition the Italian church tries continuously to improve the interaction among the bishops, especially by gradually reducing the number of dioceses; now already some bishops are in charge of combined dioceses. The greater the number of bishops, the more difficult national consultation becomes. Nowadays no new bishops are appointed to the small Italian dioceses. "It is a difficult road," R. Tucci (1966) writes, "on which only slow progress is made. But it is already important that this road was chosen."

Since Vatican II the bishops' synod has been the principal attempt to continue the council. The judgments of it have not been very favourable. R. Laurentin (1972), the well-known synod expert, points out some weak spots: the lack of realism; the complete disregard of results of research as ignoble means of pressure; the want of appreciation of movements that wanted to "coach" the synod: the pretence that obedience can be exacted, as in medieval times; and the misjudgment of the opinions of the public. Reading the World Panorama offered to the bishops' assembly on 30 September 1971 by Msgr. Bartoletti at the request of the synod's secretary, one cannot but draw the same conclusion. Competent evaluation and expert inventory were lacking. There were no contacts with experts and the mass media. Bartoletti (1971) himself said that his study was based on the reports of the bishops' conferences, but that from many conferences he received no reports at all. As a possible excuse he suggested "lack of time." Even to this kind of thing no professional time is devoted! The reports, he said, are not scientific research, but rather a brotherly exchange of experiences and observations. Even more striking is his remark that important observations or necessary additions could be offered during the synod session, but "not in general discussion, which would be impossible, but through a more ripened personal reflection." In this way, hardly any interaction among the bishops themselves proved possible. Nor was this possible at Chur during the second European bishops' conference (1969). Much time was spent discussing whether the few experts there should be allowed to attend the meetings. The media and the action groups present were kept at a far distance. Local authorities had organized so many social engagements for the bishops that, joined with the overly long monologues of the speakers, hardly any time remained for discussion and the development of common insights.

An analysis of the International Laity Congress in Rome at the end of 1967 might also provide interesting data for the assessment of the amount of interaction among bishops, experts, publicists and laity. *Katholiek Archief* (1967, 1292 ff.) studied the representativeness, the freedom of public speech, and the relations with authorities. Concerning the last item J. Stalpers writes: "For me it was refreshing to observe that the actual developments in the Dutch church province, in this field, too, were appreciated and admired by the laity everywhere in the church. They gave encouragement and hoped for possible changes in situations elsewhere. This also convinced me that our problems are not typically Dutch (*De Stem*, 4 Nov. 1967).

4. Bishops and Theologians

For a good understanding of the interpretation scheme for renewal we are offering it is necessary further to describe the position and interaction between authority and scholarship, between hierarchy and theology.

Shortly before Vatican II the credit balance of creative theology in Catholic circles was below the assets of the great Protestant theologians. T. Schoof, who in recent years made several assessments of the relations between theology and hierarchy, was first (1968) hesitant to blame this on what he calls the traditional scapegoat of restraining religious teaching authority. Rather, he thinks the slow-down is caused by the Catholic hierarchy's evident preference for a peculiar philosophy, namely neo-scholasticism. New ideas must always be expressed in categories of the old system of thinking. A Catholic theologian does not claim the position of a bearer of authority. But in his freedom of research he has a clear relation to authority: he offers his interpretations as suggestions. These suggestions are only implemented when the church community gives its consent which "is ultimately sanctioned by the leaders of that community." After Vatican II the theologians were given more freedom, and the external control on renewal theology by the Congregation for the Doctrine of the Faith in Rome has decreased. The need for what Schoof called a "built-in brake" concerning the interpretation of the Gospel and the world would become greater.

Two years later, as Schoof himself said, he had probed the situation a little deeper. In the meantime scrimmages had again occurred between church authority and theology. Schoof's own master, Schillebeeckx, was one of the victims. There was a growing tension, and people were getting tired of waiting. "Apparently an open escalation is no longer avoided, not even in 'Rome,' even though sensivity seems to have grown with regard to the mass media and their influence on world opinion." Together with all those professionally engaged in church events, the theologians were having "a difficult time," and the demand for balanced models was so great that even working overtime they could not be supplied. Authoritarian structures of government having disappeared only patient consultation could lead to a new consensus (T. Schoof, 1970).

Three years after this Schoof had to admit that the majority of church leaders not only reject this new theology, but do not even tolerate it as an alternative. Attempts are being made "to restrain the renewal that set in with the council, and to turn it back. This automatically means a return to the authoritarian patterns which are every leader's temptation; moreover, according to traditional theology those patterns were directly approved of by God himself." Contrary to what he thought five years ago, Schoof now (1973) says that modern theology, although it is "only a theology," has the right to defend its views, "even if these run counter to the policy of the ecclesiastical authorities." He would not regret it if the image of the theologian as a well-behaved functionary faded away. Through the wish for a built-in brake, and the refusal to occupy the position of authority, this author has developed a theology of opposing church government.

The relevance of the interaction between the authority and the scholarship factors with a view to church renewal is becoming more and more evident. There is a continuous endeavour to continue the discussion about the course to be followed, in mutual respect for each other's autonomy, with patience, and in critical solidarity. This continuous dialogue between the driver of the vehicle and the theologian in the "dead man's seat" should not be interrupted. The prohibition to talk with the driver should be turned into a command for the church to journey through modern society. At the beginning of Vatican II Y. Congar quoted St. Bernard: "Ecclesia ante et retro occulata" (A church with eyes in front and rear). In its journey through history the church is always looking forward and backward. Both the driver and the theologian in the seat beside him have rear-view mirrors, but as a matter of fact must first of all look forward. In dangerous traffic situations their attention is divided, which makes the going slower. Looking left and right, forward and backward are becoming, in the church, a kind of sacred cybernetics, aimed at piloting the church safely through a crisis situation. The church's strategic manoeuvering must prevent "accidents." Openness to change, both for the driver and the theologian is moderated continuously by the reality of steering (accelerating and braking) and the traffic situation. Traffic jams (collegiality with the world episcopate) are sometimes extremely irritating for vehicles that can go very fast and now must drive as slowly as old-fashioned models. The theologians offer the interpretations, they assess the surroundings, the position of the church "in the world." It is very clear: the nature of interaction between the two important factors, authority and scholarship, is decisive for the contents and pace of church renewal.

Two comparisons confirm this. The relation between political praxis and scientific study shows that civil authorities, too, often use science to protect their positions of power. Formally speaking science is independent and free. Meanwhile a scientific ethics is developing: "tolerance with regard to alternative hypotheses, with freedom of opinion as its social counterpart; public control balanced by the rejection of authoritarianism, censorship and power; and respect for partners, honesty and unpretentiousness" (O. Diuntjer, 1970). Science often works only for the power elite. This makes scientists the servants of power rather than the "new men of power." "They do not set the political objectives, but they are allowed to justify these, and to determine the means to reach those ends" (B. van Houten, 1972). There are theologians who always agree with authority. For church leaders they are useful and at the same time harmless. Others criticize authority. They feel unhappy about authoritarianism in the church. In the eyes of the leaders they are dangerous and not serviceable enough. Sometimes renewal theologians are "scotched" by authorities via defamation. Or they are sidetracked. As Butler once wrote to modernist von Hügel: The only freedom of a biblicist or a theologian is the freedom of a streetcar.... "You may run along the rails as quickly as possible; but when you try to get to a station which is not on the line, they let you be derailed" (T. Schoof, 1968). The resignation of many renewal theologians is ascribed by A.

Müller (1972) to the fact that in their "dead man's seat" they are often hard put. "The fact that theological progressivists... are again and again disavowed by the church leaders, and gradually are really made scapegoats, fosters radicalization, destroys the last remnants of 'prestige' and willingness to obey, or leads to the loss of the reform zeal." The credibility of authority is not enhanced when it is imposed absolutely. Whoever threatens the freedom of his nearest collaborators also destroys the commitment to joint responsibility. As the unpretentiousness of authority increases "its pronouncements will also have more prestige" (S. Ysseling, 1969).

Another comparison can be made with Protestant theology. In the Dutch Protestant churches the relations between hierarchy and theology have always remained a subject of discussion. Sometimes the strongly centralistic and hierarchical governmental structure of Catholicism has aroused jealousy in the more loosely organized Protestant churches. The problem was put very clearly by Dr. A. Kuyper, the great leader of the Reformed Churches in The Netherlands. He sees hierarchy, or, as he calls it, the "papal system" as opposed to the "presbyterian system." He admits that "presbyterian church government is the most awkward one can imagine. It functions excellently and smoothly as long as one has exemplary and pious ministers and lay people, but the difficulties are immense as soon as one is confronted with the reality of a number of churches whose ways of life, members and ministers have fallen short of this ideal." Then good church government becomes almost impossible, and the presbyterian forms of government nearly everywhere display "a distressing image of impotence." But, he says, even though the hierarchical system is much better in many respects, practical reasons of this kind do not allow us to give up the ideal presented in the Holy Scriptures. Rome has however declared the hierarchical system to be the ideal one, and doctrine has had to accommodate itself to it. "In every church it is necessary, and Rome also admits this, for doctrine and church government to be in harmony. If tensions or differences occur, one of two things must happen: either church government must adapt to doctrine, or doctrine must adapt to church government." (A. Kuyper, no date).

5. The Outlook

Dutch Catholicism will certainly take to heart the counsel offered by German theologian J. Metz (1970) at his address to the theological congress on the future of the church in modern society (Brussels, September 1970). This counsel is a close confirmation of our interpretation scheme for church renewal. "The inner-church processes that have started with regard to enlightenment, responsibility, the promotion of a pluralist critical openness, the change from emphatic to organized freedom, and more generally, with regard to an inner-church 'freedom culture,' should be continued courageously and constructively."

The reality however is that the renewal process is being hindered more and more. Through Roman interference exactly the opposite process has started, the three relevant factors having been turned into a regress methodology. Episcopal appointments, disapproving and correcting the renewal policy of the Dutch episcopate, frustate the interaction horizontally. Bishops who do not want personal power and are open to change become isolated. The vertical and centralistic system of communication with Rome becomes ever more prominent. The recent Vatican document "Directives for the pastoral ministry of the bishops" emphasizes this line of communication. Bishops should be bound to the Pope "in a brotherly community of love and obedience." His doctrinal statements should be "acknowledged respectfully, spread and defended." These are very legitimate wishes, but the same thing is also required concerning documents from the Roman Curia, mentioned in almost the same breath. The bishops' personal autonomy is strongly underlined, also within the national episcopal conference. Others have only advisory tasks. Decisions of a national bishops' conference only bind the individual bishop if they are approved by the central government (*De Volkskrant*, 21 June 1973).

The dangers of this development have been made quite clear by F. de Grijs (1973). An increasing number of people, and especially the young, will turn away from the church. "To an ever-increasing extent the church will show the features of a medieval fortress, inhabited by a small, well-organized group of disputatious grey-haired old people." For The Netherlands he puts his hopes on the large middle group of priests, laity and religious who do not let themselves be driven out by vertical power pressure. "They keep asking for priests, bishops, a Pope who are willing to act as the humblest man, servants of the brethren, refusing any position of domination." In the Netherlands vertical Vatican influence is so strong that the Jesuit provincial recently announced that his fellow-member H. van der Meer, chosen by Bishop Gijsen as his vicar-general, will keep this post "according to the personal wish of Pope Paul." In this respect Rome is very consistent. Priests who have publicly defended the Roman views of authority are "rewarded" by the Vatican with an episcopal candidature or even with an appointment whereby neither the resident bishops nor the chapter are consulted. This was the case in the recent episcopal appointments at Rotterdam and Roermond, and, in the latter case, also with the initially suggested candidate Dean Joosten. This practice also met the wishes of the small right-wing minorities in The Netherlands that used the post-conciliar regress movement and, just after the publication of the encyclical *Humanae Vitae*, broke off the dialogue within the Dutch Catholic Church.

Discord among the renewal theologians was also caused by the nomination of certain theologians for the International Theological Commission set up by the Vatican, or by the promotion of theologians to the cardinalate. What H. de Lubac, at one time an outstanding French renewal theologian, wrote on the "craving for renewal" and criticism of authority, is a far cry from the views he held before (H. de Lubac, 1969). The renewers are divided and their endeavours end in failure because they are isolated and have lost all influence on the policy of most of the bishops (M. Becker, 1967). The recently settled conflict between H. Küng and K. Rahner testifies to the division among renewal theologians. In The Netherlands the defenders of the "long" and "short" ways to renewal also got into conflict with each other over the position of the Amsterdam student parish. The influence of these contesting movements has already been studied extensively by P. McCaffery (1971) and was largely left out in our study. Polarization within the progressive camp may lead to

revolutionaries losing their impact in a splintered sectarianism, and reformists on the rebound becoming more and more moderate, finally alighting in the conservative encampment.... Certainly in a prosperous country like ours the main thing most people ask of the established order is that it meets their wishes for quiet and stability — those being the conditions for an undisturbed, or at any rate a not too brutally disturbed enjoyment of the fruits of that prosperity. If a revolutionary opposition, not strongly supported and balanced by a resolute reformism, creates too much unrest and disorder, the seed is sown for a particularly harmful kind of counter-revolution (C. Lammers, 1971).

Thus a Catholic reform movement, which has entered into a polarization process, can evoke absolutist counter-reformation.

Bishops and theologians appointed by Rome in the context of such a process, experience their nomination not so much as a policy-prompted act, but as a "sacred" command to exercise authority in an autonomous and personal way. Accordingly, they will fight the "dangers" of the reform movement and meet the demand for religious certainty. They will even tend to minimalize the difference between fallible and infallible papal pronouncements, and will consider attempts to explain this difference as showing a lack of respect and faith (J. Girardi, 1970). In such a situation many renewal theologians will lose courage. Already now studies are being published about "Why we are not leaving the church." The continual study of renewal possibilities is sometimes experienced as a powerless ritual (R. Italiaander, 1972; B. Willems, 1972).

The publicity factor is least affected by regress. This is a good omen for church renewal, although many media have lost interest in a church that is no longer dynamic. Meanwhile, publicity can as well serve regress by publicly giving countries like The Netherlands or renewal theologians guilt feelings after they have been disavowed by the Vatican. In the same way in which The Netherlands became internationally known as a pastoral laboratory for renewal, they also had received the public role of a pastoral cemetery in which by orders of Rome all renewal initiatives had to be buried. In a study about church images and mass media J. Gritti (1971) wrote: "France loses its monopoly of the avant garde: Holland, the country of the 'enfants terribles' of the faith, and South America, the homeland of the hagiographic figure of Dom Helder Camara and also of the revolutionary figure of Camillo Torres, are stepping into the footlights." In that public forum The Netherlands was also slandered (as in the *Times* article mentioned at the beginning of our first chapter) in order to defend the acting secretary of state Msgr. G. Benelli against the attack launched against him by P. Hebblethwaite S.J. in *The Observer* of 11 and 18 March 1973. This defense was justified, and such attacks on people who are always criticized because they bear great responsibilities play into the hands of the opponents of church renewal. But it is irresponsible to defend Msgr. G. Benelli by attacking church renewal in The Netherlands or the United States. There are, of course, also voices defending The Netherlands by suggesting that Rome has started a well-considered crusade against The Netherlands. "Against an entire national episcopate, such as the Dutch one, an ideological crusade is launched because theological thinking is too consistent there. Theologians of world status are made the targets of unremitting insinuation." This was said by Swiss convert Hans Kühner (1972) who for years was director of the Bibliotheca Germanica in Rome, and who is a well-known historian. In this way the Catholic renewal movement in The Netherlands will, also because of the often sensational image-building of the mass media, remain the subject of discussion between supporters and adversaries.

Today is 21 June 1973. Ten years ago Pope Paul VI was chosen as the supreme pastor of the Catholic Church. The only journalist ever to be granted an extensive interview once called this Pope a "conservative reformer." He combines the progressive and regressive elements of church renewal. History will eventually judge him. He tries to change the system without weakening it. That is an operation requiring time and gradual development (A. Cavallari, 1967). In the Dutch Catholic Church Cardinal Alfrink also tries to unite divergent views, "obeying Rome and giving up one's own conscientious pastoral responsibility; disobeying Rome and risking a schism; preserving the closest possible bonds with Rome and yet, by way of experiment, giving the particular local church its own local shape" (T. Oostveen, 1972). Cardinal Alfrink has never considered a schism, not even when it was almost imposed from the outside. The only reliable opinion poll (*Elseviers Weekblad* and NIPO, 5 April 1969) asked: "Do you or do you not believe in an imminent schism, a breaking away of the Dutch Church Province from Rome?" Only 17% of the respondents believed in a schism, 78% did not, and 5% gave no answer.

Despite all the attempts at reconciliation and harmonization some church officers and authors do not shun a conflict. Dutch sociologist L. Laeyendecker (1967) would like to see rules for the consultation between Rome and the local churches, but on the condition that no partly is *a priori* dominant. "Several times, for example, the wish has been heard that the Dutch bishops take an unmistakable position against the Roman authorities. This is not likely to happen soon, because this is seen as the beginning of a schism. But no one has ever attempted to find out what consequences such a step would actually have. This conciliatory attitude has estranged many people from a church which does not pay enough attention to their objections." Till this very day some high ecclesiastical authorities are also urging this kind of resistance. We are referring to the statement of the superior general of an international missionary congregation. Their canonical position enables these functionaries to take a relatively independent stand toward the Roman Curia. As a rule they are also chosen along democratic lines. In a London interview the superior general of the White Fathers, Dutchman T. van Asten said: "It may sound a bit revolutionary, but I am of the opinion that local bishops' conferences lack the courage to assume their own responsibility in opposition to Roman centralism." He thinks the Dutch bishops should continue their resistance, but he blames bishops from other countries, who have the same basic convictions, for remaining silent and letting their Dutch colleagues go it alone. "Even if I were alone, I would be inclined to go on. And although I am an outsider, I would like to see the Dutch bishops do the same" (J. Rogier, 1973).

An extensive research programme could be set up to assess the strategic manoeuvrability of the Catholic Church in times of change. Blind spots regarding the relations between renewal-fostering and renewal-obstructing factors should be more structurized. What kind of organizational policy is needed to bring together functions and categories of need without "conflicts"? Application of the requirements for good governmental strategy on the Dutch bishops' policy would show that the decision-making, communication and learning processes have developed very much. It will be very important that church members continue providing the financial means needed for the guidance of change processes from grassroots to top levels. Individual striving for power will always have to be corrected by collegial action. Enough "management risks" have been run. The learning process will mainly concentrate on the Holland—Rome dialogue, because a negative image-building from both sides is still a hindrance and because the nontheological contrasts are great. As long as within the Dutch Catholic Church room remains for a form of church membership in which critical distance and joint responsibility can work together, no one need give up looking for a Christian interpretation to the ultimate questions because of the Church's institutional shortcomings.

The three factors that, in their permanent interaction, proved to be relevant for church renewal in The Netherlands will remain influential. But even continuing church renewal will not reach perfection. "To live is to change, and to be perfect is to have changed often" (John Henry Cardinal Newman).

The Pastoral Council: Survey, Theses on Authority, Resolutions.

I. Structure and Organization of the Pastoral Council

The Pastoral Council of the Dutch Church Province was held in the years 1966—1970, after the Second Vatican Council and under the authority of the Dutch bishops; it was intended as a pastoral consultation to implement the Vatican Council, to discuss in an open exchange the situation of the Roman Catholic Church in The Netherlands, and to offer to this community, with the cooperation of many people, suggestions for the future. This broad purpose was not suitable for the form of a Provincial Council, which is a canonical legislative meeting of bishops. On 18 January 1966 the Pastoral Institute of the Dutch Church Province was put in charge of preparation and further organization. The official opening was on 27 November 1966. Extensive discussion resulted in a "working formula" approved by the bishops on 18 July 1967. This consultation, activated through a number of post office boxes for individual contributions, through discussion groups, internal cooperation of Catholic organizations and societies, study committees and publicity work, had its focus in the plenary assemblies. There were six three-day meetings, held from 1968 to 1970 (at the beginning of January and around Easter) at Noordwijkerhout. They had to decide whether the reports and suggestions offered, particularly by the study committees, reflected the faith of the church community, and to assess the desirability of drawing practical consequences from the convictions expressed. The assemblies were composed of the bishops, who were the presidium, seventy members chosen by the pastoral councils of the seven dioceses, ten religious, fifteen additional seats whose occupants were appointed by the bishops with a view to balanced representation, and finally

143

five people in charge of daily affairs. The chair was held by a successive number of lay people, and a group of experts always attended. Via their representatives other churches and denominations and also the Humanist Association, cooperated in those general meetings and in the study committees. The following subjects were dealt with: authority in the church, missions, development work, Christian ethical attitudes, marriage and family, room for youth, Christian faith today, renewing religious practice, secularization, the religious, the functioning of the ministry, Christian unity, relations between Jews and Christians, the promotion of a peace mentality. The results of the Pastoral Council are mainly in accord with the function it has in the church community. The reports and discussions offer a good survey of the opinions, wishes and expectations among the Catholics, even if not always unanimous. Authority in the church was a very delicate issue and, as a consequence, also the matter of uniformity, imposed or not, in church life. This was made very evident in the recommendation to make priestly celibacy optional, in the statement that the papal encyclical *Humanae Vitae* was not judged convincing in its rejection of contraceptives, and in the wish for more intercommunion with other Christians. It also came to the fore in repeated appeals for experiments, for pluralism, and for room to search for new ways in many areas. To a large extent the Pastoral Council was made possible by the bishops' willingness to enter into open dialogue. Nevertheless this Pastoral Council, set up as an experiment, was not appreciated by all Catholics at home and abroad according to Dr. R. Huysmans, one of the staff members of the council secretariat for the *Winker Prins Encyclopedia*. The attitude towards the Pastoral Council was almost exclusively determined by the impression the mass media gave of it. Therefore it is of great importance to offer a systematic list of the *recommendations* and *resolutions* that were *passed* by the general assembly of the Pastoral Council. They have been printed in the reports (*Kath. Archief*, 1968ff.), but these have not been made available in the bookshops. Moreover, they have never been translated in this form. Yet it is the resolutions that were *passed*, not the draft reports or draft recommendations, on which judgments concerning the contents, the ideas and the opinions of the Pastoral Council, and consequently also those of a large section of the Catholic population of The Netherlands, should be based.

In the Dutch Catholic Church the changed views of authority play an important role. The first plenary assembly was devoted to this subject, and after the discussions the draft report was considerably altered. This rewritten report on authority is published here in full. Then follow the *resolutions that were passed* through voting or that were *re-edited* by order of the assembly. Because the recommendations on the ministry and ecumenism have not been re-edited, they are not printed here. But we do include those recommendations from both reports that strongly marked the discussions and that were put to a vote. Recommendations that are rather motions and are less important from the point of view of their content were omitted. On some resolutions, of a delicate character with regard to central authorities in Rome, the bishops did not vote. They were given the status of *advice to the bishops*. These exceptions will be clearly marked.

The recommendations concerning the priestly ministry are followed by the press communiqués of 19 January and 30 July 1970 presenting the position of the bishops.

II. Theses concerning the Functioning of Authority

A. Causes of the authority crisis in the church

1. *Authority crisis in the church*. Also in the church the functioning of authority has got into a crisis. Ecclesiastical authorities find their decisions are no longer accepted as self-evident, and opinions and practices are very often held and continued which conflict with canon law. They also find their position of authority is less esteemed than their personal qualities. Those under authority appear very sensitive to anything they experience as an incorrect exercise of authority. In particular they do not accept authorities using their power to enforce their decisions and to carry them out against the will of the people concerned.

2. *Authority crisis and faith*. In part the authority crisis ensues from differences of opinion regarding the contents of the faith. Diverging opinions on central doctrinal issues result in certain pronouncements by ecclesiastical authorities no longer being accepted as correct by many.

3. *Different views of the church*. A special cause of the authority crisis is to be found in contrasting views of the church. Against the belief that the ultimate essence of the church is found in its origins in Christ and its being borne by His Word and His Spirit, there is the opinion that it is exclusively founded in and borne by the common convictions of the people. In the former view the

145

bishops have a special inherent responsibility, in the latter the bearer of authority is only a spokesman for the community.

4. *A divergent appraisal of ecclesiastical tradition.* The development of the authority crisis has been stimulated by the divergent appraisals of the ideas, customs and rules in which the common belief has been expressed, and also of the concrete organizational features of the church as an institution. Many people think the prevailing ideas, customs and rules, as well as the existing structures and in particular their underlying mentality are making Christ's real church unrecognizable and are discrediting ecclesiastical authority. Many others, however, consider these ideas, customs, rules and structures very valuable and sometimes identify the real nature of the church with these traditions. The former group stimulates rapid and thorough renewal and tends to blame the authorities for lack of drive. The latter experience renewal as a tearing down and tend to blame the authorities for offering insufficient resistance.

5. *Divergent views on the exercise of authority.* Divergent views on the way authority in the church should be practised also contribute to the crisis. Most of the faithful want the authorities to take more into account their individuality, and to offer more possibilities for consultation and joint responsibility. But there are also members of the flock who, on the contrary, ask for more frequent and vigorous action by the authorities.

6. *Authorities and the lack of unanimity among the faithful.* Because the leaders are exercising their authority over a community in which the members are not of the same mind as to prevailing norms and values, they cannot act as representatives of the entire community; their leadership lacks the indispensable support of the community.

7. *Lack of unanimity among the bearers of authority.* The authority problems are made worse by the appearance of important differences of opinion among the authorities themselves, especially as to the relations between the bishops and the central Roman government, or between bishops and their priests. For some of the faithful these differences lead to a new confidence as regards the continuation of renewal, but others experience them as an undermining of the value of authority.

8. *Crisis and renewal.* In the renewal process an authority crisis is unavoidable. The phenomena that cause this crisis are indispensable conditions for renewal. Clearly overcoming this authority cri-

sis is not only a task for the bearers of authority themselves, but also for the church as a whole.

B. Authority relations within the church

1. *The church as a community*. The church is a community of people who know they have been called together by God around Christ in order to give as many people as possible a share in Christ's salvation, and to work for such structures in human society as foster the salvation of everyone. This distinguishes the church from communities, organizations and societies whose members work for each other's well-being, for the common good, for their own interests or for humanitarian objectives.

2. *The church as an institution*. Because it is an institution of people in this world the church necessarily assumes organizational features. To experience, preserve and transmit the faith, the church as an institution is indispensable. But the concrete shape of this institution is time-bound and accordingly can differ and change with times and places. This is also true for the formulas, customs, rules and the forms of worship in which the common belief is expressed.

3. *Community and institution*. There exists an unmistakable tension between the church as an institution and the church as a community. This tension may not be removed through a denial of either of these aspects. But within this field of tension the organizational aspect should always remain subordinate to the community aspect. If the institution is seen as something with an independent meaning or value, the church as a community always suffers.

4. *Relations between the community members*. As Christians all church members, whatever their functions, are equal. Each of them and all together they have only one Lord, Teacher and Master, Jesus Christ (Matt. 23: 8—10). All are in the same way subjected to the authority of Christ and His Word. As equals they respect and uphold each other's freedom and joint responsibility. Within internal church relationships this fundamental equality always remains foremost.

5. *The authority of the community*. Authority in the church is not the monopoly of church officials. The New Testament shows that also the local community as such delegates ministerial tasks to its members (Acts 11:22), administers discipline (Matt. 18: 15—18) and takes decisions, albeit together with its pastors and leaders (Acts 15: 4.22; I Cor. 5: 4—5).

6. *Authority over the community.* As a community of the faithful the church needs leaders of the faith, in charge of preaching and teaching the faith, the administration of the sacraments, the presidency of liturgical meetings, and the establishment of the church as a service to the world.

7. *Authority within the organization.* Like other organizations the church cannot exist without governors who maintain and in time adapt church order, who look after the necessary unity, and who are responsible for the execution, assignment and coordination of the various tasks.

8. *The authority of ecclesiastical ministers.* The church was built on the foundation of Peter, the apostles and the prophets (Matt. 16: 18; Eph. 2: 20). The apostles appointed ministers who are called surveyors (*episkopoi*), elders (*presbuteroi*) and servants (*diakonoi*) (Acts 20: 28; Tit. 1: 5). The church believes that these ministers and their successors have been given a special mission by Christ, to preach and interpret His Word and to guide His church. Therefore authority in the church has special links with the pastoral ministry of the bishops. Although they do not possess the fullness of Christ's authority, they really have a share in it. Therefore, besides the authority they have as representatives of the community, they also have an inherent responsibility toward and control over that community.

9. *The relation between ministers and the other church members.* Notwithstanding the fundamental equality of all the faithful there are, also within the leadership relations, differences and distinctions. This gives the community an order which in the New Testament is compared with the structure of a body of which Christ is the head (I Cor. 12: 12—30; Eph. 4: 11—16), and with a building of which Christ is the cornerstone (Eph. 2: 19—22).

10. *The practice of authority.* In Christ the bearers of authority find the model for the exercise of their authority. His behaviour was marked by humility and simplicity, by the absence of any wish to assert or obtrude himself. He did not give orders, but he showed the way, his words were not enforcing but inviting, he did not repel people but established communion, he did not shut out but invited to enter. Pomp and exhibition, and the creation or maintenance of a distance from one's fellow-Christians run counter to Christ's example.

11. *The limits of authority.* Since the bishops have a voice of their own, theirs is the right, after consultation, to speak the decisive word in matters regarding church order, preaching, religious

instruction, the administration of the sacraments and celebration of the liturgy. In matters concerning personal belief and personal attitudes, conscience remains the decisive factor for every Christian.

12. *Church and society*. But outside its own boundaries the church has no other authority than Christ's Word. It can detract from this authority through insincerity, arrogance, complacency, alienation from the world, and particularly through real or apparent striving for power. The authority of Christ's Word can only be exercised if the church is clearly recognizable as the serving church the Gospel intends it to be. Because in social matters the church has no governing powers, it cannot lay down the rules here. Yet it must not remain silent. In its preaching it points to those values which, on the basis of God's Word, it esteems, promotes and protects.

C. Guidelines for a good functioning of authority.

1. *The attitude of the bearers of authority.* A smooth functioning of authority is only possible if a community recognizes in its leaders acceptable attitudes. Therefore these authorities should show themselves sincere in their motives, intentions and arguments, admit mistakes, revoke decisions that have proved incorrect, and make up for injustice caused by those decisions. Their actions should be marked by a positive attitude and they should prefer preaching the truth over condemning errors, fostering the good rather than repelling the bad, inviting discussions rather than rejecting criticism. A healthy attitude is also shown in a willingness to listen, to consider seriously all arguments, and to revise earlier positions. Finally, their behaviour should express a pastoral attitude. It should be possible for people to experience that for authorities, too, the people who they care for are more important than the rules of the institution.

2. *The attitude of those under authority.* A smooth functioning of authority also requires a correct attitude of those under the authority. They should take a positive stand with regard to the bearers of authority. Before making objections they should collect sufficient information, and their criticism should preferably be constructive. In discussions they should keep an eye on the common good, they should seriously study the matters to be discussed, offer reasonable and constructive suggestions, and acknowledge the bishops'

right to speak the decisive word. Finally, they should show their willingness to accept and carry out the decisions taken.

3. *Attitudes towards each other.* In relation to each other the bearers of authority and those under authority should be patient and admit their own limitations, they should display faithfulness and sincerity, respect each other's motives and intentions, and show understanding for mutual mistakes and shortcomings.

4. *Dialogue.* The most important condition for the smooth functioning of authority is the continuous and public dialogue between leaders and community.

5. *Consultative bodies.* Dialogue is guaranteed through the establishment of public consultative bodies composed of the bearers of authority and representatives chosen by the community. In order to ensure a balanced representation of the entire community, it should be possible for the authorities to appoint one or more members from those groups that otherwise would not be represented sufficiently. The composition, power and procedures of those consultative bodies should be outlined in a national charter.

6. *Subjects of discussion.* Joint consultation should not be limited to matters of internal policy, but also deal with the way in which the church realizes its service to the world. And because the contents of the preaching can only be understood by a joint listening to and discussion of the Gospel message, the contents, meaning and formulation of doctrine should also be discussed.

7. *Doctrinal pronouncements.* As spokesmen for the community the bishops interpret the faith of the community. Therefore they should listen very carefully to what is alive in the Christian consciousness of the church members. Besides this, the bishops have also an inherent task to preach the faith, and for the sake of clarity it can be necessary for them, as religious leaders, to take a stand against public theories and practices which they consider incompatible with the Gospel.

8. *Acceptance.* The complement of a clear doctrinal statement by the bishops is the approval of the community, which, however, does not necessarily preclude a continuation of discussion. The individual church member can only freely confirm to this agreement. If anybody thinks he cannot in conscience do so, he should only disregard such a statement after serious thinking. In their official preaching ministers should keep within the boundaries of prevailing doctrine. If this should be impossible, they should place their preaching mandate at the disposal of the bishop.

150

9. *Communications media.* Because the communications media stimulate the formation of opinion needed for dialogue, an give all interested parties a share in the consultations, the authorities should have an open and positive attitude towards these media, However, this openness does not extend to matters which in the interest of a third party or of the common good should not be made public.

10. *Democratization.* Dialogue and openness will foster the democratization of the church. This will lead to new structures in which it will be normal for the community to have a say in the appointment of its leaders, special attention being paid to the prophetic, pastoral and liturgical capabilities of the candidates. In transfers, too, the community will be consulted as much as possible, and justified complaints about ministers will be considered. On the other hand the community will understand that not all particulars with regard to persons can be published, so that the motives for a different decision cannot always be made known.

11. *Decentralization.* In the interest of a fruitful consultation between authorities and the community, and of forms of preaching and policy adapted to the national or local church community, a general decentralization is to be stimulated. But in certain cases the mutual solidarity of Christian communities and the efficiency of government may require centralization. Demarcation of the areas in which either decentralization or centralization is to be preferred will take place through joint consultation between the authorities and the community.

12. *Pluralism.* Democratization and decentralization enhance the pluralism in the shaping of the common faith. This pluralism should be judged positively, but it does demand intense and frequent contact between the various groups and the local churches. Experiments intended to realize pluralism deserve support. In the last analysis they are the responsibility of the bishops, who have an inherent task to preserve unity. To insure this unity mutual information from the bishops and continued contact with the world episcopate are of great importance.

III. Resolutions of the Pastoral Council

A. Authority: views and attitudes

1. *Calling in expert advisors.* On all levels the bearers of author-

ity should not only consult the faithful entrusted to them, but also request the advice of experts. Generally speaking this advice should not be set aside by the authorities without explaining this to the advisors.

2. *Planning and coordination on the national level.* Planning on the national and diocesan levels, with intensive cooperation and participation of bishops, religious superiors, priests and laity, is urgent if the organizational elements in the Dutch Church Province are to function in the best possible manner.

This planning and consultation should cover, among other things, appointments, missions, training for the priesthood, in-service pastoral training, catechesis, youth and adult education, finances.

3. *Developing consultative bodies.* On the various levels of pastoral care consultative bodies should be developed.

It is absolutely necessary for these bodies to be given clear instructions, insofar as possible identical throughout the country.

4. *Appointments.* It is advisable to develop, for all ministerial functions, appointment procedures in which the existing consultative bodies can also cooperate.

5. *Participation in ordinary pastoral work..* In order to prevent alienation and isolation it is desirable that all ministers have informal contacts with the faithful, among other things through participation in the ordinary pastorate. The faithful should themselves extend the invitation.

6. *Decentralization.* The plenary assembly of the Pastoral Council is of the opinion that both the discussions at the European Bishops' Symposium and its own discussions show that decentralization on all levels is of fundamental importance for the Catholic Church both in this country and elsewhere.

7. *Concerned dialogue among the movements in the church.* To promote unanimity among Dutch Catholics, and consequently to provide the room for the more efficient exercise of authority, we recommend that forms of consultation be sought which foster mutual understanding, respect and appreciation of the values cultivated by the various movements in the Dutch Church Province.

8. *Introducing renewal.* Care should be taken that the renewal of church life is carefully introduced and explained, in particular via good adult-directed catechesis and formation projects.

B. Missions

1. For the propagation of a responsible vision about the "mission," as formulated in the report "Our Missionary Task Today," the Dutch Missions Council is requested to create a study secretariat which will offer its services to preaching, catechesis and information work. In the teamwork of this bureau of the Dutch Missions Council with all other institutions working in this area, further forms of cooperation should be developed for the training, instruction and re-orientation of all people assisting young churches in their pastoral, missionary and social work. Through this level of consultation between the Dutch Church Province and the young churches themselves should be stimulated.

2. The plenary assembly of the Dutch Pastoral Council expresses its satisfaction with the coordination of missionary activities as planned by the Dutch Missions Council, and expresses its hopes and wishes that this council acquire a clear status through the recognition and cooperation of everybody concerned.

3. Central consultation concerning the supply of missionary personnel is urgent, also with a view to modern methods and conditions for development cooperation, particularly in the field of group work, specialized training and project development. Cooperation should be sought between the bureau for missions of secular priests and the personnel bureau for ecclesiastical development workers who do not belong to a religious order or congregation. Possibilities should be developed for Dutch lay people and secular priests to offer their services, either temporarily or permanently, to young churches; existing missionary institutions should, insofar as their structures allow this, cooperate. The Dutch Council is commissioned to create a committee to study this matter and to advise the Missions Council.

4. It is necessary for the Dutch Church Province to be informed about the systems of recruiting, training and sending out missions, as well as of the financial aspects. On the basis of such a survey a team of experts, appointed by the Dutch episcopate on the recommendation of the Dutch Missions Council, is to offer suggestions to the Missions Council aimed at further coordination and, if necessary, concentration of those systems, and at a financial plan in which the burdens are equally divided.

5. It is necessary that national Catholic organizations coordinate both their campaigns and their support programmes to be of better service to the work of the young churches. The Dutch Missions

Council should see it as one of its tasks to realize this cooperation as quickly as possible.

6. To maintain a high level of interest and generosity centralization should leave room for missionaries to appeal directly to the parish or groups with which they have a special relation. But these individual activities have their limitations. They should take place in such a way that they do not harm the big national collections for missions, and, in general, they should not overstep the boundaries of a local action. For bigger projects no action should be undertaken before it has been made clear that national organizations can offer no help. Actions with a wider scope should only be started after consulting the Missions Councils on the deanery, diocesan or national levels. In influencing mentalities the importance of the church universal will have to be made clear via responsible publicity and adequate propaganda techniques, so that the faithful really feel involved in the work of the missionary church.

7. The churches in The Netherlands should give concrete shape to their wishes for cooperation and real unity both in their country and in those areas of the world where their missionary activity is directed. The cooperation of the Protestant and Catholic Missions Councils is a welcome first step. As regards the future, the Pastoral Council considers it a task of the forthcoming Council of Churches in The Netherlands to organize and supervize this cooperation. Among other things this cooperation, which is an expression of the undivided faithfulness to the one Lord, will be directed towards:

—common study, reflection and experiments with a view to discovering in how far a unanimous witnessing of Jesus Christ and the kingdom to come is possible;

—common efforts, in behalf of the world diaconate, among other things through the coordination of similar activities in the various churches;

—unifying missionary activities in The Netherlands;

—cooperation with Christians working in developing countries;

—common financial support for the missionary projects of the Dutch churches;

—common training and instruction of the priests, ministers and experts sent out by the Dutch churches.

8. National planning and coordination will also have to include the integration of assistance to young churches and to missionary personnel.

Good information should quickly be made available concerning the financial situation of the Dutch Church Province in its broadest sense.

C. Development work

1. The plenary assembly of the Pastoral Council declares the report on "Development Work" because of its tenor and mentality to be an excellent starting point for a good insight into the requirements for development assistance.

The plenary assembly asks the secretariat to have this report discussed in as wide a circle as possible (council discussion groups, organizations, educational institutes).

2. The assembly seconds the proposal to offer this report to the forthcoming Council of Churches in The Netherlands, with as a goal the issue of a common statement on development cooperation.

3. Considering the importance of a change of attitude in the sense of the new conscience described in *Populorum Progressio* the plenary assembly of the Pastoral Council expresses its appreciation of the educational activities already displayed by various organizations in this field.

It asks the organizations and associations, especially those represented at the Pastoral Council, to plan a training programme for attitude change which could already be implemented during the coming winter.

Moreover, it asks that the development issue be integrated into all educational programmes, especially those of teachers colleges and theological faculties.

4. Consequent to the preceding resolution we should like to emphasize that in the programmes of the theological faculties in The Netherlands so far very little attention has been paid to the problems of man and his world in the light of change and development, to the issues of mission and development work, of wealth and poverty, war and peace, etc.

If we do not want to degenerate into a "theology of prosperity" these matters will have to be included in the study programme of every future priest, whether he is going to work in this country or elsewhere. Furthermore, we think theological training centers and faculties should be open to the whole world and should show this openness through;

—an exchange of teachers from all over the world;

—offering exchange possibilities to students of all theological training centers and faculties both nationally and internationally.

5. The plenary assembly, well aware that the encyclical *Populorum Progressio* has not reached all members of the Catholic Church and that, generally speaking, they little realize the necessity of development work, proposes the establishment and execution, in and for The Netherlands, of a systematic and efficient programme for in-depth education, in order to make our entire people conscious of the real dimensions of the development problem and to foster personal commitment. This kind of education will have to penetrate into the work of parents, schools, churches and training centers. Such contacts will have to be established between actual projects and the vital groups of our people so that they become fully acquainted with development work.

6. The plenary assembly considers it urgent, considering the scarcity of expert personnel and financial resources, that private organizations for development aid set up efficient cooperation and coordinate their activities both nationally and internationally.

7. The plenary assembly, realizing that a real education in world-wide thinking is not possible without contact and dialogue with people from developing countries, urgently requests all groups and authorities wanting to work for development cooperation to ask, if possible, non-western workers and students staying in The Netherlands to take part in their consultations, discussions and activities.

8. The plenary assembly ascertains that the necessary steps toward an international legal order, toward a just international economic order, and toward such changes in our own economic structures that enable developing countries enter our markets are essentially political steps.

Therefore the Pastoral Council appeals to all Catholics for a personal political commitment in order to realize these ends as best as possible.

D. Ethical attitudes of Christians in this world

1. *Basic convictions*
    a. The church should with an open, but critical eye, face the changes of our times. It must again and again examine these changes in the light of the Gospel, reflecting on its own nature

and structures, and through the Gospel approach the world in order to humanize it.

b. Changes should be actualized in dialogue with all people of good will, so that the positive contributions of all concerned can be realized. This applies also to those norms and rules for moral life that are acceptable from the point of view of the Gospel.

c. In all this we should recognize man's autonomy as inherent in the plan of God who is the origin and the destiny of man and his world.

d. Not the rules nor the norms should dominate: Christ's self-giving and self-sacrificing love is for the Christian the only absolute norm, from which he should, in his Christ-centered freedom, develop his norms and rules of conduct.

2. *Subjects*

a. Ethical growth asks each of us to commit himself on two levels: the level of developing personal life-styles, and of the building of a just and merciful society. In his personal life a Christian should, guided by Christ's teachings and example, and in living contact with Him, develop himself and be formed as to his conscience and his deeds. In Christ's spirit — based on the Gospel — the church can offer guidance and help, and bring reconciliation when humans fail.

b. Parents and other educators have the task and the right to help form the conscience. Those in charge of the forming of the conscience of others should show their ideals in their own lives and themselves, too, be open to criticism.

c. Conscience formation by the parents will only be effective if — wherever possible — the "how" and "why" are also explained. It should not be forgotten that the consciences of parents or other adults can also be influenced by the norms and values emphasized by the young.

d. The concern for a just world demands that everybody live a just life himself. For it is often our engrossment in private and group interests (power, possessions, career) which retards the development of a just society. This hinders cooperation between nations, help to underdeveloped countries, sharing of all in the prosperity, the recognition of minority groups.

e. The solution of these problems asks for procedures which are discussed below. Good will is not sufficient. Giving meaningful and lasting help presupposes knowledge of good methods.

3. *Methods*

a. In matters of ethics the church, preaching the way of Christ, should avoid two extremes:

—it must not allow itself to be led passively by actual developments. For there is no guarantee that these actual developments will be salutary.

—it must not pretend it can dictate developments. For moral decisions also depend on the many factors occurring in the development of life itself, with its ever new opportunities and limitations, its tensions and conflicts. On the other hand the church should contribute to this development, through the personal lives and personal commitments of its members and also through the preaching of the biblical ideals.

b. Accordingly the church can only give directives after studying the development of human life, using all available methods.

c. More concretely, this means that the church's directives should be based upon:

—a reflection on the Gospel and church tradition;

—the opinions of experts based, among other things, on scientific research;

—opinions and feelings as they exist among the people concerned, if possible also outside the Catholic milieu.

d. This requires a dialogue between experts and representatives of the groups involved, in all stages of consultation:

—in collecting opinions and data;

—in formulating questions and alternatives;

—in drawing conclusions.

This model of decision-making is already used profitably in the fields of community organization, social work, modern business management, etc.

e. In case the situation is not ripe for pronouncing judgments ecclesiastical authorities should refrain from giving definite directives and wherever possible leave room for experiment. In such cases taking risks is justifiable, and even necessary, if the church is to remain faithful, in multiformity, to its fundamental vocation to be God's people on the march.

E. *Marriage and family*

1. a. As the community of the faithful the church has been given the task of preaching the good message, also as regards marriage. This preaching proclaims the selflessness of love as it was made manifest in Christ.

It is a matter of conscience for all the faithful, both married and unmarried, to make this love visible. Christian preaching is an appeal to reorient our moral attidudes on Christ's love, in a continuous conversion from egotism and laziness.

b. The changing cultural patterns make us aware of a new relationship between men and women, now firstly experienced as a looking for and giving shape to human communication. Thus, put in the wider context of human encounter and cooperation, it is a partnership and friendship, in which men and women develop through the appeal they direct to each other.

2. a. The preparation for marriage should receive much more attention; by this we do not only mean sex instruction, but the whole of education in the personal sphere, in which full light is thrown upon the meaning of the man—woman relation and upon both their relations to society. Closer study should be made of the exact task of the parents, but also of the competency of others in sexual education in this wider sense.

This includes naturally the preparation in a stricter sense which is already being handled on the diocesan and national levels by those who have the task and responsibility of educating and guiding the young.

b. Men and women should acknowledge each other as equal partners with their own responsibilities. This must be expressed in their mutual relationship, the care for their family, in their professional lives, and also in their relations with society and church. Christians should encourage the positive elements in this development.

c. The family is of foremost importance as the first circle of contacts in which people of different generations learn how to live together. Dialogue is indispensable for this. Conflicts can be useful for the establishment of a new peace and a better world.

3. a. The plenary assembly asks for further consultation with the world episcopate, the Pope, married people and experts about a presentday Christian view of marriage.

b. The plenary assembly considers the absolute rejection of artificial means of birth control by the encyclical *Humanae Vitae* unconvincing in its arguments. The well-considered personal and conscientious decisions of married people should be acknowledged.

c. Therefore the plenary assembly is of the opinion that the discussions about married life are not closed, and that the activities in pastoral care and mental health care can be continued taking this into account.

4. a. Husbands and wives have the right to receive every kind of support the church can give to their married life, through prayer, mutual help, pastoral care and preaching. People who are jointly responsible for the offering of advice and help are urgently requested to acquaint themselves with the new views on sexuality, marriage and family that have gradually emerged, also within the Catholic community.

Insofar as the existing institutions for mental health cannot yet offer adequate help with regard to the problems of birth control, we express the hope that they will be able to extend their indispensable help as soon as possible.

b. For those Catholics whose marriages have been disrupted irreparably, the plenary assembly advocates solutions that are more than compromises or stop-gap solutions on the pastoral level. It urgently requests that qualified people and/or authorities in the church:

—seek an answer to the theological and practical problems concerning the indissolubility of a Christian marriage;

—strive for the necessary amendations and simplifications in the prevailing canonical regulations regarding marriage, the wedding ceremonies, marriage suits, and the juridical aspects already regulated by civil authority.

c. The plenary assembly appreciates the revisions now being prepared in the Dutch divorce law, and asks the qualified authorities to raise this issue as well with the National Council of Churches.

5. It is necessary that various organizations within the Catholic community study the variety of specific problems connected with the man—woman relationship, in cooperation with other churches and ideological groups.

F. Christian faith today

1. *Preachings.* In its preachings, to which all are called, the church should begin with the testimony of the Gospel about Jesus Christ, "who is the same yesterday and today and forever" (Hebr. 13: 8).

The church only has a clear understanding of its pastoral mission if, in modern language, it passes on the faithfully preserved Gospel message. Because in Christ it finds redemption and real life,

160

it must, as God's people on the move, give guidance in the variegation and confusion of spiritual attitudes. Through this it makes clear what it really means to have faith, a searching faith in Him who is called "the reflection of the glory of God," "the author and perfector of our faith" (Hebr.1: 3; 12: 2). Especially those who were called to ministerial preaching should consider themselves the faithful "stewards of the mysteries of God" (compare I Cor. 4: 1—2). For those who, because of the modern religious crisis, hardly find themselves inspired by the Gospel to carry out this task in a responsible way, it may be advisable to take some distance from this task.

2. *Multiformity*. The Gospel content is so rich that no single person, no single period, and no single church can ever give an adequate answer. For this reason the Pastoral Council acknowledges on principle multiformity as an effective and Scripture-inspired starting point; therefore both experiences which are mainly based on tradition and ones that are mainly directed by new values, have a right to exist. It is of great importance that a dialogue between the various ways of faith experience is started and continued. Everyone who still wants to call himself a Catholic should be welcome in the church.

3. *Openmindedness*. Therefore the Pastoral Council consciously chooses in favour of openmindedness and dialogue with everybody, with a view to the future of the church community and its individual members (compare Vatican II, constitution *Gaudium et Spes* on the Church in the modern world, n. 43: "They should always try to enlighten one another through honest discussion, preserving mutual charity and caring above all for the common good").

This openmindedness includes a willingness to listen to all who have this common good at heart, and a refraining from fanaticism.

4. *A sense of history and the critical mind*. It is the opinion of the council that mutual tolerance will be strengthened and that a more relaxed manner of religious experience will be furthered if the various currents in the Catholic faith are on their guard against one-sided theses and evaluations, and also against false dilemmas. Attempts should be made to realize both the importance and the relativity of the actual situation: a real assimilation of Christian preaching and Christian experience only makes sense if it includes frank criticism of presentday society and its structures.

5. *Experiments*. Ample room should be allowed for well-considered experiments regarding forms of religious experience.

Inventiveness and creativity should be stimulated, without treating the Gospel in an arbitrary way. Therefore experiments should be conducted within the religious community, in a continuous interplay of pastoral policy and actual life (compare Vatican II, "Decree on the Apostolate of the Laity," n. 3).

Experimental forms of Christian life should, accordingly, be a normal feature of the pastoral scene; this prevents isolation. To the extent that an experiment appeals to the community, it loses its uncommitted character, with all consequences of this, also with regard to the authorities.

Experiments are of special importance with regard to the church's ecumenical task, which is firstly one of renewal (compare Vatican II, "Decree on Ecumenism," n. 6). Here the churches can help one another, first of all on the local level. The various churches bear a common responsibility for making room for all who are in search of new ways to experience their faith. This should be taken into consideration by the Council of Churches in The Netherlands when it conceives of its tasks.

N.B. Innovations and experiments can only bear fruit if they take place under optimal conditions (i.e. if they are explained, motivated and supervised by experts) and are followed by critical evaluation.

6. *Applications*

a. *Liturgy*. Liturgy can assume several forms, and this requires consultation between the community (in whatever sense) and the ministry. This also applies to sermons, which should be given very special attention. It should include, among other things, a careful study of both Scripture and modern life. A good preparation for liturgy should, however, also show such a concern for expressiveness in words and gestures that their intention is clearly understood.

Alongside the celebration of the Eucharist, and possibly as a preparation for it, prayer services and "instruction services" should receive more attention, as they can systematically bring a better understanding of the Scripture to the community and lead to sympathetic forms of piety which are concretized into service to society, in particular to those in need.

b. *The life or prayer.* For many Christians praying is difficult nowadays. We need time to develop new praying habits, after a period in which prefabricated prayers may have held too dominant a position. Sermons and instructions should pay more attention to the development of a new prayer culture. Here the wealth of the Christian praying tradition can still offer its good services. It shows that, alongside supplication, thanksgiving and praise, disinterested meditation, admiration and wonderment have important roles to play.

If a new prayer culture is to develop, account should be taken of the peculiarities of modern secularized man, of the requirements of intensive ecumenical cooperation, and also of the wealth of Jewish piety.

c. *Religious formation of youth and adults.* The family, being the primary social unit, has the task of creating a fertile climate for religious experience. This asks of both parents (for religious education is not the task of a mother only) that they develop an ever stronger religious feeling and sensibility. Praying must be learned in the family. As the children grow up, the ways, in which the faith is experienced will change, in dialogue and in consultation. Religious observances in the homes are very important. Both the priests and the other members of the community can and must promote them. They need not lead to isolation from the rest of the parish, but they may, provided they are celebrated in the proper atmosphere, further a more active and resourceful participation in community life.

In educational institutions the religious formation of the pupils does not only depend on well-prepared and re-thought-out instruction, given in separate religious classes, but even more on the absorption of the religious attitudes of the teachers in the various subjects and groups.

Training courses on all levels deserve more explicit attention in pastoral policy, because they can help parents and teachers, young people and adolescents develop an adequate understanding of the signs of the times. Experts in this field, with a pastoral or theological training, can certainly play a role here.

Discussion groups, too, can make valuable contributions if they take up subjects that are of actual importance for the church and for mankind at large, and if they encourage public opinion at grassroots level through the publication of the summaries and results of their talks.

d. *Structures of the pastorate.* These will have to become increasingly differentiated. Only a team of pastoral workers with different orientations and adequately trained (priests, laity and religious) will be able to serve both youth and adults, both the more conservative and the more progressive, to stand at their side, to prepare them for a mature faith and thus to form a missionary community. Generally speaking pastoral guidance will only be effective if it is flexible and variegated, if it is done competently, and if it is attuned to the varying needs of the various sections of human society.

e. *The mass media.* They can be given a task of interpreting and critically selecting the large amounts of information and impressions in the field of ecclesiastical/social change. Moreover, a systematic study should be made of how they can stimulate, in their own way, the receptiveness to religious experience and religious attitudes. More specifically, great value should be attached to the possibility of directly presenting, on radio and television, the Christian message and the Christian experience. The specific requirements for such a presentation should be scientifically researched bearing in mind the practical applicability.

f. *A study of spirituality.* It would be useful to commission a study of the contents of modern religiosity and contemporary forms of piety. The Titus Brandsma Institute, opened in December 1968 at Nijmegen, deserves our attention in connection with this matter.

G. *The renewal of religious practice*

1. *Liturgy*

a. Liturgy should be simple and unpretentious, so that human distress and misery are not obscured by luxury and display of power, but rather made visible. The elements of person- and ministry-worship which have obtruded themselves into liturgy should be removed as unevangelical.

b. The liturgy need not be adapted to God, who is content when we address ourselves to Him "in spirit and truth." Therefore there is every freedom to adapt it to the variety of people who through the liturgy must be oriented to God and their fellowmen. The ensuing multiformity of liturgy is, accordingly, not a matter of permissiveness, but of principle: the liturgy should grow out of and remain rooted in human communities with their different cultures and needs.

c. In the past centuries Christian liturgy has been an important source of cultural inspiration and creativity. Gradually, however, it has lost this inspiring power, and its form-giving has degenerated into form-preservation. The modern Christian must seek authentic forms in which he can realize his service to God and his fellowmen. In doing this, he will again create a new culture. Besides this, the liturgy can also be a framework in which old cultural attainments are applicable.

d. In the course of the centuries the celebration of the Eucharist has developed too much of a character of passive presence rather than of active participation. One cause of this was that "hearing mass" on Sundays became a church commandment. In its pastoral work the church should shift the emphasis from canonical obligation to spirited and motivated invitation to share the celebration of the Eucharist. Celebration on "the Lord's day," as a commemoration of the resurrection, deserves permanent and special attention.

e. The usual masses in large churches are certainly not the most suitable way of celebrating the Eucharist. Little groups in small rooms, where solidarity, personal participation and creativity can be developed are to be preferred. Ecclesiastical practice should adapt to the weakening of territorial allegiance in our society, which in fact also affects the parish structure. As a consequence, parish church masses should not be more than one of the possible forms for celebrating the Eucharist. Besides this, ample opportunities should be offered for the celebration of the Eucharist in nonterritorial formations. On the one hand these possibilities should focus on existing communities and groups: family, associations, school classes, etc. On the other hand they should focus on certain categories: youth, the aged, etc. Liturgical forms will have to adapt to this variety of groups and categories.

2. *The sacrament of penance.* The very rapid decline of the traditional practice of private confession shows how exhausted this form was. A revival of the sacrament of penance will only be possible if new forms are created in which this sacrament regains its original community character or, in its private form, is freed from the oppressiveness of the confessional.

3. *Prayer*

a. The modern use of varying and suitable prayers of intercession in the celebration of the Eucharist has as a rule met with a favourable reception. Renewal should be continued in this direction, also as regards praying outside the eucharistic celebrations: we should turn to God from the real human needs of this moment, from our personal needs, and from those of our community and the whole world. In this way prayer will also be interwoven with care and action.

165

b. Prayer in the family has badly fallen into a rut: a continual and enforced repetition of routine texts. Renewal in this field must be inspired by the successful renewal of liturgical prayer. On the one hand emphasis must be placed on good concise texts (the Our Father, prayers for morning, evening and meals) that are not repeated endlessly. On the other hand people must learn how to pray for their own needs, for those of their friends and of the world. A booklet on family prayer should be composed.

4. *Preaching*

a. Christian preaching does not only mean sermons, i.e. talking to others; it also means talking with others. Discussion, as a common discovery of God's word and its meaning for this world, must be given much more space. This holds good not only for private discussion — Catholics never had the courage to talk to each other about religious subjects — but also for group discussion, in which the communications media also play a role.

b. The dull round of Sunday sermons in the parish church, in which the same man is always discussing the same things in the same way, must be broken through. Nor should the sermon be the exclusive individual business of the priest who contrives what he is going to preach, but rather it is the end of a dialogue. This can be realized through preparatory talks in a group composed of the preacher and other church members. In addition it is also possible to give the sermon a more communicative character through contributions by several people, dialogue, forum, open discussion. But we should be alert for technical tricks which may hurt more than help the real atmosphere of receptivity and authenticity.

5. *Service and action*

a. In the promotion of human well-being, in the field of charity as well as of the pastorate, expertise is playing an ever greater part. This does not alter the fact that help given on the basis of neighbourly love will always remain part of the normal life pattern of every Christian. Sometimes he can do this through his own professional activity, sometimes through voluntary assistance to professional workers. But he will always have to do it through sympathizing with his neighbors in need and through helping them wherever he can.

b. Beside care for those in need Christian practice also requires that we try to establish social structures in which the peace of Christ, the freedom of God's children, and the brotherhood of all men can become living realities.

166

c. The church must play its role in the reform of the world through the word it speaks and the example it gives, not through the accumulation of power. It must inspire the faithful, not weld them together. The faithful must be prepared to co-operate openly and extensively with all people that are sincerely striving for human well-being in the spirit of the Gospel.

d. Solidarity within the community and openness towards the needs of the world are both parts of the heritage left by Christ. Solidarity should not lead to parochialism, nor should cosmopolitanism lead to the neglect of one's direct neighbours. Love in the spirit of Christ extends to both those who are near and those who are far.

6. *Community building*. The great changes in social life, through which many traditional allegiances have disappeared, make loneliness one of the big threats to our society. Therefore one of the main tasks of the church in the modern world is caring for the lonely and creating new communication forms. The unattached, the aged, people with individual or social problems are now among the poor to whom Christ's good message is especially directed (Mt. 11: 5).

7. *Personnel and buildings*

a. The historical development in which ecclesiastical activities are concentrated in the one figure of an official priest should not obstruct necessary renewal. The possibilities that exist in a general priesthood of the faithful should be worked out once again into a division of functions and appointments: ordained people alongside the laity, married people alongside celibates, full-timers alongside part-timers. This is even more urgent because an open and multiform Christian practice, in which people partake freely, is not likely to ask for fewer personnel, but rather for more. Inviting and accompanying take more time than commanding and organizing. This is no reason to choose an authoritarian way, but it is a reason to extend the range of fellow workers. Functional specialization, for that matter, should always be combined with team cooperation that can be permanent or temporarily, depending on the task. It is absurd that even within the same parish priests should work alongside each other without a functional delegation of tasks and without teamwork.

b. In the past hundred years the church has invested most of its money into buildings. It is now time to invest it in people, especially in the training, salaries and equipment of the church staff. The building of imposing and sumptuous churches must be stopped. Wherever new churches are needed they should be simple, of multi-purpose design and not larger than is necessary. In planning them cooperation should be sought with other denominations and with the local community.

H. The ministry

1. *The specific tasks of the ministry.* Within the development of present-day society the specific task of the ministry should ever more clearly become: religious leadership in inspiring a Christian life, as God's emissary and responsible witness to the ultimate salvation in Jesus Christ.

2. *Women in the ministry* It is necessary that as soon as possible women are further enlisted in all those fields of church activity in which their appointment is not or barely is problematic. Further developments should go towards admitting them to all ecclesiastical functions, that of presiding over the eucharistic celebration not excluded.

3. *Optional celibacy*

a. For future priests celibacy should no longer be a requirement for admission to the ministry.

b. Priests who intend to marry or have already married should — under certain conditions — be given the opportunity to remain in office or to be readmitted to it.

c. Married people should be given the opportunity to be admitted to the ministry.

d. Compulsory celibacy as a condition for ministerial work should be abrogated.

e. The bishops are requested, if these recommendations are accepted, to carry them out in such a way that attention is not only given to item (c), which seems easiest to realize, but that within a short time items (a) and (b) as well are implemented.

On this resolution concerning celibacy the bishops did not vote. On 19 January 1970, only twelve days after the council meeting, they published the following press communiqué, with an additional comment by the secretariats of the bishops' conference and of the council:

> The fifth plenary assembly of the Pastoral Council has made clear the opinions of a substantial part of the Dutch Catholic community as to the binding between celibacy and the priesthood.

The bishops also know that another part of this community holds different views.

They hope that the entire community of the faithful will show understanding for this complicated situation, in which the bishops stand as pastors of their whole flock.

The same differences of opinion also exist in other parts of the church.

One section of the Dutch church community, however large it may be, cannot and may not demand that its views are shared, without further discussion, by the entire church.

The tradition of priestly celibacy is not uniform in the Catholic Church; the Eastern Church has married priests.

Pastoral policy in one church province will, of course, have repercussions in other parts of the church, certainly today when through the mass media the whole of mankind has become one community. The bishops are responsible for their own section of the church, but at the same time they bear responsibility for the church universal. That is the real meaning of collegiality as it was discussed at the Second Vatican Council.

Considering this responsibility the bishops believe that their first task is to inform the Holy Father of the exact situation in their local church, and of the opinions and wishes that exist here, convinced that they are not only existant in The Netherlands.

The bishops think that their religious community would be better off if, beside a celibate priesthood clearly chosen in freedom, married priests could be admitted to the Latin Church, i.e. if married people could be ordained priests, and if, in special cases and under certain conditions, priests who have married could return to the ministry.

But no single church province can do this alone, without consulting the Holy Father and the world church. A deliberation of the entire church about such important and urgent matters, that regard the whole church, would certainly be beneficial for the church.

The bishops want to act in communication with the Holy Father, and to consult him about the interests of the church in The Netherlands.

Before long Cardinal Alfrink will get in touch with the Holy Father in order to inform him about what is happening here, and to discuss with him what, in this situation, must be done for the benefit of the church.

The accompanying comment ran as follows:

As is known, during the plenary session of the Pastoral Council the bishops did not vote, in order to be able to formulate as clearly as possible in their conclusions their specific responsibility as bishops.

They have now expressed these conclusions in this statement of 19 January.

This means that the Dutch bishops' conference will, regarding the celibacy problem, develop a pastoral policy that is in line with the recommendations of the Pastoral Council.

The implementation of this policy will have to take place in consultation with the Pope and the other bishops.

In many parts of the world church a solution to the problem of the priesthood is being studied. The statement by the Dutch bishops is the first public pronouncement of a bishops' conference about a solution to this problem in the direction of a new form of ministry in which, besides a freely-chosen celibate priesthood, a married priesthood is very explicitly requested. This statement of principle, made public after the bishops had consulted their religious community, is a clear and important step; public discussion of the celibacy problem has now been brought to the level of pastoral policy.

This starts a new phase in the dialogue, which has been given a new content and an open character. The bishops' policy can only be realized if it is supported by the whole community.

It also means a rejection of those activities, by whatever individuals or groups, that oppose this policy and in doing so might undermine the authority of the bishops both within this country and in the world church. They might also thwart, if not make impossible, the concrete implementation of the policy now announced. For naturally in this new phase concrete implementation is subject to discussion.

The bishops' statement that it should be possible for married people to be ordained priests implies that both their personality and their training, and also their marriage and family situation should be paid attention to. One can here think of what St. Paul wrote to Titus, Bishop of Crete (Tit. 1: 5—9). This offers of course new perspectives for those people who, after pastoral training and apprenticeship, prove to be suitable candidates for ordination, even if they do not feel called to the celibate state.

For theology students who choose the celibate priesthood a trial period in pastoral work will also be desirable before they are ordained.

Priests who have married and want to return to the ministry are evidently facing a new situation, which also implies a number of conditions. Inquiries will have to be made regarding: the candidate's motives to continue his priestly work, his religious attitude and his professional capabilities, his pastoral concern — criteria applicable to every priest — and the situation of his marriage. In addition, the question will have to be answered whether the congregation to which he is appointed is willing to accept and pay a married minister.

The first steps towards implementing this new policy have already been taken. Discussions with the central government in Rome and with representatives of the bishops' conferences in other countries have already started or are being prepared. The Union of Religious Priests in The Netherlands (SNPR) has been informed at a meeting with the bishops about the plans as explained in the bishops' statement. The abbots and provincials present have consulted with the bishops about the consequences this new policy may have for members of their communities. The policy itself is the bishops' own responsibility. The abbots and provincials have offered their loyal support for the implementation of the plans.

As to developments in the weeks to come, the bishops will go on giving the fullest possible information.

On 30 July 1970 the Dutch bishops published the following communiqué:

> In the past days the bishops have discussed the recent visit of Cardinal Alfrink to Rome and the talks he had there.

170

The cardinal has spoken in detail with the Pope and his nearest colleagues — Cardinals Villot, Seper, Willebrands and Wright, and Bishops Benelli, Casaroli and Schröffer — about the situation of the Dutch Church with regard to priestly celibacy and the ideas of the bishops as explained in their statement of 19 January. In it the bishops expressed their opinion that "their community would be better off if, besides a celibate priesthood clearly chosen in freedom, married priests could be admitted to the Latin Church, i.e. if married people could be ordained priests, and if, in special cases and under certain conditions, priests who have married could return to the ministry."

In this view the important value of a celibate priesthood was and is fully recognized. But ways were sought to provide the Dutch Church with a sufficient number of priests, also in the future, and to meet the actual needs of many priests. There was no question of a plea to abrogate celibacy, and the bishops have more than once expressed their great appreciation of those priests who, for the sake of the Kingdom of God, remain celibate in a spirit of dedication and sacrifice. It is to both groups that the bishops extend their sympathy and their concern.

Cardinal Alfrink has twice had long talks with the Pope, during which the Pope, with great interest, benevolence and understanding, listened to what the cardinal told him about the situation in The Netherlands and about the bishops' solicitude. On the other hand, in these talks the cardinal was again confronted with the delicate and extremely difficult position of the Pope whose pastoral ministry encompasses the whole church. Within that church he is, also with regard to celibacy, approached with opposing wishes and views. In the midst of those he stands with his own responsibility as Pope. Every Catholic will understand this.

Without ignoring the problems presented by the cardinal, the Pope considers that the arguments for maintaining the traditional juncture of priesthood and celibacy in the Latin Church are still valid today, and perhaps even more than before. The Pope sees it as a serious and imperative task of his apostolic ministry to adhere to this opinion. For the Pope this is a well-considered obligation of conscience in which he feels he has the general support of the bishops, although he knows there are bishops with different opinions.

The Pope abides by what he wrote, on 2 February of this year, to the cardinal secretary of state, concerning the possibility of ordaining married man of maturer age, in order to provide for exceptional situations. This is a subject which, according to the letter mentioned, could be discussed and studied in collegial consultation.

The bishops' synod of 1971, at which the priestly ministry will be an item on the agenda, might be a suitable opportunity for a further discussion of this subject.

Both sides have expressed the wish that the discussions between the Dutch Episcopate and the Holy See be continued.

I. The religious

1. *The specific function of the religious.* In the draft report the word "religious" is not used in its general sense of: devout, god-fearing, expressing faith. The report adheres to the usage which applies the term to certain groups within Christ's church. As a rule these groups have their origin in the religious experience and conversion of an inspired person, and the members are expected to realize this experience in their own lives. This does not mean that the choice of a religious life is a choice between God and man. On the contrary, in this life God is seen as loving mankind, who gave us his Son that we should live. Therefore religious life is as much service to mankind, a service of care, of building up society, of preaching, of prayer for the people, a prayer that can also inspire others to believe and to pray.

This service to God and mankind can be summarized as a service to the kingdom of God, which is the promised and now-developing communion of love and peace which God gives to us and which we may build up through his grace. A religious group within the church can remind us of the group of disciples surrounding their master, if it really serves and gives shape to the kingdom of God. In their conversion to this kingdom of God the religious criticize church and society. In this way they can be a token of the peace promised by God.

In the report the life design of the religious is mainly characterized by the unmarried state for the sake of the kingdom (compare Matth. 19: 12), for the sake of Christ and the Gospel (compare Mark 10: 29), for the sake of "the things of the Lord" (ICor. 7: 32). These characteristics do not exclude the possibility that other evangelical movements arise when married or unmarried people come together for the sake of the kingdom. In the opinion of the writers of this report it is only less desirable that such movements also assume the name "religious." Earlier developments in the life pattern of the religious themselves have led to the search for new names ("regulars" next to "monks"; "congregations" next to "orders"; "houses" next to "monasteries"). We think it important that today, too, this be done, in order to avoid confusion by deviating from common usage, in order not to gloss over the specific vocation to unmarried life, and in order to clarify the new element in these forms of Christian living.

2. *Recommendations*

a. Besides their other tasks the religious have the special vocation of keeping the spirit of contemplation and prayer alive in the church and the world. Private prayer and liturgy in their various forms will have their special attention. Their principal service remains, in the midst of our modern world with all its questions, an unremitting belief in and hope for God who reveals Himself in Jesus Christ. Religious communities which consider their main task to be meditation and prayer and an openness to our times are of great value, particularly as places of hospitality and quiet.

b. The prevailing differences of spirituality should be assessed critically. Insofar as they are based on really prophetic personalities and movements in the history of the church, thus representing an authentic biblical witnessing to Jesus, they not only have a right to exist, but can still be of eminent service to the church and the world. As a matter of fact this is only possible if, in the religious communities that profess a certain kind of spirituality, this prophetic-biblical witnessing is actively perceived.

c. The religious will work wherever the most appeal is made to the evangelical inspiration of their lives. This applies especially to missionary and development work and to the needs in our affluent society. Religious who, either on their own initiative or after being asked, do pastoral work will, as a matter of fact and as far as these activities are concerned, work under the responsibility of the bishops.

d. The religious may be expected to show an evangelical and modern life-style in their attitudes towards work, money and property. This requires an observable practice of soberness and mortification within our society, and the readiness to make their work and the wages earned available, as much as possible, to the really poor and destitute, wherever they may be.

e. In their work for the church and society the religious, too, are confronted with the obstacles caused by the divisiveness of Christendom. Bringing about the unity of the churches will be an urgent task for them. Daily prayer for unity and the promotion of ecumenical contacts are among their very first tasks. Now that in other churches there is a growing openness to religious life, study should be made of forms of living and working together with those members of other churches who want to follow the vocation to religious life.

f. The responsibility of all religious for each other and for the group should find clear expression in a democratic form of government. What can be decided at a lower level should not be regulated from above (the principle of subsidiarity). From this it is obvious that ecclesiastical authorities and the groups' own governing bodies, both nationally and internationally, retain a certain amount of decisive power; they are however first of all expected to offer evangelical inspiration and to promote communication.

g. An important element in the renewal of religious life lies in the promotion of opportunities for the female religious to shape their religious lives based on their own responsibility, both canonically and actually. This personal responsibility does not exclude contributions made by male ministers and religious. On the contrary, given the necessity of mutual complementariness of men and women, contributions from the male side — in dialogue — are very important for a balanced development of the lives of women religious, whereas the female approach can enrich the religious lives of the men.

h. All religious, but the younger in particular, should be given chances to seek new life forms. In this renewal of religious life the well-being of the religious and their vocation in this world should carry the most weight; the survival of religious institutions is only relevant insofar as they contribute in this direction. This will require breaking through existing barriers and promoting mutual contacts, in particular for the young.

i. Presentday developments ask for various forms, of community life, ranging from larger units to a union of members that live alone, with an exchange of inspiration, particularly in periodical meetings. The renewal of religious life should not be limited to certain forms. A real religious and brotherly life is also possible in larger groups. Room should be allowed for smaller communities, in which the members have much to offer to each other and, because of the inevitability of their daily contacts, can also demand much from each other. Thus religious life, in whatever form, can be present in the secular city, offering service and inspiration.

It should not be forgotten, however, that smaller living units can also lead to the adoption of a bourgeois style or to a continuation of the bourgeois style that was formerly hidden behind the institutions. If this should happen, smaller groups would sooner spoil the development of religious life than foster it.

j. In this time of change it is understandable that many people find that religious life no longer helps them to fulfil their vocation. This asks for an open and fair dispensation policy. The community of the faithful and especially the order or congregation concerned will have to consider it their duty to offer new possibilities to those that leave, to show recognition for their commitment and loyalty of many years, and to disavow every kind of discrimination against those that leave. It is unchristian to let these people fend for themselves. Pastoral and social aid meets a real need.

k. We must expect a decreasing number of people to enter religious life. We are right in expecting that those that do apply are led by authentic evangelical inspiration. At the same time there is a risk that people who feel ill at ease in modern society will try to take refuge in religious life. Therefore it is desirable that religious communities select critically, that candidates make a well-considered choice, especially as to the group they want to join, and that they are given a chance to get acquainted with this group in a realistic way.

l. Consideration should be given to developing forms of temporary commitment to a religious community. This may be a short-range commitment, intended to be followed by a different way of life, or a commitment that is continued without being made explicit and unconditionally permanent. The explicit life time commitment remains the essence of religious life. It seems important also that forms are developed for the association of married people with religious communities.

m. A common service institution for the deepening, renewal and shaping of religious life would seem necessary, although as a matter of fact the religious themselves must decide upon this. The existing associations of the religious could be a starting point. But it is necessary that these associations not only be structures for cooperation between higher priors and governing boards, but also be developed into vital and future-directed contacts among members of those religious institutions. The issues already raised concerning total or partial mergers, federations or other forms of association, can be worked out in this way.

n. The continuation or withdrawal from certain activities, the settlement in or departure from certain areas, the tackling of other activities, all of this will have to be done according to criteria in which the common good is served: good planning is necessary. Here, too, the aforementioned institution might offer its services.

o. Expert advice is indispensable for the renewal of religious life. Therefore much attention should be paid to the training and appointment of staff members and the selection of expert advisors. Again, the abovementioned bureau might be of service.

The existing system of officially or privately appointed rectors, vicars or other advisors will have to be critically examined and, if necessary, revised.

p. If religious life is to bear full fruit both for the religious themselves and for all who have contact with them, care should be taken that, especially in community life, there is a healthy psychological climate in which people are left free to remain themselves, so that on this basis they can serve the kingdom of God. Adequate counseling techniques are necessary in this connection.

q. The problem of the aged weighs heavily on an increasing number of religious groups. Joint consultation of the religious, together with experts, is necessary; it has already started and should be extended. This consultation will deal with the common problems, but also especially with the common elaboration of solutions and with mutual help. First of all the responsibility of the religious to care for their own aged fellow-members should be acknowledged and lead to practical results. But the church community as a whole should also try to find ways of helping those who for years have done valuable work for the community and are now in difficulties.

r. The present life-form of the secular priests makes it necessary that a number of them, who for the sake of the Gospel want to live their priestly lives as celibates, be offered the possibility for an acceptable form of religious life. A new way of fulfilling the religious ideals may be expected from this.

J. Ecumenism

The following advisory recommendation was presented to the bishops:

> The plenary assembly of the Pastoral Council presents to the bishops the following statement of opinion:
> Room should be allowed, or at least not be denied, for mutual participation in the Eucharist: if unity in Christ is the foundation and motivation for a real community of Christians from different denominations; if, on this basis, the ministers are mutually recognized as called by the one Lord in the one Church; and if, in a unanimity of faith, the Eucharist is commonly recognized as the sanctified commemoration of Christ's death and resurrection.

(One thinks, for example, of inter-church marriages, discussion and action groups, and local communities, provided the above requirements are fulfilled.)

This does not imply that the churches as such already fully recognize each other's existence — that is, the community around the Word, the sacraments and the ministry in service to the world. The presence of this re-established unity in certain situations is an indispensable factor in the dialogue between the churches.

The plenary assembly of the Pastoral Council urges the bishops to conduct their policy along these lines.

Already on this same day (8 April 1970) Cardinal Alfrink on behalf of all the bishops reacted to this recommendation with the following: "The bishops will consider this recommendation together with the other churches united in the National Council of Churches. And they will also consult with the Secretariat for the Promotion of Christian Unity."

The recommendations were not put to a vote. The report on "The Unity Made by the Lord" was accepted in its general meaning.

K. On preaching the Gospel (preaching and catechesis)

"The plenary assembly again expresses its appreciation of The New Catechism in its original form and declares that it can be a safe guide in the catechesis for youth and adults." (This was a vote of confidence in the policy of the bishops who, as a matter of fact, did not participate in the voting, January 1969.)

Recommendations. (The following recommendations express the general attitude of the assembly.)

1. *Introduction.* In the actual preaching of the faith — in whatever form — the polarity of preaching should always be considered. Room should be made for, and attention should be paid to the message given to us by the Bible and by tradition and already expressed and formulated in many ways by the Christian community; but attention should also be given to man himself for whom the message is intended, to his experiences, his faith, his search for an individual and responsible way of life.

We should especially guard against the tendency to emphasize one of the aspects at the cost of another; the tendency to look upon the Christian message as a series of unchangeable truths, given once and for all; the tendency to accept as valid only those aspects which are considered a credible attitude among the people concerned and which can be put into words as a common belief.

These tendencies diminish the special character of the message as a witnessing and a promise, the special impact of the message through the power of the Spirit, and consequently also the real event of the preachings.

Attempts to find a solution for the questions and problems involved in preaching the Gospel should not be limited to a search for new methods, new forms and new words. They must also always take the spiritual climate into consideration, which should be characterized by the allegiance of partners concerned with the one message. Methodologically speaking both teaching and discussion can be used. The object should be that the receivers of the message are also actively involved in the process. Every preacher of the Gospel should stimulate and realize this.

The plenary assembly expresses the wish that the text of the report, and in particular chapters 2 and 4, be given a place in Christian preaching, so that in consultation with everybody concerned it can contribute toward mutual understanding, toward the avoidance of misunderstandings, "short-circuits" and breakdowns of communication.

2. *Adult catechesis, sermons and liturgy*

a. In Christian preaching more attention should be paid than in the past to a specific approach toward adults. Adult catechesis cannot be a mere repetition and brushing up of what was taught in youth; nor can it only be seen as a necessary but incidental refresher course. New approaches also requiring new forms are necessary. In these, attention should be paid to the individual in the entirety of his private, ecclesiastical and social situation. Besides the traditional point of contact such as birth, marriage, death etc., other issues also require attention, particularly socio-economic stress situations (industrialization, war and peace) and matters concerning political responsibility. Special attention is needed for a catechesis of the "signs of the times": help should be offered for the religious interpretation of what is happening around us, for the discovery of God's presence in presentday reality, so that on this basis we can understand what tasks these phenomena put upon our shoulders.

b. The sermon in the Sunday Eucharist still offers many possibilities. To be sure, there are difficulties: the time is limited, and so are the themes, because too much consideration must be given to the widely differentiated audience, because there is no opportunity for repartee. Preparatory discussion with others (priests and laity) as well as subsequent evaluation are good means for the ministerial preachers to develop the so-desirable dialogue attitude. This dialogue attitude is a prerequisite for the establishing of contact and the raising of questions with those who receive the message.

Wherever the attitudes of those attending and the structure of the church building make this possible, varying forms of liturgy should be considered. One can think of more elaborate or independent "word services," in which everyone gets the chance to speak, and also of services in which the main emphasis is on music and singing, on imagery, play and silence.

c. In all forms of preaching and catechesis there should be respect and openness towards everyone who, in whatever manner, wants to take the Gospel testimony as his or her life's guide; this means openness towards all traditions within this common framework since each of these can in its own way bear witness to that testimony; openness also in the sense that real contacts are possible with all who ask, seek and hope.

d. The New Catechism is a good starting point for an adequate system of adult catechesis, also in this sense, that it does not claim to be a "unitary catechism." It will be necessary to follow this road ever more consistently. It is important that other possibilities regarding form and content be created.

e. The very fact that this Pastoral Council is held creates a fertile climate for preaching the Gospel. Ways should be studied to continue this process, so that not only a limited group but the largest possible circle is reached. In addition the council reports may be used as materials for the preaching.

3. *Preaching the Gospel to the young; schools*

a. Also when bringing the Gospel to the young we shall have to make it clear — both through our words and our actions — that the Gospel is an offer and an invitation to which the only real answer is a free and personal one, coming from within. For the young in most cases this will not be a stand taken once and for all. Their experience is that man is always in search of new answers in the ever-changing situations of human history.

b. The religious education of children is first of all the parents' task, no matter what kinds of school their children attend. Parents have a right to expect the help of the Christian community in accomplishing their educational task. On the other hand parents may be expected to play an active role in the religious instruction and education which others have taken upon themselves at the parents' request. Therefore the plenary assembly appeals to the parents:

179

—to give attention themselves within the family to religious education;

—to maintain good contact with those to whom they have entrusted a part of their children's religious education, either at school or elsewhere;

—to make serious efforts to develop personal religious convictions and practices.

c. Preaching the Gospel to the youth, and even more so to children requires great prudence and carefulness regarding an explicit catechesis, in the sense of laying down strictly worded rules and obligations. For young children the emphasis should be on experience rather than on explication. Even more than with adults, it is here the atmosphere that is decisive, the genuineness, the openness and the room needed for growth towards a real attitude of belief.

d. The Pastoral Council advocates a positive approach towards all forms of religiosity found nowadays among the young. The decline in church attendance, especially among the young, does not necessarily point to a decline of religiosity. In connection with this, attention should be paid to alternative expressions of the religious experience such as mysticism and meditation, "political evening prayer," etc. The Pastoral Council is of the opinion, therefore, that the appointment of youth-pastors on the regional and local levels is of great importance.

4. *The preacher himself*

a. The Pastoral Council is of the opinion that those who are professionally engaged in preaching the Gospel will benefit from a training in diagnosing the situation in which they participate as preachers. Staff and financial facilities should be made available for this. Such training is a prerequisite for the efficient use of catechetical materials.

b. The Pastoral Council expresses the wish that those who preach or otherwise announce the Gospel message shall be provided with good and varying projects to be used with children, adolescents and adults, if possible coordinated with each other.

c. Besides being an expert, the preacher of the Gospel should also have the conviction of being vitally involved in the message that Jesus Christ is the salvation of the world; in this conviction he is bound to the entire community of the faithful.

d. Preachers of the faith may be expected to consider it their duty to consult with colleagues, and to take part in experiments and refresher courses.

e. The Pastoral Council expects that communication in the field of catechesis will be promoted through a clear definition of the tasks of the various pastoral centers, in their mutual relations, as well as in their relations with the National Council for Catechesis.

f. An efficient policy in the field of religious instruction and education demands a yearly collection of data concerning the catechetical situation at schools and elsewhere.

5. *Recommendations concerning further study and consultation*

a. It will be good to keep in mind that the shifts of accent occurring in catechesis also have consequences and raise questions regarding the position of the sacraments within religious instruction and education. Imagine the problems concerning the administration of baptism, first communion, school masses, confirmation and confession. Studies, investigations and consultation of all people concerned will be necessary.

b. A thorough study is desirable of the religious experience of children and adolescents, in particular with regard to such questions as: how do they experience the phenomena with which they are confronted by the church and religion; what psychological aspects can be observed in the actual practice of religious education in schools and elsewhere? On this basis criteria might be formulated for possible methods. Likewise, new suggestions might be offered for catechetical training in teachers' colleges.

c. Since the basic questions concerning preaching and catechesis are not bound to one particular church only, we suggest that good contact be established with other churches for the exchange of information, for a coordinated study and approach.

6. *Mass media.* It is desirable that at our coming National Pastoral Consultation — in connection with the report "On Preaching the Gospel" and other statements of the Pastoral Council — attention be paid to the important role of the mass media in preaching the good message; special study should be made of the question how these media can best be used — recognizing their specific responsibilities.

L. The relationship between Jews and Christians

1. The Pastoral Council asks the Dutch Church Province to let its attitude towards the Jews also be inspired by the declaration *Nostra Aetate* (n. 4) of the Second Vatican Council. This entails that:

a. Because of the Patriarchs, the Jews always remain especially dear to God (Rom. 9: 4—5; 11:28);

b. Christ's church was grafted on the root of the Jewish people (compare Rom. 11: 17—24);

c. Jews and Christians have a common spiritual heritage.

2. The Pastoral Council acknowledges that the biblical message has come to the church in and from the Jewish world of thinking and beliefs. Therefore:

a. A thorough knowledge and a good understanding of the Bible as the proclamation of God's approach to mankind is not possible without a familiarity with the Jewish belief in God and the Jewish understanding of biblical ideas;

b. It should be acknowledged that not only the Old Testament but also the New Testament is part of Jewish writing, and that the New Testament cannot be understood without a knowledge of the Jewish backgrounds;

c. A common Jewish—Christian study of Holy Scripture is desirable;

d. The church has the duty to reflect on the entire history of the Jewish people both before and after the coming of Christ, and also on the manner in which this people understand itself; Christian churches a collective reorientation on the common Jewish origins is necessary.

4. The Pastoral Council rejects any form of anti-Semitism and specifically declares that:

a. Proceeding from the declarations of Vatican II, it not only deplores any form of anti-Semitism, but also emphatically denounces it;

b. It wants to repeat that Christ's passion cannot be blamed upon all the Jews then living, nor upon the Jews of today, and that consequently the Jews should not be presented as cursed or repudiated;

c. The discrimination against Jews as a peculiar group within the world community, and also discrimination against Jews as adherents to a certain religion and philosophy of life, should already both be condemned on humanitarian grounds;

d. The church has the duty to reflect on the entire history of the Jewish people both before and after the coming of Christ, and also on the manner in which this people understands itself;

e. The joint reflection of Jews and Christians about their common origins and about the causes of their growing apart is necessary, in light of presentday Jewish and Christian thinking.

5. The Pastoral Council wants to testify that, together with all Christians and Jews, the Catholic Church of The Netherlands desires:

    a. to live based on God's promise of justice and peace;

    b. to be of service to the well-being of the whole of creation;

    c. to seek answers to the questions concerning the images of God and man, and the hopes for the future, so as they at this moment affect the general and the religious crisis of western civilization.

6. The Pastoral Council emphatically requests the responsible authorities to pay serious and continual attention to the implementation of these convictions, and of the results of further study and reflection, in theological training, preaching, catechesis, liturgy and publications.

M. Peace

1. All parishes should consider it their task to inspire the faithful through the preachings of the Gospel — in sermons and in prayers, in liturgy and religious instruction, in discussion groups and adult education — to work for peace and justice. The Pastoral Council hopes that the theme of the forthcoming Peace Week "Unite the Nations" will be given much attention in the parishes, and that these parishes will also offer opportunities for large groups to receive information about the fundamental purpose of the peace week theme.

2. The faithful should make it possible for their parishes to set apart a fixed amount of money yearly for the support of local and national peace work, so that — among other things through the appointment of professionals — the necessary change of mentality and structures can be effected.

3. The Dutch Church Province should work together with other local churches in the world whenever these fight against injustice, lack of freedom, racial prejudice and war. In such cases the Dutch Church Province should offer to those local churches and groups in need the help they are entitled to ask. This entails as well that the faithful take a critical stand against those structures in their own community that cause and continue injustice and strife by and in other countries.

4. The Pastoral Council believes that the information about military service offered in the schools should be complemented by a discussion about the problems of war and peace. For this, people

should also be invited that can give expert information about the problems of peace from different points of view and positions (e.g. the Dutch Institute for Peace Problems and the Peace Movements).

5. The draftee is facing the question whether or not his military service really serves the peace. Not everybody will have the same opinion on this. But both those who enter military service and those that refuse should do it on the basis of a well-considered and personal decision.

A real choice, however, is only possible if the person concerned receives political education and expert guidance, and if service to the community can also be performed in other ways.

6. A further discussion, in which representatives of all types of army chaplains (of all denominations) can participate should be held concerning the question of how the army pastorate can best use the criticism and inspiration of the Gospel in relation to their own position in the armed services, and also with regard to the issues of war and peace.

Bibliography

Abbink, G., "Van isolement naar openheid. Een vergelijkende analyse van het katholicisme in Nederland en in de andere westeuropese landen," (From isolation to openness — a comparative analysis of Catholicism in Holland and the rest of Western Europe), *Bijdragen*, 4, 1970, 368—369.

Adams, G., Bijdrage tot verheldering van de situatie in het bisdom Roermond (A contribution to clarifying the situation in the Roermond Bishopric), 24 Jan. 1973 (pro manuscripto).

Alting von Geusau, L., et. al., *Het Dossier van de Nederlandse Katechismus* (The dossier of the Dutch catechism), Utrecht, 1968, 25.

Aukes, H., *Kardinaal de Jong*, Utrecht, 1956, 82.

Auping, J., "Verzuiling en ontzuiling. De huidige kerk-crisis in historisch, godsdienstig-sociologisch perspectief" (The contemporary crisis in the church in historical and religious-sociological perspective), *Streven*, June, 1972, 864—865.

Auwerda, R., *Dossier Schillebeeckx. Theoloog in de Kerk der Conflicten* (The Schillebeeckx dossier — A theologian of the church in conflict), Bilthoven, 1969, *passim*.

Baechler, J. *Les Phénomènes Révolutionnaires*, Parijs, 1970; *Vormen van Revolutie*, Utrecht, 1972.

Bartoletti, Mgr., "La vie de l'église cinq ans après le concile" (The life of the church five years after the council), (*Osservatore Romano*, 2 October, 1971), *Documentation Catholique*, 19 Dec. 1971, 1114.

Bea, A., "Kerkvader van de openheid" (An open-minded prelate of the church), *De Heraut*, July—August 1964, 203—205.

Becker, M., *Die Macht in der Katholischen Kirche* (Power in the Catholic church), München, 1967, 90 vv.

Benelli, Mgr. G., Referat Bischofssymposion in Leitershofen b. Augsburg, 1 July 1973.

Berger, P., *The Sacred Canopy*, New York, 1967, 145.

Beveridge, W., *Managing the Church*, London, 1971, 10.

Bless, W. en J. Roes, Literatuur over "De Nieuwe Katechismus" (Literature about the new catechism), in *Jaarboek van het Katholiek Documentatie Centrum*, Nijmegen, 1972, 129—149.

Borne, E., "Regards sur quelques antécédents," *Réinventer l'Eglise, Esprit*, 408, Nov. 1971, 646.

Bright, L., "The quiet revolution," *New Christian*, 21 March, 1968.

Bunnik, R., *Dienaren van het Aggiornamento. Het kerkelijk ambt in een tijd van evolutie* (The servants of the Aggiornamento. The duty of the church in a time of evolution), 1967, 242 pages.

Caporale, R., *Les Hommes du Concile. Etude sociologique sur Vatican II,* Paris, 1965, 207 vv.

Catholica, door A.M. Heldt, s.v. *Theologie,* 1968, 2620.

Cavallari, A., *Het oude Vaticaan is dood — het nieuwe nog niet geboren* (The old Vatican is dead but the new not yet born), The Hague, 1967, 242.

Cohen, A., *Het waarnemen van de veranderingen* (The perception of changes), Rede Dies Natalis Universiteit Leiden, 1973, 6.

Congar, Y., *Vraie et fausse réforme dans l'église,* Paris, 1950, 231, 356.

Congar, Y., quoted in brochures *Vaticanum II,* Heeswijk, 28 March, 1962.

Cornelissen, R., "Heeft de confessionele organisatie nog een toekomst? " (Does the confessional organisation still have a future?), *Politiek Perspectief,* 2, 1973, 34—43.

Cornelissen, R., "Kerkelijke organisaties en de veranderde samenleving 1: Een hiërarchische kerk in confrontatie met de democratische samenleving," (Religious organisations in a changing society 1: Hierarchical church and democratic society), *Tijdschrift voor Effectief Directiebeleid,* January 1973, 12—14.

Cornelissen, R., (ed.), "Kerk en organisaties. Inventarisatie-nota van de commissie 'Kerk en Samenleving' inzake de problematiek van de maatschappelijke organisaties op konfessionele grondslag" (concept pro manuscripto), 1973, 39.

Dansette, A., *Destin du Catholicisme Français 1926—1956,* Paris, 1957, 493.

Dijk, J. van, "Actiegroepen aan de slag," (Action groups at work), *Wending,* June 1973, 237—244.

Divendal, H., *Roerige Kerk* (The Church astir), A.O. Dock, 19 May, 1972, 5.

Dombois, H., *Hierarchie. Grund und Grenze einer umstritten Struktur,* Freiburg, 1971, 110—111.

Doorn, J. van, "Toekomstoriëntatie en prestatiemoraal. Over een klassiek thema van actueel belang," (Ambition and careerism: a classic theme of current significance), *Onderzocht en Overdacht* (special issue of the journal *Mens en Maatchappij*), Rotterdam, 1972, 299—320.

Duintjer, O., "Moderne wetenschap en waardevrijheid," (Modern science and value freedom), *Algemeen Nederlands Tijdschrift voor Wijsbegeerte,* 1970, 1, 38—39.

Dukker, G.; Peters, J. and Smits, L., *Een nieuw beleidsklimaat. Pastorale gesprekken in het bisdom Den Bosch onder leiding van Mgr. W. Bekkers* (A new policy climate: Pastoral dialogues in the diocese of Den Bosch), Hilversum, 1966, 241.

Dunk, H.W. van der, "Crisis en crisisbewustzijn" (Crisis and crisis-consciousness), *Tijdsein,* Alphen aan den Rijn, 1972, 11—28.

Estruch, J., "L'Innovation réligieuse," *Social Compass,* 2, 1972, 242.

Euser, B., "Multinationale ondernemingen" (Multinational corporations), *Intermediair,* 28 July, 1972, 7.

Faber, H., *Buigen of barsten. Gedachten over "planning of change"* (Bending or breaking. Thoughts on the concept of "planned change"), Meppel, 1970.

Girardi, J., "Infallibilità e libertà," *Aggiornamenti Sociali*, 1970, 255—280.

Goddijn, H. en W., *Sociologie van Kerk en Godsdienst* (Sociology of church and religion), Utrecht, 1966, 121—123.

Goddijn, W., *Katholieke Minderheid en Protestantse Dominant. Sociologische nawerking van de historische relatie tussen Katholieken en Protestanten in Nederland en in het bijzonder in de provincie Friesland* (Catholic minority and Protestant majority. A sociological view of the historical relationship between Catholics and Protestants in The Netherlands), Assen, 1957.

Goddijn, W., "Le concept sociologique de minorité et son application à la relation entre catholiques et protestants," *Revue d'Histoire et de Philosophie Religieuses*, 1961, 252—262.

Goddijn, W., "Kirche und Sekte II. Soziologische Betrachtungen über Gruppendifferenzierungen innerhalb des Christentums," *Probleme der Religionssoziologie*, Hrsg. D. Goldschmidt und J. Matthes, Keulen, 1962.

Goddijn, W., "Nederland — Rome. Wederzijdse groepsbeelden en toekomstperspectief" (Holland and Rome. Mutual group images and perspectives of the future), *Kosmos en Oecumene*, 1969, 327—337.

Goddijn, W., "Nederland als koploper. De ontwikkelingen in Katholiek Nederland sinds 1945" (The Netherlands as front runner. Developments in Catholicism since 1945), *Onze jaren 45—70*, Amsterdam, 1973, 2201—2204.

Goddijn, W., en C. Thoen, *Het Katholiek Sociaal-Kerkelijk Instituut. Researchcentrum en Planbureau, 1946—1956*, The Hague, 1956.

Goudsbloem, J., *Dutch Society*, New York, 1967, 1—6.

Greeley, A., *Unsecular Man. The Persistence of Religion*, New York, 1972, 240 vv.

Grijs, F. de, "Geloofsvragen rond macht en onmacht in de kerk" (Questions of belief regarding power and powerlessness in the church), *Theologie en Pastoraat*, 1973, 106—121.

Gritti, J., "Images de l'Eglise à travers les mass média," *Esprit*, Nov. 1971, 612.

Grond, L., Het Katholicisme in Europa (Catholicism in Europe), *Katholiek Archief*, 1960, 1169—1208.

Groot, J., "De voorzitter van de Nederlandse bisschoppenconferentie" (The chairman of the Dutch conference of bishops), *De Heraut*, July—August 1964, 205—109.

Groot, C. de, "Moeizame katholieke bevrijding" (Laborious Catholic liberation), *De Bazuin*, 14 Jan., 1973.

Groothuis, L., "Der Beitrag der Bischöfe Bekkers und de Vet zur Erneuerung der Pastoral in der Katholischen Kirche der Niederlände" (pro manuscripto), Münster, 1971, 357.

Gustafson, J., *Treasure in Earthen Vessels. The Church as a Human Community*, New York, 1961, 102.

Haarsma, F., "Over de gezagsuitoefening in de kerk" (Regarding the excercise of authority in the church), *Tijdschrift voor Theologie*, 1969, 367.

Haarsma, F., "De doorwerking van het tweede Vaticaans Concilie" (The influence of the second Vatican council), *Wending*, April, 1972, 112.

Hadden, J., *The Gathering Storm in the Churches*, New York, 1970, 1—38.

Harrison, P., *Authority and Power in the Free Church Tradition. A social case study of the American Baptist Convention*, Princeton, 1959, 130 vv.

Heek, F. van, *Het geboorte-niveau der Nederlandse Rooms-Katholieken. Een demografisch-sociologische studie van een geëmancipeerde minderheidsgroep* (The birthrate among Dutch Catholics. A demographic study of an emancipated minority), Leiden, 1954.

Heek, F. van, *Verzorgingsstaat en sociologie* (The welfare state and sociology), Meppel, 1972.

Hertog de Baena, *Het Raadsel Nederlander* (The riddle of the Dutch), Den Haag, 1968, 17, 18, 73, 80.

Hoekendijk, J., "De missionaire struktuur van de gemeente" (The missionary structure of the community), *Gereformeerd Theologisch Tijdschrift*, Nov., 1963, 225—238.

Hoekstra, H., "De pastorale biechtgesprekken in het bisdom Den Bosch. Een onderzoek naar hun gesprekstechnische vormgeving" (Confession in the diocese of Den Bosch. A study of the design of the conversation technique), (doctoraalscriptie pro manuscripto), Leuven, 1967, 4—17.

Hoeven, P. ter, *Charisma en Politieke Vernieuwing* (Charisma and political renewal), Alphen aan den Rijn, 1971.

Hoger Katechetisch Instituut, *De Nieuwe Katechismus. Geloofsverkondiging voor Volwassenen* (The new catechism. Explaining the faith to adults), Hilversum, 1966, V.

Holk, L. van, "Progressie en regressie in de R.K. Kerk (probleem van dubbelzinnigheid)" (Progression and regression in the Catholic church), *Tenminste*, October, 1972, 4—10.

Hoof, J. van, "Organisaties en hun omgeving: verandering in openheid" (Organisations and their environments — changes in openness), *Tijdschrift voor Effectief Directiebeleid*, Dec. 1972, 402—410.

Houten, B. van, "Wetenschappelijke Theorie en Politieke Praxis" (Scientific theory and political practice), *Civis Mundi*, June—July, 1972, 175.

Huisman, J., "De Kerk van Morgen," in: H. en W. Goddijn, *De Kerk van Morgen. Een postconciliair toekomstbeeld van de katholieke kerk in Nederland* (The church of tomorrow. A post-council view of the future of the Catholic church in Holland), Roermond, 1966, 185—215.

Huysmans, R., "Het Pastoraal Concilie in canoniek perspectief" (The Pastoral Council in canonical perspective), *Bijdragen*, 4, 1970, 373—389.

Huysmans, R., "Internationaal-kerkelijke aspecten van de kerkelijke veranderingen in Nederland" (International aspects of the changes in the church in The Netherlands), (pro manuscripto), 13 October, 1972.

Huysmans, R., en Y. Snabel, "Buitenlandse literatuur over de katholieke kerk in Nederland, 1965—1970" (Foreign literature about the Catholic church in Holland 1965—1970), in *Jaarboek van het Katholiek Documentatie Centrum*, 1971, 149—163.

Instituut voor Toegepaste Sociologie. *Ambtscelibaat in een veranderende kerk. Resultaat van een onderzoek onder alle priesters, diakens en subdiakens in Nederland* (Celibacy in a changing church. Results of a study of priests of all ranks in Holland), published by Pastoraal Instituut van de Nederlandse Kerkprovincie in conjunction with Katholiek Archief, Amersfoort, 1969, 134 vv.

Italiaander, R. (Hrsg.), *Argumente kritischer Christen. Warum wir nicht aus der Kirche austreten.*

K.A. = Katholiek Archief, Amersfoort.

Katholiek Sociaal-Kerkelijk Instituut, *Kerkelijkheid en kerksheid in Nederland. Kommentaar op de gegevens der kerkelijke registratie-1960 en de eerste uitslagen van de volkstelling-1960* (Church attendance and religious feeling. A commentary on the ecclesiastical registration and the census of 1960), The Hague, 1963.

Katholiek Sociaal-Kerkelijk Instituut, *De katholieke bevolking van Nederland. Kanttekeningen bij de voorlopige uitslagen van de volkstelling 1971* (The catholic population of Holland. Remarks on the provisional results of the population census 1971), The Hague, 1972.

Kenntner, G., *Die Veränderungen der Körpergrösse des Menschen*, Karlsruhe, 1963, 112—121.

Kilsdonk, J. van, "De noodzaak van een loyale oppositie" (The necessity of a loyal opposition), *Adelbert*, Nov., 1962, 143—151.

Kirk, Dudley, *Europe's Population in the Interwar Years*, League of Nations, 1946, 49.

Klingen, J., *Strategische manoeuvreerbaarheid en strategische besturing* (Strategical manoevrability and strategic management), Alphen aan den Rijn, 1973, *passim.*

Klostermann, F., in: Der Zustand der römisch-katholischen Kirche. Eine Enquête unter Christen, *Sonderheft von Wort und Wahrheit*, March—April, 1972, 147.

Klostermann, F., et al., *Handbuch der Pastoraltheologie,* Band V, Lexicon, s,v. Aggiornamento, Freiburg, 1972.

Kok, J. de, *Nederland op de breuklijn Rome — Reformatie. Numerieke aspecten van Protestantisering en Katholieke Herleving in de Noordelijke Nederlanden 1580—1880* (Statistical aspects of Protestantisation and Catholic revival in the northern Netherlands 1580—1880), Assen, 1964.

Kok, J. de, Het Modernisme: Leer van de "Grote Komst," *Bijdragen*, 1971, 255, 236.

K.R.O. (Catholic Broadcasting Organisation), Broadcast of 20 Jan. 1970 after the communiqué from the bishops about celibacy (transcript).

Kühner, H., "Die römisch-katholische Kirche als konservative Grossmacht im 19. und 20. Jahrhundert," *Rekonstruktion des Konservatismus* (Hrsg. G. Kaltenbrunner), Freiburg, 1972, 384.

Kuyper, A., *E Voto Dordraceno. Toelichting op den Heidelbergschen Catechismus* (Information about the Heidelberg catechism), Part 2, 3rd Impression, 43—46.

Laan, H., *De Rooms-Katholieke Kerkorganisatie in Nederland. Een sociologische structuuranalyse van het bisschoppelijk bestuur* (Catholic church organisation in Holland. A sociological and structural analysis of management by the bishops), Utrecht, 1967.

Laarhoven, J. van, "Een land vol kerktorens" (A country full of church towers), *De Bazuin*, 1 April, 1973.

Laeyendecker, L., *Religie en Conflict* (Religion and conflict), Meppel, 1967, 305—309.

Lammers, C., "Democratisering; evolutie of revolutie? (Is democratization evolution or revolution?), *Sociologische Gids*, Jan.—Feb., 1971, 15—16.

Lammers, C., "De professionele vereisten van een sociologische opleiding" (The professional requirements of a sociological education), *Sociologische gids*, March—April, 1973, 75.

Landes, D.S. and Ch. Tily (Eds.), *History as Social Science*, New York, 1973.

Lange, A. de, "De crisis van het nederlands katholicisme" (The crisis of Dutch Catholicism), (Pamphlet by *De Gids*), Amsterdam, 1966, 25—26.

Laurentin, R., "Après le synode, où va l'Eglise? " *Informations Catholiques Internationales*, 1 Jan., 1972, 12—14.

Lewin, Kurt, "Group Decision and Social Change," in: *Readings in Social Psychology*, edited by Th. Newcomb and E. Hartley, 1947, 340—344.

Lindqvist, M., *The Crisis of the European Churches and Their Efforts for Functional and Organisational Reform*, Helsinki, 1971.

Lubac, H. de, "Die Kirche in der gegenwärtigen Krise," *Theologie der Gegenwart*, 1969, 201.

Luckmann, Th., *Das Problem der Religion in der modernen Gesellschaft*, Freiburg, 1963.

Manning, A., "Uit de voorgeschiedenis van het Mandement van 1954" (The prehistory of the mandate of 1954), in: *Jaarboek van het Katholiek Documentatie-Centrum*, 1971, 138—148.

Marrau, H., in: *Réinventer l'Eglise*, in *Esprit*, 408, Nov., 1971, 522—527.

McCaffery, R., "Some groups at present seeking to influence the development of Roman Catholicism in the Netherlands," May, 1971 (pro manuscripto).

McCready, W. and A. Greeley, "The End of American Catholicism? " *America*, 28 October, 1972, 338.

Metz, J., "Over de tegenwoordigheid van de kerk in de maatschappij" (The presence of the church in society), *De Toekomst van de Kerk*, Bussum 1970, 91.

Moberg, D., "Religion and Society in the Netherlands and America," *Social Compass*, 1, 1961, 17—19.

Moberg, D., "Social Differentiation in the Netherlands," *Social Forces*, May, 1961, 333—337.

Moberg, D., *The Church as a Social Institution. The Sociology of American Religion*, New York, 1962, 118 vv., 295.

Müller, A., in: *Der Zustand der römisch-katholischen Kirche. Eine Enquête unter Christen*, Maart—April, 1972, 177—178.

O'Connor, J.P., *A National Pastoral Council: Pro and Con.* Proceedings of an Interdisciplinary Consultation August 28—30, 1970, in Chicago, III, Washington, 1971, 139—140.

O'Dea, Th., The role of the intellectual in the Catholic tradition, *Daedalus*, 2, 1972, 181.

Ogborn, W. and M. Nimkoff, *Sociology*, New York, 1946, 814 vv.

Oostveen, T., *Bernard Alfrink, Katholiek*, Den Bosch, 1972, 151, 154.

PC = Pastoraal Concilie van de Nederlandse Kerkprovincie (Pastoral Council of the Dutch ecclesiastical province), Report under editorship of W. Goddijn, O. ter Reegen, A. van Dijk en H. van Santvoort, published by Katholiek Archief and the Central Commission.

Perlmutter, H., "The tortuous evolution of the multi-national corporation," *Columbia Journal of World Business*, Jan.—Feb., 1969, 9—18.

Poulat, E., *Histoire, dogme et critique dans la crise moderniste*, Paris, 1962, 696 blz.

Poulat, E., *Intégrisme et catholicisme intégral. Un réseau secret international anti-moderniste: La "Sapinière"* (1909—1921), Paris, 1969a, 627 blz.

Poulat, E., "Modernisme" et "Intégrisme". Du concept polémique à l'irénisme critique," *Archives de Sociologie des Religions*, 27, 1969b, 3—28.

Rahner, K., De verhouding van de kerk tot de situatie in het algemeen (The relationship of the church with the general situation), in: K. Lehmann e.a., *Kerk in moderne samenleving*, Hilversum, 1968, 17—26.

Remy, J., "Innovations et développement des structures," *Lumen Vitae*, 24, 1969, 201—228.

Remy, J., "Open informatie in de kerk: om uit ongelijkwaardige dialoog te komen" (Open information in the church to avoid onesided dialogues), *Concilium*, no. 3, 1971, 87—96.

Rogier, J., "Concordaat bindt Vaticaan aan Portugal" (Portugal and the Vatican are bound by a concordat), *Vrij Nederland*, 14 April, 1973, 17.

Rogier, L.J., *Het verschijnsel der culturele inertie bij de Nederlandse katholieken* (The phenomenon of cultural inertia among Dutch Catholics), Amsterdam, 1958.

Rogier, L.J., "De historische achtergrond van de secularisatie" (Historical background to the process of secularisation), in: G. Puchinger, *Christen en Secularisatie*, Delft, 1968, 30—31.

Rogier, L.J., "Evolutie van het cultuurbegrip der Nederlandse katholieken in de nieuwste geschiedenis" (Evolution of the concept of Dutch catholicism in contemporary society), *Geneeskunst en Levenshouding*, Eindhoven, 1969, 16—24.

Rogier, L.J., "Op- en neergang van het integralisme" (The rise and fall of integralism), *Archief voor de geschiedenis van de Katholieke Kerk in Nederland*, 1970, 257—357.

Schelsky, H., "Ist die Dauerreflexion institutionalisierbar," *Auf der Suche nach der Wirklichkeit*, Düsseldorf, 1965, 157 vv.

Schillebeeckx, E., "Kirche nach dem Konzil. Ausblicke für Holland," *Diakonia*, 2, 1967, 1—15.

Schillebeeckx, E., "L'église catholique aux Pays-Bas," *Septentrion. Revue de Culture Néerlandaise*, no. 1, 1972, 25—39.

Schmidtchen, G., *Zwischen Kirche und Gesellschaft*, Freiburg, 1972, 56 vv.

Schoenmaeckers, E., "Die katholische Kirche der Niederlande in der Krise der Gegenwart," *Orientierung*, 1964, 19—26.

Schoof, T., *Aggiornamento. De doorbraak van een nieuwe katholieke theologie* (Breakthrough of a new catholic theology), Baarn, 1968, passim.

Schoof, T., "Theologie in de katholieke kerk: op zoek naar een nieuwe koers" (Theology in the Catholic church — in search of a new approach), *Wending*, 1970, 421—436.

Schoof, T., "Opstand der theologen. De ontwikkeling van de rooms-katholieke theologie sinds 1945" (The rebellion of the theologians — development of Catholic theology since 1945), in: *Onze jaren 45—70*, no. 69, 1973, 2186—2189.

Schreuder, O., *Revolution in der Kirche? Kritik der kirchlichen Amtsstruktur*, Düsseldorf, 1969, 49, 95—96.

Siefer, G., *Die Mission der Arbeiterpriester. Ereignisse und Konsequenzen. Ein Beitrag zum Thema: Kirche und Industriegesellschaft*, Essen, 1960, 291 vv.

Simpfendörfer, W., "Kirchliche Experimente in Westdeutschland," *Concept* (Wereldraad van Kerken) III, Winter 1963—1964, 5.

Smulders, P., "Een poging tot theologische reflectie" (An attempt at theological reflection), *Bijdragen*, 1970, 399—400.

Suèr, H., *Niet te geloven. De geschiedenis van een pastorale commissie* (Unbelievable. The history of a pastoral commission), Bussum, 1969, 27.

Szczesny, G., *Afscheid van Links? of: Het zogenaamde goede. Over de onmacht van de ideologen* (The powerlessness of the ideologists), Amsterdam, 1972, 86 vv.

Tellegen, F., "De lotgevallen van de confessionaliteit" (The vicissitudes of confessionalism), *Geneeskunst en Levenshouding*, Eindhoven, 1969, 25—35.

Thompson, K.A., *Bureaucracy and Church Reform. The Organizational Response of the Church of England to Social Change 1800—1965*, Oxford, 1970, XXIII, 212 vv., 243.

Thurlings, J., *De Wankele Zuil. Nederlandse katholieken tussen assimilatie en pluralisme* (The shaky pillar. Dutch Catholics between assimilation and pluralism), Nijmegen, 1971, 208.

Tucci, R., "Voraussetzungen zu schaffen. Bilding einer echten Bischofkonferenz bedeutet für Italien einen ersten Schritt," *Wort und Wahrheit*, December, 1966, 784—787.

Verbeek, H., "Nieuwe structuren voor de R.K. Kerk in Nederland. Het ambt zoekt zijn plaats" (New structures for the church in Holland. The clergy has to find its place), *Vox Theologica*, Dec. 1967, 292—320.

Vidler, A., *A Variety of Catholic Modernists*, Cambridge, 1970, 82, 86, 91, 92.

Vleck, J. van, *Our Changing Churches: A Study of Church Leadership*, New York, 1937.

Vogel, C. de, *Aan de Katholieken van Nederland. Aan allen* (Address to the Catholics of the Netherlands. To everyone), Nijmegen, 1973, 79.

Warwick, D., "Personal and organizational effectiveness in the Roman Catholic Church," *Cross Currents*, Fall 1967, 401—417.

Weima, J., "Authoritarianism, Religious Conservatism, and Sociocentric Attitudes in Roman Catholic Groups," *Human Relations*, no. 3, 1965, 233—234.

Willems, B., "Misschien hebben we een heel lang moratorium nodig" (Perhaps we need a very long moratorium), *Kosmos en Oecumene*, 8, 1972, 288.

Williams, C., *Where in the world. Changing Forms of the Church's Witness*, New York, 1963, V.

Winter, G., *The New Creation as Metropolis. A Design for the Church's Task in an Urban World*, New York, 1963.

Ysseling, S., "Gezag en vrijheid" (Authority and freedom), *Tijdschrift voor Theologie*, 1969, 268.

Zijderveld, A., "The future of organized religion: Analysis of a taken-for-granted opinion," *Mens en Maatschappij*, 1971, 24—41.

Zizola, G., "Democratische vorming van het volk van God" (Democratic education of the people of God), *Concilium*, 1971, 122.

Zulehner, P., *Säkularisierung von Gesellschaft, Person und Religion. Religion und Kirche in Österreich*, Wenen, 1972, 217.

Author Index

Subject Index

Action Française, 52, 63, 110, 111
Adelbert Organization, 78
Adaptation, 22, 26, 55, 56
Aggiornamento, 5, 23, 51, 54, 56
American Institute of Management, 36
Americanism, 55
Anglican Church, 21, 28
Army Chaplains, 79, 184
Austria, 80, 125, 126
Authority (exercise of), 10, 12, 15, 19, 23, 24, 26, 32, 38, 41, 50, 51, 56, 57, 59, 76*ff*, 84, 102, 113, 117, 122, 128—130, 135, 145*ff*
Auxiliary Bishops, 80

Baptist, American, 20
Belgium, 80, 118, 121, 125
Bishops, 6—10, 15, 32, 63, 64, 68, 74, 79*ff*, 86—88, 91, 100—102, 112, 115, 117, 121, 122*ff*, 134*ff*
Bureaucracy, 19, 102
Brazil, 125, 132

Canada, 125, 126
Canon Law Society, 37
Cathechesis, 86, 91, 92, 95, 177*ff*
Cathechetical Institute, 62
Catholic Broadcasting Corporation, 74, 106, 120, 122
Catholic Central Bureau for the Promotion of Mental Health, 78
Catholic Documentation Center, 93
Catholic People's Party (KVP), 75
Celibacy, 6, 60, 120, 168*ff*
Centralization, 20, 44, 51, 108, 142
Church Universal, 68, 89, 104, 122, 131*ff*, 159, 169, 170
Collegiality, 28, 45, 88, 104, 125, 136
Communication, 80, 94, 128, 130
Communications Center, 114
Communism, 33, 60, 61

Conflict, 9, 10, 12, 19, 20, 30, 65, 106, 113*ff*, 117*ff*, 119*ff*, 142
Congregation for the Doctrine of the Faith (Holy Office), 60, 93
Conservatives (alarmed), 13, 19, 68, 105, 106, 110
Conservative reaction, 61, 115—117
Conservatism, 28, 52, 60, 109
Consumer society, 33
Contemplation, 32
Contesting, 130
Cybernetics, 136

Decentralization, 44, 104, 108
Democratization, 31, 63, 76, 82, 102, 123, 130
Denominational organizations, 33ff, 63, 104
Development work, 155*ff*
Dioccsan density, 80, 133
Discussion groups, 104, 129, 143
Dutch Catholics, 76, 77
Dutch Catholic Sports League, 74
Dutch Episcopate, 38*ff*
Dutch Institute for Public Opinion Research (NIPO), 98, 141
Dutch Pastoral Council, 8, 15, 20, 68, 73, 81, 82, 85, 86, 89, 90, 94, 96, 97, 101, 103, 107*ff*, 111, 118—120, 122*ff*, 143*ff*

Ecumenism, 10, 29, 39, 73, 76, 78, 80, 83, 86, 90, 95, 176, 177
England, 45, 67, 68
Ethical attitude, 156*ff*.
Europe, 5, 29, 80, 95, 122
European Bishops' Conference, 44
Experts, 69, 74, 83, 86, 100, 108, 109, 113, 131, 134*ff*.

Faculties of Theology, 86